BOUDICCA'S HEIRS

BOUDICCA'S HEIRS

Women in early Britain

Dorothy Watts

HQ
1137
· G7
W 38
2005
West

Routledge
Taylor & Francis Group

LONDON AND NEW YORK

First published 2005
by Routledge
2 Park Square, Milton Park, Abingdon, Oxon OX14 4RN

Simultaneously published in the USA and Canada
by Routledge
270 Madison Ave, New York, NY 10016

Routledge is an imprint of the Taylor & Francis Group

© 2005 Dorothy Watts

Typeset in Garamond by
Newgen Imaging Systems (P) Ltd, Chennai, India
Printed and bound in Great Britain by
MPG Books Ltd, Bodmin

British Library Cataloguing in Publication Data
A catalogue record for this book is available from the British Library

Library of Congress Cataloging in Publication Data
A catalog record for this book has been requested

ISBN 0–415–28068–0

OPTIMO ET CARISSIMO AMICORVM

CONTENTS

CONTENTS

PLATES

TABLES

PREFACE

Some years ago, when carrying out research for *Christians and Pagans in Roman Britain* and analysing cemeteries from the fourth century AD, I was struck by the absence of burials of infants or neonates in many of the cemeteries, while noticing at the same time an imbalance between the numbers of males and females. I was prompted to further research, but at that stage my interests were focused elsewhere. Now it has been possible to return to those questions I first asked on burials, and to look beyond them to an assessment of the overall position of women and their place in the Romanisation of Britain.

It became quite obvious that the research should not deal only with the Roman period, and nor should it deal only with women. The immediate pre-Roman period had to be investigated and, in order to assess the position of women, the data for men's burials had to be compared. The Roman period is well served with carefully produced cemetery reports, but for the Late Iron Age only a handful of reports was available. However, because of the quality of recent reports and the size of the relevant cemeteries, there was sufficient material to make the necessary comparisons.

From there the overall concept grew, and my teaching interests in Roman political and social history made the integration of the historical and prosopographical material a logical next step. *Boudicca's Heirs: Women in Early Britain* is the outcome. It will, I hope, be as enjoyable for the reader as it was for me to research and write.

During this project, one of the difficulties I have had is in handling reports of such varying quality and depth of information. Since almost half of this book deals with cemetery remains, I would like to take the opportunity which this personal note affords to make a plea to archaeologists to provide certain basic information in their reports. These include: sex to be confirmed if two experts differ, so that in the report both male and female are not given to the same remains; method of sexing explained at the outset; heights to be given (in centimetres); age parameters to be uniform, and clearly stated, for such terms as neonate, infant, child, adolescent, young adult, adult/mature adult, old adult (it would also be helpful if ages beyond 45 could be refined, but I realise that this is very problematic); dimensions of grave to be given – length × breadth × depth: even if these are somewhat 'rubbery' they can be used in working out averages; drawings of all burials, complete with grave cut and goods shown; bone reports to give individual burial numbers for all pathologies, and for such conditions as cribra orbitalia and dental enamel hypoplasia; fractures of ribs to indicate which side of the body; record of grave goods including coins to indicate burial number.

I realise that most of this information is in some reports, but for the potential researcher nothing is unnecessary. I also realise that the inclusion of such detail, particularly drawing of all burials, adds greatly to the cost of a paper report; but the use of a CD-ROM for such material would be relatively inexpensive, contain a great deal of information, and be far better than the dreaded microfiche sheets, which invariably get scratched or lost in university libraries, and are usable only with equipment which is not easily transportable.

Having said this, I must thank the authors/editors of all the reports used in this study for their attention to detail, for their generally comprehensive covering of the archaeology of their sites, and for specialist reports which are clear and understandable to the non-specialist. The reports are a mine of information, and still provide the basis for considerable analysis in the future.

Research for this work was completed during study leave from The University of Queensland. Funding for the project was provided by The University of Queensland and the Australian Research Council and this is acknowledged with thanks. I am also most grateful to a number of people who have given information, advice, criticism and encouragement: Mr David Wilson for information on Ancaster cemetery; Messrs Brian Dix, Steve Parry and Ian Meadows for the Ashton data; also Mr Philip Crummy, Mr Michael Jones, Emeritus Professor Philip Rahtz and Professor Paul Corby Finney.

Colleagues and graduate students have also played an important role in the production of this book by their critical comments and enthusiasm for matters Romano-British. My special thanks are offered to Mrs Penny Peel for her meticulous attention to detail during many hours of research assistance, and for preparing the index. To Emeritus Professor Robert Milns, fine scholar and good friend, I give my grateful thanks for reading the last draft, and for drawing to my attention the most glaring errors. All views expressed in this work except where acknowledged, and any errors, are mine alone.

To my family members who have provided their support throughout the project – my husband, son and daughter who, despite their own commitments, have taken on tasks to allow me time for completion, have given emotional support when the odds seemed stacked against me, and have patiently sorted out computer problems – I express my heartfelt gratitude and love.

While the writing of this book has been a personal challenge, I have been inspired by the many great scholars who have gone before me, and by the ancient Greeks and Romans, from whom we have inherited so much. Apollo still plays his lyre and the Muses sing.

Dorothy Watts
University of Queensland
Brisbane, Australia
July 2004

ABBREVIATIONS

BAR	British Archaeological Reports
BMC	*British Museum Catalogue of Coins of the Roman Empire*
CBA	Council for British Archaeology
CIIC	*Corpus Inscriptionum Insularum Celticarum*
CIL	*Corpus Inscriptionum Latinarum*
FOS	*Prosopographie des Femmes de l'Ordre Sénatorial (Ier–IIe siècles)*
IG	*Inscriptiones Graecae*
OUCA	Oxford University Committee for Archaeology
RIB	*Roman Inscriptions of Britain*
RIC	*Roman Imperial Coinage*
SHA	*Scriptores Historiae Augustae*

1

HISTORICAL BACKGROUND

There is a tide in the affairs of women,
Which, taken at the flood, leads – God knows
where.

(Byron: *Don Juan* 6.2)

Britain became part of the Roman Empire in AD 43, with the arrival of the emperor Claudius and the subsequent surrender of the British chiefs. The province of Britannia was set up and pacification was complete by about the end of the second century, by which time the major Romano-British towns were well established and Roman practices widely adopted. Yet this adoption of Roman ways did not start with the Occupation. Even before Julius Caesar's campaigns of 55 and 54 BC, the attractions of Rome were known in Britain, mainly because of Roman advances in Gaul and Spain. In the following century, Roman imports and luxury goods, and native coins with Latin inscriptions or with designs which reflected those of the Graeco-Roman world became widespread; and, even if diplomatic influence waned along with the links set in place at the time of Caesar's invasion, increased commercial contact showed that Britain was coming more into Rome's sphere of influence. British entrepreneurs, leaders in their own societies, in turn provided Rome with various commodities.[1]

Close ties existed with the tribes across the Channel, and they increased in the century before the Conquest. The ties were both commercial and social. Considerable trade had been carried on between Gaul and ports on the southern British coast, especially Hengistbury Head. It was probably controlled at the continental end by the Veneti (Caes. *B.G.* 3.8; Strabo 4.4.1), and conducted out of their ports on the south Armorican coast.[2] There was also contact with the Gallo-Belgic tribes. This was revealed in the archaeological record of the tribes of the Trinovantes, Catuvellauni and Cantii, those people of the south-eastern part of Britain, formerly believed to be of Belgic origin, but now seen as native and referred to as the 'Aylesford-Swarling' culture or, more commonly, the 'Aylesford' culture.[3]

The influence from the Continent may have increased political tensions in Britain, as the aggressive Catuvellauni came to dominate their neighbours, moving from Verulamium to take over the territory of the Trinovantes and their capital near

Colchester. This was in contravention of the settlement of Caesar in 54 BC. In the central south, the 'Belgic' Atrebates formed a pro-Roman bloc based on an area from Chichester to Winchester and north to Silchester, with Roman or Gallo-Roman influence progressively diminishing to the north and west.

Contact with Rome was through the native leaders, and even at this early stage there would be considerable *kudos* in being able to demonstrate their familiarity with Roman ways. Nevertheless, it might be questioned to what extent Roman influence filtered down to the lower classes.

By the beginning of the first century BC, Britain had settled into a tribal society, although the situation was sufficiently fluid that some of the tribes Caesar mentioned had disappeared before the Occupation. Society seems to have become fairly peaceful, with the result that many hill forts of the previous period were deserted, and fortified or unfortified *oppida* replaced them as tribal *foci* in locations more conducive to trading activities. These *oppida* could not always be considered proto-towns, but centres such as Colchester had some of the features of a town, with comparatively large-scale industry (see below) and a mint; and Silchester has yielded evidence of a Roman-style street system about 60 years before the Claudian invasion. Besides these larger centres, there were many settlements ranging from villages to hamlets of two or three houses. Such settlements were often of very long standing, and it was here that most of the population were to be found.[4]

As land control and ownership replaced communal use, the hierarchical nature of society was strengthened, and the ordinary native Briton was less able to see himself as the equal of his wealthier fellows. Only the leaders of society would be able to indulge in the trappings of wealth: imported pottery, wine, oil and fish sauce from the Continent, and the gold and silver coins which played little part in the economy but probably had more of a political use as payment of tribute, for mercenaries, or as means of gaining support.

The economy was centred on the land and its produce. Industry was generally cottage based (such as the wool 'industry' at Danebury), and any mass-production was still small-scale as compared with Roman times. Even so, regional resources could provide the impetus for some specialisation or production beyond subsistence requirements: salt, glass, bronze, copper-alloy, silver and gold works are known at sites ranging from north to south. Some areas were particularly productive, so much so that the scale of industry may have necessitated the use of slave labour. This is suggested for the ancillary 'industrial' zones of pre-Roman Colchester, which yielded metal working of various types, much glass, bone and pottery.[5]

The Claudian Conquest, while resulting in the conspicuous changes brought about by presence of the Roman Army, may not initially have had a great impact on the lives of ordinary Britons – although hardship and bloodshed did occur in some parts.[6] A number of chieftains submitted at once to Rome's authority; and Tacitus' oft-quoted passage from *Agricola* 21 illustrates the willingness of the native aristocracy to adopt Roman customs, language and dress; yet the revolt of the Iceni as early as AD 47 shows that, even of this class, not all welcomed the conquerors. Tribal disturbances continued sporadically until the end of the second century.

Roman legions built forts and roads, and probably had input into the planning of some towns which were often, but not always, established on the site of earlier tribal or *civitas* capitals. The major towns were constructed in the wake of the army's advance on its way to conquering Britain and parts of Wales. A wall begun in the reign of Hadrian separated the pacified areas from those in the north which were unable to be conquered or were hard to hold. The towns were an important factor in spreading Roman culture and customs and the Latin language. Smaller settlements sprang up along the main roads and around forts. The governor was based first at Colchester (*Camulodunum*), and then London, and a large administrative base set up there. In the *civitates*, it was not practicable to have large Roman establishments, and so Rome made use of the services of the former tribal leaders and local aristocracy. Local senates or councils were established, and magistrates appointed. The reward for service as a local magistrate was Roman citizenship, so there would have been no shortage of offers, at least at the outset. This was to change by the fourth century, when civic duties became a burden to be avoided if possible. The emperor Diocletian then made positions on local councils hereditary.

The amenities offered by the towns were commonly a market place (*forum* or *macellum*), an administrative building (*basilica*), public baths, and a temple or temples to various deities, all built on a street grid. Water was reticulated by aqueducts to baths and, for the lucky few, to houses. These facilities were provided by the civic leaders in their capacity as members of the local council. They also erected arches, statues and columns, as appropriate for a Roman town. In the second century, town walls appeared. The houses of the ordinary people were both inside and outside these walls.

Wealth was, as it had been in the pre-Roman Iron Age, in the land, and the wealthy – almost certainly the same local aristocratic families as before – who probably had already built town houses for themselves in the Roman style, now spent vast sums on converting their primitive homesteads into villas. This was for some an on-going process over many generations, with the most elaborate and best-appointed emerging by the end of the third and the beginning of the fourth century. Improved farming techniques had increased production and created surpluses for local consumption or export.

Organised industry, previously rare, now became more widespread and varied. Salt production and mining increased at the source as did ironworking, but some also occurred in the towns. The wheel was now used for pottery, and what might be seen as mass-production for the ancient world occurred where the clays were of the highest quality, south-east of the Jurassic ridge. The military was a major market. But that does not mean that Britain became an industrialised nation in the modern sense. Home-based industries continued: villas in particular were probably self-sufficient in basic needs. Wool-working by women would continue to be done in the home, although a late development was a 'factory' staffed by women wool weavers set up by an imperial official at 'Venta' (either Caistor-by-Norwich or Winchester),[7] probably for the purpose of making the *birrus Britannicus*, a popular hooded coat exported to the Continent.

The process of Romanisation was slow and at times superficial, especially in rural areas. However, it can be traced to some extent in the classical sources and the inscriptions from Roman Britain. These sources, together with archaeological evidence, can be used to build up a picture of Romano-British society. On the other hand, very little can be extracted from the ancient writers about life and society in Britain before the coming of the Romans. The evidence we do have is second hand, selective, frequently generic, and often little more than propaganda.[8]

When we look specifically for women from the immediate pre-Roman period, there is even less material. The notable exceptions are Boudicca and Cartimandua whose lives spanned the pre-Roman/Roman divide. They must be considered as pre-Roman. The best and in most cases the only evidence for other women is archaeological.

There is little published modern research on the women of Roman Britain, apart from the studies by Allason-Jones and the more specialised works by Johns and Redfern.[9] For the pre-Roman period, there is still less: a handful of scholars have dealt with various aspects of the topic, but no overall study has been made. The women of early Britain have usually been dealt with as part of general research on European Iron Age communities, or on women in antiquity.[10]

This present study looks at the available literary and inscriptional sources, but it is also to a considerable extent based on archaeological evidence, in particular on material from the remains of burials. The period covered is generally from about the first century BC to the beginning of the fourth century AD, but some pre-Roman material has been drawn from earlier centuries. It is hoped to produce a clearer picture of the women of early Britain, and to assess the effects of the Roman occupation.

The identity of a number of women from Roman Britain is known from the inscriptions, and others can be gleaned from prosopographical studies. They are introduced according to their rank and origin, or their religious affiliation. The position of such women in society is not difficult to ascertain. But for the majority of women whose names and backgrounds are lost and who are only known through cemetery archaeology, determining their status is much more difficult.

According to the first century BC writer Posidonius, quoted in the third century AD by Athenaeus (4.152b), status was achieved by martial skill, family nobility or wealth. How status in the Late Iron Age and Roman period could be determined with regard to burial evidence is not so clear cut, since the first two would not be readily apparent. The obvious equation would be status = wealth, but one has only to look at that most famous of Roman *poseurs*, Trimalchio (in Petronius' *Satyricon*), to acknowledge that having extraordinary wealth did not necessarily equate with what modern society would term 'high class'. Even so, to some Romans – slaves, freedmen and the poor free, who made up a large percentage of the population – a real-life Trimalchio would seem the epitome of success. 'Status' is thus a subjective term.

It does appear, however, that the display of wealth was equated with status by both pre-Roman and Roman societies. The well-known possession and wearing of gold torcs by British leaders and their families (shown even on the Ara Pacis at Rome, where a small boy, presumably a Celtic high-status hostage at the court of the emperor Augustus is depicted wearing not only Roman dress but also this distinctive neck-wear), and barrow burials with complete chariots, may be compared with the jewellery, *objets d'art* and splendid mausolea in the possession of upper class families at Rome. In other words, manifestations of wealth and status are very hard to separate.

The relationship between status in life and burial practices in the immediate pre-Roman period has recently been examined,[11] and it was concluded that, in areas where the social structure was unstable and there was need for strong 'native' leadership, burials would demonstrate status in a non-native or Romanised way; whereas in those areas which were already familiar with the ways of Rome, status would be defined in the more traditional way of barrows and impressive imported grave goods, especially pottery.

Difficulties arise when one has to determine what constitutes items of value and status to society. In the pre-Roman period, certain objects, especially imported Roman pottery vessels (and presumably the oils, wines and sauces which filled them), dinner ware and glass, were highly desirable commodities and are found in what can be assumed to be high status graves. After the Conquest, and particularly as the exclusiveness and novelty of Roman imports gave way to availability and familiarity, these types of grave goods became less common. It could well be, too, that the economic situation at certain times reflected a reluctance to consign to the earth perfectly usable objects for a purpose which might or might not ensure a happy afterlife for the deceased. Practicalities might dictate that only fragmentary glass, broken pots and dress pins, small-value bronze coins or similar modest items be included in burials. Fashions also change: an unfurnished rural grave in the late second century AD may have a different significance from an urban one in the fourth.[12]

Moreover, there is the problem of not being able to determine with any degree of certainty what religious beliefs, if any, underlay the deposition of certain types of grave goods or influenced burial practices, and to what extent these relate to status. Some foods such as the imported wines and oils might be seen as demonstrating wealth, rather than religious beliefs. But others, such as the cheap cuts of pork found in British chariot burials, suggest a deeper meaning – after all, if conspicuous consumption was the purpose, why not deposit a whole pig? Once more the practicality of the situation probably meant that, if conspicuous consumption were the motive, then the choice cuts would have been consumed at a public funerary feast, the piece deposited being a discard but still acceptable as a burial offering. However the fact that in earlier Iron Age burials the same types of animal remains have been found in a number of graves suggests that there was, indeed, a deeper meaning for the grave deposit.

The use of grave goods as an indicator of status may be questioned, as it has been by various scholars in the past. Like elaborate graves and burial monuments, grave deposits may have been intended to impress the living (e.g. Lucian *Dial. Mort.* 24); they reflected the wealth and status of the people who were burying the dead rather than that of the deceased; but then again, wealth and status was probably the same for both the living and the dead. Toynbee says that the purpose of grave goods was 'partly to honour the dead, but mainly to serve them and help them to feel at home in the afterlife'. She does not enter into the question of status, but she does point out that Roman legislators attempted to restrict the amounts spent on funerals.[13]

Other criteria have had to be developed to determine status in the burials of women in pre- and Roman Britain. The following are suggested: use of burial structures or graves which involved particular expense or physical effort; evidence of focal burial or grave with spatial significance; presence of 'valuable', rare or numerous grave goods;

the evidence of the bones themselves – on the assumption that remains which demonstrate good nutrition are more likely to come from the classes which have access to an adequate and balanced diet; and the relative numbers of males and females and the implications of this. These criteria are developed in Chapters 2 and 4.

Women from all strata of society have been studied here. Besides their identity and status, aspects of their lives and death, their religion and their everyday activities are examined. It will be obvious that the evidence is heavily slanted in favour of those who could afford houses with mosaics or frescos, tombstones with inscriptions, and jewellery or other items of value to be deposited in graves. It is very difficult to identify the poorer classes, and even more difficult to ascertain their attitudes to Rome and to Romanisation.[14] The historian, reliant on the archaeologist to tease out this information from the dwellings of the ordinary people, must admit to some little frustration when attempting a study in which it is hoped to give a general overview of women in early Britain.

Apart from the information from inscriptions, limited literary material and prosopographical evidence, little is known about women in the Late Iron Age and Roman Britain. Archaeological evidence helps greatly in filling in the picture. 'Putting flesh on the bones' is not an easy task – especially when many of the bones have been cremated or destroyed. But if this work expands knowledge of the life and death of some of those who theoretically would have formed 50 per cent of the population of early Britain, it will have achieved its objective.

Notes

1 The first century AD writer, Strabo 4.5.2, tells of the export of slaves, cattle and hides, hunting dogs, grain, gold, silver and iron. Tin was also exported from Cornwall.
2 Rather than out of Alet, as has been previously thought (cf. Cunliffe 1984b: 98–191, 1991: 543, fig. 20.7; deJersey 1993).
3 For example, Fitzpatrick 1997: 208; cf. Cunliffe 1991: 130, fig. 7.1.
4 A brief examination of Britain in the Late Roman Iron Age will suffice here, as the reader is directed to the comprehensive coverage by Cunliffe 1991 on the British Iron Age for full background and appropriate references. On Silchester street system, see Jones 2004.
5 Henderson 1991; Ryder 1993; Thompson 1993: 97; Crummy 1997a: 16.
6 The dramatic description of the Conquest by Hingley 1997: 81 needs some tempering.
7 *Not. Dig.* 11.60.
8 Issues such as contemporaneity, genre and intended audience for the work, the background of the author, and his skill as a writer and researcher must be taken into account, and we discover, as do all first-year university students, that all sources are not equal in quality.
9 Allason-Jones 1989, 1999, 2004; Johns 1996; Redfern 2002.
10 For example, the works by Rankin 1987; Ehrenberg 1989; Ross 1992; James 1993; Cherici 1994; Berresford Ellis 1995; Green 1995a, etc.
   It is not my intention to become involved in the controversy regarding an acceptable nomenclature for the inhabitants of pre-Roman Britain (see Megaw and Megaw 1996; Collis 2003, etc.). Thus the term 'Celt' will be avoided where possible.
11 Struck 2000. See also Barber and Bowser 2000: 325–9.
12 So Philpott 1991: 231.
13 Ucko 1969–70; Toynbee 1971: 53–4; Morris 1992: 104–27.
14 See Hingley 1997: 84–5.

2

IDENTIFICATION, NUMBERS AND STATUS IN THE LATE IRON AGE

The difficulties of discovering the women of early Britain are considerable. The logical place to start is with the written material: the classical sources, and the Irish myths and legends.

The main problem with the first is that they were written entirely by Greek or Roman men, and very often themselves from secondary sources; and it is a common failing amongst ancient writers that they are willing to repeat, embroider or invent tales of barbarism and debauchery, incest and cannibalism, in their efforts to portray the 'otherness' of a people with whom they had had no known contact. Even writers who did have contact with them are not necessarily reliable or without errors of fact. A notable case is Julius Caesar and his *Gallic Wars* (*B.G.*): he was, after all, first and foremost a general and politician, and his role as ethnographer and anthropologist came a very poor second. Any attempts to reconcile the contradictions in the *Gallic Wars* with regard to British women are generally unsuccessful. It would seem better to take the view that he was actually wrong on some aspects, as he was on other topics, and has been proved so by archaeological excavation. A further problem is that, in the main, the classical writers restrict their references to women of the upper classes of society – a situation which is familiar to any researcher on women in early civilisations. These sources must, therefore, be used with care.

If the later Irish myths are used, difficulties arise with the reworking of the oral material by Christian monks, who tended to paint women characters as supernatural, saintly, or as sinners of the worst kind. It is a fairly easy task to peel away the Christian veneer but, as with the classical material, many aspects of life and society have been omitted, even from the original tales. Little detail on the lower classes is given, in particular on women of those classes. There is also no way of knowing the sources the Irish poets themselves used, or how familiar they were with the works of the Greek or Roman writers.

With regard to the inscriptions from Britain, some material relates to 'native' women, but this actually applies to the Roman period. For the British late pre-Roman Iron Age, apart from the few references in the classical sources, archaeological evidence is all there is.

Archaeology brings its own problems, the most significant being those of sex determination. Recent research now permits some confidence in the generally accepted methods of sexing skeletal remains. A discussion of the techniques currently in use lists the criteria which are seen as giving the most accurate results based on osteological examination, and shows that ongoing research using DNA – yet in its infancy for sex identification in archaeology – appears to confirm the accuracy of the conventional methods.[1] The accuracy of these methods will thus be assumed in this present work.

Identification

We know the actual names of only two British women from late pre-Roman/early Roman period, and they are from the upper or ruling classes: Boudicca and Cartimandua.

The tale of Boudicca is well known to us from Tacitus (*Ann.* 14.31–7) and Dio Cassius (*Epit.* 61.1–12). The version by Tacitus is more immediate than that by Dio, in that Tacitus was writing only a couple of generations after the revolt and may have had access to records or even to people who actually remembered the events. Dio, writing more than a century later, had to use transmitted sources; and while the two accounts generally agree, in some details there are disparities. Dio's account is certainly the more colourful.

In the narrative, Boudicca becomes Queen of the Iceni on the death of her husband, Prasutagus, a client king of Rome. She is driven to revolt when, instead of inheriting her rightful share of her husband's kingdom in partnership with Rome, she receives a beating from Roman soldiers, her daughters are raped, and her property attacked. The vast army she raises attacks Colchester, a particular target for British hatred because it was a Roman *colonia* and also boasted a temple to the emperor Claudius which was seen as a symbol of Roman oppression. Verulamium and other smaller towns are burnt on the way to laying waste London. The Romans rally under their general, Suetonius Paulinus, and in the final battle the native forces are defeated and Boudicca dies. The method of Boudicca's death varies from Tacitus (suicide by taking poison) to Dio (fell ill and died), but the outcome was the same: the failure of the revolt.

Our information on Boudicca's northern counterpart, Cartimandua, queen of the Brigantes, also comes from Tacitus (*Ann.* 12.40.2–7; *Hist.* 3.45). Cartimandua was a client ruler, and had a formal association with Rome by which she was bound to have the same friends and enemies as her ally; in return she could expect the Roman army to come to her assistance if her rule were threatened. Even at the outset, however, it is doubtful that her position was totally secure. She would most certainly have been seen by the disaffected in her tribe as a collaborator with Rome, the more so when she handed over the fugitive – or patriot, depending on one's viewpoint – Caratacus to Rome after he sought asylum with her.[2] When Cartimandua divorced her husband and competent general, Venutius, and took as her lover his squire, Vellocatus, this caused a crisis in the tribe and the queen only escaped from their wrath with the help of the Roman army. Tacitus tells us, 'Venutius retained the kingdom, and we (the Romans) had the war on our hands'.

Numbers

While the actual identity of women in the Iron Age is impossible to recover, it is possible to determine the composition of the population of the period and their likely position *vis-à-vis* men by examining the archaeological record, particularly that of cemeteries. It does seem that there is a link between the percentage of women in the population of Late Iron Age Britain and their status, a point to be taken up later.

The evidence can be problematic. A major stumbling block is the nature of Iron Age burial practices. It was not usual for people to be buried in designated areas set aside for the purpose, so that actual cemeteries were few and far between. Until the 1970s and early 1980s, no substantial sites of multiple burials had been carefully excavated and reported. Furthermore, many Iron Age burials have disappeared through the advance of farming techniques or urbanisation, or are 'archaeologically invisible': it has been estimated that between 90 and 95 per cent of all British Iron Age burials have disappeared without trace. Bodies were not normally interred in cut graves and in coffins, as in the Roman period. The dead could be disposed of in ditches, wells, middens and other convenient places, or exposed to the elements and scavengers and the subsequent disarticulated remains then scattered, deposited in streams, or in the various ditches, wells and middens.[3]

With the introduction of cremation – a rite which appears to have come from Europe or, less likely, was a reversion to a practice of the British Bronze Age – there is a further obstacle: the location of cremated remains when not placed in a permanent receptacle, such as a ceramic pot, prior to burial. No doubt remains were gathered up using skins, woven cloths, wicker or wooden boxes and containers of other organic material, but these have not stood the test of time, thus thousands of late Iron Age cremations will forever remain undetected.

A related problem in cemetery studies is that the populations of some burial sites may not present a true demographic picture. This has frequently been remarked in respect of the absence of adolescents, children or infants,[4] and the burial of infants in habitation sites rather than in cemeteries is well recorded.[5] More important for this analysis, the relatively small populations of some cemeteries may not reflect accurately the ratio of males to females. That has influenced the methodology employed here, and ways of reading the data.

The archaeological reports analysed have been of varying quality, and lack of detail a handicap. But it is fortunate that there have recently been a number of well-published reports of cemeteries or cemetery groups. The more comprehensive publication of some larger sites such as the barrow cemeteries in East Yorkshire, the cremation burials of King Harry Lane, Verulamium and the Westhampnett Bypass at Chichester, and the inhumation cemetery at Mill Hill in Kent has allowed a reasonable analysis to be undertaken (Table 2.1).[6]

Burials in the Late Iron Age could be inhumations or cremations,[7] and most were in very small cemeteries when such common burial grounds existed. For example, the Baldock burials number only four, but are included here because of the later ones

Table 2.1 Sexed burials in Iron Age cemeteries

Site	Date	Approx. number of dated burials	No. sexed	% of identifiable adults sexed[a]	No. of M/?M and % of sexed adults	No. of F/?F and % of sexed adults	Unsexed adults identified	Adolescents/children/infants[b]/neonates identified
Arras culture:								
Cowlam[#]	C2–1 BC	5	4	100	2/50	2/50	—	1
Garton Slack/Kirkburn[#]	C3–1 BC	18	17	100	8/47	9/53	—	N 1; *in utero* 1
Rudston/Burton Fleming[#]	C3–1 BC	252	185	75	87/47	98/53	—	C 5; I 1
Wetwang Slack[#]	C3–1 BC	446	193	98	79/41	114/59	4?	13
Baldock*	Mid-end C1 BC	4	—		—	—	—	
Bledlow[#*]	C1 BC–AD C1	5 (#4; *1)	2	100	1/50	1/50	—	C 2; I 1
'Central Southern England'[#]	Late IA	341	109	48	56/51	53/49	120	A/C 18; I/N 92
Chichester, West-hampnett Bypass*	90–50 BC	121	26	26	4/15	22/85	75	14
Danebury Late Period[#]	300–50 BC	28	16	100	8/50	8/50	—	12
Deal, Mill Hill[#*]	C2 BC–AD C1	47 (#42; *5)	30	86	14/47	16/53	5	A/C 10

Dorchester Dorset Poundbury #	Late IA	58	23	85	11/48	12/52	4	C 5; I 22
'Durotrigian':								
Maiden Castle #	C2 BC–AD mid-C1	68	57	100	34/60	23/40	—	11
Litton Cheney #	AD C1	6	5	83	3/60	2/40	1?	A/C 1
Whitcombe #	AD C1	10	9	100	6/67	3/33	—	
Owslebury #*	C1 BC–AD C1	31 (#23; *8)	6	30	4/67	2/33	14?	C 1; I 7; N 11
Verulamium King Harry Lane #*	AD 1–60	489 (#17; *472)	97	35	72/74	25/26	201	A 5; C 12; I 9; N 3
Totals		1929 (#1443; *486)	779	65	389 =50%	390 =50%	424	298

Notes

If cemeteries with fewer than 50 per cent of adults sexed (including 'Central Southern England' and Verulamium) are eliminated, M = 51 per cent, F = 49 per cent.

If cemeteries with fewer than 30 sexed burials are eliminated, M = 51 per cent, F = 49 per cent.

If sexed cremations are eliminated, M = 48 per cent, F = 52 per cent.

* Cremation.

Inhumation.

a Those over about 15 yrs, and adolescents/sub-adults able to be sexed.

b 'Adolescent', 11–14 yrs; 'child', 1–10 yrs; 'infant', younger than one year but older than neonate.

from the Romano-British period. Also included are some multiple-site groupings: a number of inhumations comprising pit burials, 'orthodox' graves, and burials in ditches, ramparts and banks from Central Southern England and listed under that heading; and the data from Maiden Castle compiled from Phases A, B and C, and the 'War Cemetery' at that site.[8]

The analysis shows that the overall percentages are the same for male and female. When cemeteries with fewer than 30 sexed burials are disregarded, the percentages vary slightly (M = 51 per cent, F = 49 per cent). If those cemeteries which have fewer than 50 per cent of all adults sexed are eliminated, then the result is still M = 51 per cent, F = 49 per cent. But this would exclude two large burial groups, 'Central Southern England' with 109 sexed burials (48 per cent of identifiable adults sexed) and Verulamium, with 97 (35 per cent). It was decided, therefore, to include the information from these in any comparison with cemeteries from the Roman period (see Chapter 4), together with all other cemeteries with more than 30 sexed burials, but to disregard individual figures from the small sites of Cowlam, Garton Slack/Kirkburn, Baldock, Bledlow, Chichester Westhampnett Bypass, Danebury Late Period, Poundbury Iron Age, Litton Cheney, Whitcombe and Owslebury.

With males 50 per cent and females 50 per cent, or even with adjusted figures of males 51 per cent and females 49 per cent, we have virtual parity between the sexes, although there do appear to have been regional differences, and some segregation of burials may have occurred. Despite such variations, and probable Roman influences already being revealed in some areas having close connections with the Continent, it seems that infants of both sexes were allowed to live and to make a contribution to society as adults. In other words, there is no apparent evidence of female infanticide in the pre-Roman period.[9]

Status: the literary evidence

'Status' is a term is used here to describe the position or standing of women in society, particularly as compared with men, and also as compared with women of other parts of the Roman Empire. On the evidence of the ancient writers and of archaeology, it is concluded that, while women of pre-Roman Britain may not have been completely equal in status to that of men, they were still considered valued members of society and, indeed, some had considerable power and influence.

There seems to be more difficulty in interpreting the status of women when dealing with the ancient sources than when using the archaeological material. The problems of using the literary evidence have already been briefly stated above, yet it should be possible to expand and refine the portrait of women in the British Iron Age by drawing analogies from Irish myths and from the evidence of Celtic women from the Continent. The written sources can then provide one view, however incomplete, which can be put alongside the archaeological evidence. The result is a reasonable assessment of the status of women in late pre-Roman Britain, one which fits into the larger view of the peoples of western Europe.

That there were similar cultures in Britain and Gaul cannot be doubted. Tacitus, one of the most reliable authorities, says:

> But a general survey inclines me to believe that the Gauls established themselves in an island so near to them. Their religious belief may be traced in the strongly-marked British superstition. The language differs but little; there is the same boldness in challenging danger, and, when it is near, the same timidity in shrinking from it.
>
> $(Agric.\ 11)$[10]

and even Caesar notes: 'Of all the Britons the inhabitants of Kent...are by far the most civilised, differing but little from the Gallic manner of life $(B.G.\ 5.14)$.[11]

Studies by modern authors on the status of women of the pre-Roman period do not differentiate between women of Britain and the Celts of Europe.[12] Their works have, however, been generally restricted to the reasonably substantial (if sometimes contradictory) literary evidence for Celtic women in Europe, and there has been no specific examination of women in pre-Roman Britain, apart from Boudicca and Cartimandua.[13]

With regard to the status of Celtic women generally, there are differing opinions. These range from 'high stature' or full equality with men, to something merely approaching equality. Cunliffe believes that Celtic women had a higher position in society than those in the Graeco-Roman world and, on the basis of the 'mirror' burials of the Arras culture, that women may have status equal to that of men in some communities; and Berresford Ellis, using the evidence of Boudicca, also takes this view. It is not shared by other scholars such as Rankin, Cherici and James, who see that the sources portray a closer balance between the sexes, but not equality.[14] Others, such as Ehrenberg, Ross and Green view the status of women as high, but have different bases for this opinion.[15]

Ehrenberg looks at the problem from an anthropological viewpoint, and believes that the Celts had a non-patrilineal society: in such systems women marry men of about their own age, whereas in patrilineal systems there is a much greater age gap between male and female. She holds that, because it was the women who sowed and harvested the crops (men being the hunters), they had higher prestige than in societies where men provided the food. Tying the two theories together, she concludes the non-patrilineal pattern of descent is quite common in agricultural societies, and is frequently connected with higher status of women.

Ross and Green concentrate on the evidence from Celtic religion. Both see the important position of goddesses in Celtic religion as reflecting the position of women in Celtic society. Green believes it is perhaps more than coincidence that, in a society where female deities are perceived as powerful, there is also evidence for a relatively high status for women, as compared with women of the Mediterranean world. Ross looks at the specific and concludes that the powerful position held by the queen of the Brigantes tribe in northern Britain, Cartimandua, may mirror that of its goddess, Brigantia. There are difficulties with these interpretations, in that there are other ancient societies where the status of male and female deities in no way reflects the position of men and women in that society.

Green is one of the few scholars, along with Cunliffe, to look also at the archaeological evidence, although restricting it to what may be seen as high-status burials. She notes that, as in Europe before the spread of Romanisation, some women of Iron Age Britain were given rich burials – evidence for their high social standing.

We turn now to the ancient literary evidence itself, which confirms that women could hold positions of power and influence in the Celtic world. Such women also seemed to have considerable sexual freedom. From Irish myth there is the powerful Queen Medb (Maeve) in the *Táin Bó Cuailgne*, and from Britain the well-known historical examples of Boudicca and Cartimandua. Medb, the daughter of a king and married to the King of Connaught, boasted that she 'was never without one man being with [her] in the shadow of another'[16] and that she had no place for a jealous husband. Cartimandua, Tacitus (*Hist.* 3.45) tells us, was driven by lust to shed her husband in favour of his armour-bearer,[17] with whom she then shared her throne and her bed. This freedom to choose one's husband is also recorded in the classical sources: the story of the daughter of a Celtic ruler in southern Gaul who at her wedding feast chose her own bridegroom, the Greek who would become the founder of Massilia (Marseilles) (Athen. 13.576; Justin, *Hist. Phil.* 43.3).

Caesar (*B.G.* 5.14) says that British women were able to have more than one sexual partner:

> Groups of ten or twelve men have wives together in common, and particularly brothers along with brothers, and fathers with sons; but the children born of the unions are reckoned to belong to the particular house to which the maiden was first conducted.[18]

It is interesting how Caesar here has the men having wives (*uxores habent*) in common, rather than that the women were free to have more than one partner and, presumably, were able to choose the one with whom they wished to sleep. But such freedom is borne out by another source: Dio (77.16.5) relates a purported conversation between the third century Julia (Domna) Augusta, mother of the emperor Caracalla, and the wife of the Caledonian chieftain, Argentocoxus:

> When the empress was jesting with her... about the free intercourse of her sex with men in Britain, she replied: 'We fulfil the demands of nature in a much better way than do you Roman women; for we consort openly with the best men, whereas you let yourselves be debauched in secret by the vilest.'[19]

Indeed, since it appears that homosexuality was widely practised among the Celtic people, this could have been one of the reasons for the sexual 'liberation' of Celtic women. It has been suggested that, because of this supposed freedom of sexual relationships, pre-Roman Celtic society had no need for prostitutes.[20] It might be argued that homosexuality was yet another topos to emphasise the barbarity of the Celts; but homosexuality was viewed in a different light by the ancient Greeks, and these references should not be seen as condemnatory.

Nevertheless, such sexual freedom may not always have been the norm among the Celtic people in Europe, even though the story by Strabo (4.4.6) of the women of the Samnitae – living without men on an island at the mouth of the Loire, and choosing to sail once a year to the mainland to have intercourse with men – shows that at least some were in control of their sexuality. There is the tale of Chiomara, as related by Plutarch (*De Mul. Vir.* 22), which indicated that amongst some Celtic tribes women were monogamous and that marital fidelity was valued: Chiomara, the wife of a Galatian leader whom she was accompanying on campaign, was captured by the Romans. She was taken and raped by a centurion, but he was bribed with a large sum of money to hand her back. She bade her captor a seemingly fond farewell and, with a nod to a nearby Celtic soldier, indicated that he was to kill the Roman. Gathering up the severed head in her skirts, she went to her husband who said in amazement as she dumped it at his feet, 'A noble thing, dear wife, is fidelity'. 'Yes' said she, 'but it is a nobler thing that only one man be alive who has been intimate with me'.[21]

The concept of female virtue and the resultant legitimacy of children is also found in the ancient sources, as in a poem by an unknown Greek *c.*200 BC:

> The brave Celts test their children in the jealous Rhine and none regards himself as being the child's father until he sees it washed by that venerated river . . . for he does not feel for it like a true father until he sees it judged by the bath in the river, the test of conjugal fidelity.
>
> (*Greek Anthology* 9.125)[22]

and in the *Second Oration* by the fourth-century emperor Julian where he describes this same Gallic practice:

> They say that the Celts also have a river [the Rhine] which is an incorruptible judge of offspring, and neither can the mothers persuade that river by their laments to hide and conceal their fault for them, nor the fathers who are afraid for their wives and sons in this trial, but it is an arbiter that never swerves or gives a false verdict.[23]

This would seem to indicate that if, indeed, women in Iron Age Britain (and presumably Ireland) had freedom to choose their sexual partners, this was not necessarily always shared by their contemporaries on the Continent. We must remember, too, that in Britain, as in Galatia, chastity could also be highly valued: as in the example of Boudicca who rallied the British tribes, not least in response to the atrocities committed on her and her daughters by Roman soldiers.

It is likely that women in pre-Roman Britain could also hold positions of influence in religion, although the only literary reference is to one Fedelm, a prophetess or

Druidess in the realm of Queen Medb (*Táin* 55a) but probably of British origin.[24] Other Druidesses were presumably Irish (e.g. *Táin* 59). From the historical sources there are references to them in Gaul in the third century AD, and to priestesses in various parts: Camma, in Galatia, and Veleda, a Celtic woman living in Germany.[25] These women held considerable status and power within their communities. Tacitus records the respect which Veleda commanded, particularly from visiting ambassadors. The women who terrified the Roman soldiers at Anglesey also held some position in the native religion, as prophetesses or priestesses. They may also have had a role in a druidic ritual in which participants would 'cover their altars with the blood of captives and…consult their deities through human entrails' (Tac. *Ann.* 14.30).

With regard to property and marriage, the evidence is somewhat confusing, mainly because of the conflicting information from Caesar. The *defixiones* from Uley, the earliest dating to the late first/early second century, give a glimpse of British women who owned property of value.[26] According to Caesar, women and men brought property of equal value to marriage and, on the death of one, the other would inherit (*B.G.* 6.19). As for marriage itself, we know from the example of Cartimandua that women could choose their husbands (at least, upper-class women could). So it comes as a surprise to be told by Caesar, in the same passage where he discusses contributions to the marriage, that husbands had the power of life and death over their wives and children. Modern classical scholars tend to see this as Caesarian propaganda, designed for his Roman audience.[27] It is not easy to reconcile it with the other information we have.

The ancient literary evidence is somewhat confusing regarding the position of women in the pre-Roman period, but the general picture is one of considerable freedom and status. That picture might now be compared with the evidence of archaeology.

Status: the archaeological evidence

Earlier in this chapter, the numbers of males and females in Iron Age cemeteries were discussed. This was also a first step in defining the status of females in early Britain. The archaeological evidence from those cemeteries and elsewhere is now analysed in more detail, in particular burials of importance/spatial significance, numbers and value of grave goods, use of coffins, size and depth of graves, and the evidence gleaned from the bones themselves.

It seems that women could be given burials of undoubted status or importance, and their very presence could also have ritual significance. This can be seen not just in formal cemeteries. An as yet unpublished example comes from Odell, in Bedfordshire, dating to the last quarter of the first century AD: a small cremation group near which the head of a woman was found cradled in the pelvic girdle of a horse is seen by the archaeologist as a burial connected with fertility, since the horse is the attribute of the Celtic goddess Epona who had both fertility and chthonic associations. The burial is similar in focus to one in Ireland, at Ballinlough, Co. Laois.

Here, with five complete skeletons, was the skull of an adult female propped upright against a large piece of human bone, and flanked by three pieces of rib bone. This, too, is interpreted as a ritual burial.[28]

Two further examples of what may have been high status women's burials come from Stanway, near Colchester, and Dorton, Buckinghamshire. In the first, dated to the late pre-Roman or very early Roman period, among a series of four large enclosures containing prestige burials was one cremation with 19 vessels, a glass phial and some glass and paste beads. In the second, a cremation burial from about the last decade BC yielded a fine bronze mirror placed in a box with the calcined bones, as well as three imported amphorae and a cup. The grave furniture of both these burials suggests they were from a woman's grave.[29]

In the formal burial grounds, about 15 cart (or chariot) burials have been found among the barrow burials in the eastern part of Yorkshire and one in west Yorkshire, and three of these are known to be of women. One, uncovered in the nineteenth century, was buried with a dismantled two-wheeled vehicle together with metal horse fittings, an iron mirror, and the foreparts of a pig. A second was found in 1984, located between two other cart burials. It was the largest of the three, probably the first of the group. The woman was buried with a dismantled two-wheeled cart, the tray apparently inverted over her body and the pole buried separately. Grave goods included an iron mirror, an iron and gold dress pin decorated with what is thought to be coral, and an enigmatic bronze container with incised decoration, 'enamelled' roundels, and a short length of chain attached. Other objects of note in the grave were horse fittings made of ornamented bronze and decorated with red coral which, unfortunately, faded to white immediately on being exposed to the air. The body was on its side, flexed, with the grave goods placed at the back behind the shoulder. Across the body were the remains of two forequarters of a pig.

The third female cart burial, discovered near Driffield in 2001, appears to be the same type of high status burial. The woman, in her late twenties/early thirties, was buried with a two-wheeled vehicle and also horse trappings, indicated by elaborate bronze rein rings inlaid with coral. Here, too, the remains of a pig were placed across the upper body. This cart burial has been dated to the fourth century BC, and is possibly the earliest of its kind yet found in Britain, although the west Yorkshire example could be earlier.[30]

Other female burials, while not as spectacular as those of the Arras culture, appear to indicate status. At King Harry Lane, Verulamium, some were seen to be of special significance either by the use of enclosures or by their relationship to other burials. There were eight focal burials with others clustered around them, all within enclosures. Three were male, one female and three of unknown sex. A further ten were spatially differentiated, and with others grouped around, but not enclosed. They included four male, one female and five unsexed. Of these last five, one was among the richest in the cemetery: it had as grave goods a copper alloy spoon and brooch, two spindle whorls, another unidentified iron object and also a mirror; and since, from the evidence to date, spindle whorls are found only in females' graves, it is likely that this burial is also of a female.[31]

The cemetery at Mill Hill, Deal, is not as rich as the previous two, with few grave goods, and those of little value. Even so, there is at least one distinctive female burial, in a grave partially enclosed by a ring gully, well separated from the other inhumations. Accompanying the skeletal remains were a brooch and a pin, and also five joiner's dogs which probably had the function of holding up a wooden slab cover. They were placed one at the head and the other four at the foot of the grave. This grave and four others may originally have been covered by barrows, in view of their fairly isolated position in the cemetery.

Similarly, in the cremation cemetery at the Westhampnett Bypass, Chichester, a number of Iron Age enclosures yielded little of note, but one, marked by a ditch and four postholes, contained in a red-slip vessel the remains of a young woman.[32] This apparent distinction was not enhanced by grave goods of any kind.

When the grave goods of the Iron Age burials are examined, it is found that there is little difference in deposits for male and female. Information on grave goods from the cemeteries in this study was limited, but the figures available show that, among the sexed burials, 63 per cent of males and 65 per cent of females were buried with some kind of grave furniture, excluding the pottery jar in which cremated remains were placed. It is clear that, while some grave goods were especially favoured for one sex or the other, there was generally no difference in the quantity or quality for males and females.

In the four cemeteries which comprised the 'East Yorkshire' burials (Garton Slack, Kirkburn, Rudston and Burton Fleming) for instance, where 75 per cent of the inhumations were sexed, grave goods were found with 65 per cent of males and 61 per cent of females. At Verulamium, while only 97 out of 489 burials (or 35 per cent of identifiable adults) could be sexed, giving a disproportionate distribution of 72 males to 25 females, the percentage having discernible grave goods beyond the pottery vessel in which cremated remains were placed was fairly even at 68 per cent of males and 72 per cent of females.

There were two sites where, unlike Verulamium, cremated remains were not normally placed in a pottery vessel but were accompanied in the grave by a pot; such vessels must then be interpreted, as with other deposits, as grave furniture. One was Westhampnett, where only two cremations were urned, and both of these were women. Of the other 22 women, all but one had at least a pot accompanying but not containing the remains. The four or five males identified were also unurned but each had a pot, or a pot and other objects, as grave goods. The percentages with grave goods are $M = 100$ per cent, $F = 95$ per cent. The second was Owslebury, where the one female and three males out of six Iron Age cremations sexed had pots in the grave. The percentages here were $M = 75$ per cent, $F = 50$ per cent.

The incidence of grave goods varied, as did the quality. Few items of value were found in the burials at Westhampnett yet, conversely, the item of greatest intrinsic value from all Iron Age burials covered in this study came from this cemetery: an early British uninscribed gold coin found in a woman's grave, together with the bones of an animal, and three locally made pots. A second female grave yielded an unusual pair of brooches with remains of a chain attached to each, a small ring, a belt hook and fragments from two pots. This grave was the largest of all the sexed burials, and in fact the third largest of the whole cemetery after a double burial of a juvenile and sub-adult (in a grave which yielded a fragment of gold foil and five pottery vessels), and that of a sub-adult or adult, all unsexed.

The Iron Age burials at Owslebury were more dispersed than those at some sites, but a late La Tène and early Roman cemetery and other burials dating to the same period were identified. Of 31 cremations and inhumations, only six could be sexed. The wealthiest burials were those of two males and a female. One of the males had twelve or more vessels, a razor and the jaw of a pig, and the other had seven vessels and three brooches. The female was buried with 11 vessels. In all three burials the pottery assemblages included a number of imported wares.

One of the most unusual finds came from a female burial at Mill Hill: the disarticulated bones of what has been interpreted as a small or lap dog, the size of which, according to the archaeologist, could only have meant it was a pet. One might well speculate on the life this little animal led, in supposedly uncivilised Britain, but quite possibly in a household where its female owner had time to lavish attention and affection on it to the extent that its bones were finally interred with her. But there may also have been a cultic practice involved here: a small clay figurine found at Canterbury depicts a dog on the lap of a figure interpreted as a mother goddess; and the Celtic goddess Sirona, a goddess of healing, is depicted seated with a small lapdog in a second century AD sculpture at Hochscheid in the Mosel region of Gallia Belgica. The burial of dogs with humans was carried out in graves from the late Iron Age onwards.[33] The dog was equated in classical beliefs with death, and in Celtic beliefs was also an attribute of Epona who was associated with both death and regeneration. It is possible, too, that a 'non-working' animal such as this may have represented a status symbol for the woman.

Overall, the types of grave goods in these Iron Age cemeteries were usually fairly standard, and some sex specific, such as weapons in male graves (19 instances, mostly from the East Yorkshire burials; none in females'), and mirrors and spindle whorls in female graves – all from East Yorkshire excepting one very rich cremation from Verulamium which had a mirror and a spindle whorl together with other deposits. Mirrors were only found in prestige burials (Plate I). The most common grave goods were items of personal adornment, usually copper-alloy or iron brooches (in 33 per cent of all sexed burials, and in 33 per cent of both male and female); pottery other than the cremation urn (31 per cent of burials: in 15 per cent of male, 34 per cent of female); and animal bones, especially those of pig and goat/sheep (17 per cent of burials: in 12 per cent of male, 27 per cent of female). Multiple pots – probable indicators of wealth and status – were deposited in both male and female graves; for example, at the King Harry Lane, one male had ten, another seven, and a female also had seven. These three are especially noteworthy because they have been dated to the earliest phase of the cemetery, and each of the assemblages contains a number of imported wares: five, seven and six, respectively. At Owslebury a similar situation occurred, with Class G ware coming in first via Hengistbury Head, and later the

Plate I Desborough mirror (British Museum).

more numerous Gallo-Belgic ware through Silchester. Clearly at this time it was not only the number of vessels deposited which was important, but also the place of manufacture. In this Iron Age community, as in others studied, there was considerable prestige attached to the possession of imported products well before the Conquest, and such symbols of status were the prerogative of both sexes.

A suggested criterion for determining status was the attention given to the burial, and whether the remains were put into a coffin. Coffins are generally found after the coming of the Romans, but there are a few examples from the Iron Age. The East Yorkshire group of inhumations is noteworthy for the use of coffins at least two centuries before the Occupation; in this respect the burials appear to be unique in Britain for this period, although 'coffins' of some type seem to have been used in a number of earlier Bronze Age burials. Of 270 sexed inhumations, 18 were found to have used wooden coffins, but there may have been more, and of these, eight were for males, and ten for females. There were a further two coffined female burials amongst the Iron Age burials at Poundbury, Dorchester.

Table 2.2 Size of sexed burials in Iron Age cemeteries

Cemetery	Males			Females		
	Maximum (m²)	Minimum (m²)	Average (m²)	Maximum (m²)	Minimum (m²)	Average (m²)
Cremations						
Chichester, Westhampnett	0.59 × 0.40 = 0.24	0.30 × 0.27 = 0.08	0.16	0.95 × 0.80 = 0.76	0.25 × 0.18 = 0.05	0.27
Verulamium, King Harry Lane	1.80 × 1.60 = 2.88	0.25 dia. = 0.05	0.51	1.50 × 1.30 = 1.95	0.40 dia. = 0.13	0.52
Inhumations						
Deal, Mill Hill	2.13 × 1.10 = 2.34	1.79 × 0.38 = 0.68	1.28	2.41 × 0.64 = 1.54	0.80 × 0.59 = 0.96	0.96
Dorchester, Poundbury IA	1.68 × 0.99 = 1.66	0.76 dia. = 0.28	0.81	2.39 × 1.32 = 3.15	1.02 × 0.61 = 0.62	1.36
East Yorkshire (excl. cart burials)	2.50 × 1.65 = 4.13	1.20 × 0.75 = 0.90	2.06	2.55 × 2.20 = 5.61	1.55 × 0.55 = 0.85	2.26

Mention has also been made of the size of the grave as a possible indicator of status, owing to the effort required to dig a hole in sometimes unyielding soil. This relationship of size to importance is borne out in mythology: at the end of the Irish *Saga of Cuchullain*, the wife of the hero orders a wide and very deep grave for him after he falls in combat, and she herself is buried with her husband. In our early British archaeological context, it is not surprising, in view of the apparent equality of burial rite given to males and females already shown, that both males and females could have large graves. In four of the five sites analysed, the average size of females' graves is larger than that of males' (Table 2.2).

The largest sexed burials of all were those containing carts/chariots. They were found in East Yorkshire: at Kirkburn (*c*.18.72 m²) and Garton Station (9.60 m²), both males. The occupant of the largest male grave, at Garton Station, appears to have been accorded some special ritual at burial: the remains were found with 11 spearheads, apparently thrust into the grave fill after the body had been interred. One was thrust into the body. Male 'speared corpses' were also found in nearby Kirkburn and Rudston. This particular inhumation was found amongst others with spears and swords deposited in the conventional place for grave goods. The attention given to the burial would suggest status rather than punishment, and the large grave cut would reinforce this interpretation.

Women were not accorded such a bizarre rite, but were given status. The rich grave goods have already been noted; and while the size of the female chariot burials was not given, it is noted that, of the three burials of this type found at Wetwang Slack in 1984, the enclosure for the woman's grave was the largest (enclosure of 9.23 m², as compared with 7.39 m² and 5.10 m²). The four largest ordinary burials in the cemetery group from East Yorkshire were also for women. The largest, at Kirkburn, was for a woman and infant accompanied by an amber and a jet bead, and a copper ring and stud; the others were at Burton Fleming and Rudston.

A woman's grave was the largest amongst the Iron Age burials at Poundbury, and hers was also the deepest of the female burials, so the size of the cut does not seem to be accidental. The largest male grave was considerably smaller, and the average size of male graves was smaller than females'.

The situation differs at Mill Hill. Male burials are consistently larger than female. This goes against the trend for the other three Iron Age burial groups. The two largest burials were for males, with the third, a female, having a grave cut considerably smaller. Grave goods were limited at this cemetery. In the largest male grave only a brooch was found; in the female's there was a pot and a coin of Eppillus, the only coin found in the cemetery.

Results from the cremation cemetery at King Harry Lane, Verulamium show that, while the average size for females was marginally greater than that for males, the largest cut is for a male. The second largest was for a female. The grave goods in the first were substantial and prestigious: seven vessels (all imported, including a Spanish amphora) and seven copper studs apparently from a wooden tray or box in which the grave goods and the cremated bones were placed. Those in the female's, while fewer in number, were equally prestigious: a pair of matching *lagenae* from Central Gaul, and fragments of copper which perhaps belonged to a wooden cover for the grave.

The cremations at Westhampnett follow the pattern of the Yorkshire and King Harry Lane burials, with the average size of females' graves greater than that for males. The largest grave cut is for a female: in this case more than twice the area of the largest cut for a male. At this site it was noted that, although the number of items deposited in the male graves at this cemetery was about the same per burial as in the females', the quality was perhaps not quite as high. However the small number of cremations sexed at this site does not make it easy to define trends.

While the size of the grave cut may give an indication of status, the depth of the burial is also relevant. Such a study is fraught with difficulties because it is not always possible to establish the upper level of the grave cut and often, too, the grave cut had been partially removed by a mechanical earth mover before the archaeologists took over. But even taking these factors into account, it was found that, apart from the very deep graves needed for the cart burials, there was little difference in the depths of graves for male and female; however the average for female graves was more often greater (Table 2.3).

In the East Yorkshire burials the deepest graves were for women: in all there were twelve of one metre deep or more, and nine of these were of women. The deepest of these was that of the young woman and infant, mentioned above. This grave also had the largest grave cut. The deepest male grave was for a warrior found with weapons and pig bones. At Mill Hill, the other inhumation cemetery where the information was given, of the three deepest inhumations, two were females (the second burial also with the largest grave cut and the pot and British coin, mentioned above), and one was male, buried with a locally made pot.

Table 2.3 Depth of sexed burials in Iron Age cemeteries

Cemetery	Males			Females		
	Maximum (m)	Minimum (m)	Average (m)	Maximum (m)	Minimum (m)	Average (m)
Cremations						
Chichester, Westhampnett	0.27	0.17	0.21	0.37	*c.*0.05	0.19
Verulamium, King Harry La.	0.80	0.10	0.27	0.65	0.20	0.28
Inhumations						
Deal, Mill Hill	0.92	0.19	0.50	0.93	0.26	0.53
Dorchester, Poundbury IA	0.99	0.10	0.56	0.86	0.18	0.56
East Yorkshire (ex. Cart burials)	1.10	0.10	0.61	1.30	0.15	0.68

Of the cremations, at King Harry Lane the deepest graves among the sexed burials were of two males, and the next deepest was of a female. There appears to be a correlation between depth and status here, as the first of the males had quite a large grave, and also an Italian wine amphora amongst his grave goods; the second had four pots, which included one imported. The female burial was also the largest in size of all the sexed females, and contained the pair of matching imported *lagenae* noted above. The deepest female cremation at Westhampnett contained two pots, a brooch, and animal bone; the largest of the males contained similar grave goods, as well as an iron nail. Neither of these burials was the richest for its sex, and the data from this site are not particularly conclusive.

The evidence that can be extracted from the skeletal remains themselves was considered, but only those aspects which might relate to status are dealt with in this chapter.[34] A major problem is the paucity of material from which to draw conclusions. From what we have, however, it appears that there was virtually no difference in the treatment of males and females. For instance, there is little evidence at all for broken bones, and none for a higher incidence of 'parry' or similar fractures in women's remains than in men's; this could suggest domestic violence was not prevalent – or at least of the type that would result in broken ulnae. As far as nutrition is concerned, in the East Yorkshire burials there were five cases of dental enamel hypoplasia, which may have been the result of dietary deficiencies in childhood. Of these, three were female, one male and one unsexed. At Mill Hill, there were one female and one male with this condition. These figures, while not conclusive, do not give any strong indicator of the less favourable treatment for females, or of any dietary deprivation during their childhood. The implication to be drawn is that, on the evidence of the bones, women were not treated as inferiors.

From the above discussion, therefore, it would appear that the women of pre-Roman Britain enjoyed relatively high status. They probably had greater freedom than their Celtic sisters on the Continent, and even more than their counterparts in classical Greece and Rome; and while it is probably true that they did not have complete equality with men, some did have positions of wealth, power and influence. The cemetery evidence also shows they were valued as human beings at birth, were allowed to live and to make a contribution to society as adults, were not physically treated as inferiors during life, and at death were given the same respect and status as their husbands, sons and brothers.

Notes

1 Keegan 2002: 42–3.
2 This son of Cunobelinus had overrun the Dobunni and later mounted raids on the Romans and their allies from south Wales.
3 For Iron Age burials, see Wait 1986: 90.
4 For example, Warwick 1968: 147; Wheeler 1985: 275; Neal 1987: 104; Crummy *et al.* 1993: 63; Dawson 1994: 29–30.
5 See Watts 1989.
6 Publication details of the 16 sites analysed are: 'Arras' burials: Cowlam (Stead 1986), the 'East Yorkshire' cemeteries of Garton Slack/Kirkburn, Rudston/Burton Fleming (Stead 1991), and Wetwang Slack (Dent 1982, 1983; Whimster 1981: 102); Baldock (Stead and Rigby 1986); Bledlow (Collard and Parkhouse 1993); 'Central Southern England' (Whimster 1981: 4–36); Chichester, Westhampnett Bypass (Fitzpatrick 1997); Danebury (Cunliffe 1984a); Deal, Mill Hill (Parfitt 1995); Dorchester, Poundbury Camp (Farwell and Molleson 1993); Maiden Castle (Wheeler 1943; Whimster 1981: 37–47); Litton Cheney and Whitcombe (Whimster 1981: 43–5); Owslebury (Collis 1968, 1970, 1977, 1994); and Verulamium, King Harry Lane (Stead and Rigby 1989).
7 For discussion on the problems of sexing cremated remains, see Chapter 4.
8 M = 4, F = 6; M = 8, F = 7; M = 22, F = 10 respectively.
9 In support of this, it should be noted that Strabo 4.4.3 comments on the 'excellence of (Celtic) women at bearing and raising children'.
10 Trans. M. Hadas.
11 Trans. S.A. Handford.
12 See note on the term 'Celts', see Chapter 1, n. 10.
13 For example, Allason-Jones 1989: 16–21; Ehrenberg 1989: 164–8; Berresford Ellis 1995: 83–93, etc.
14 Cunliffe 1995: 81, 1997: 109; Berresford Ellis 1995: 182. Cf. Rankin 1996: 253: '(the sources) testify not so such to a species of sexual equality, as to a more equitable balance of the functions of men and women in society'; Cherici 1994: 21: '(women) did not enjoy full equality with men. But neither was Celtic society a patriarchy'; James 1993: 66: 'women were not treated as equals in Celtic societies, although compared especially with their Greek equivalents, noblewomen enjoyed considerable freedom of action and even power'.
15 Ehrenberg 1989: 158–9; Ross 1992: 452–6; Green 1995a: 17–18, 27, 1996: 27.
16 Trans. A. Gregory 1902: 142.
17 Cherici (1994: 21–7) believes, on the basis of the Irish myths, that both males and females used their sexuality to control the other.
18 Ehrenberg (1989: 160–1) proposes that the large round-houses common in Britain confirms that Celtic women in Britain practised polyandry – the houses were large enough to accommodate several family units.

19 Trans. E. Cary.
20 For example, Arist. *Pol.* 2.6.5–6; Strab. 4.4.6; Diod. Sic. 5.32. On absence of prostitution Cherici 1994: 27.
21 Trans. F.C. Babbit.
22 Trans. W.R. Paton.
23 Trans. W.C. Wright.
24 So Rankin 1996: 253.
25 Gaul: SHA *Alex. Sev.* 59.9; *Numer.* 14; *Aurel.* 63.4.5; Galatia: Plut. *De Mul. Vir.* 257–8; *Amat.* 22; Polyaenus *Hist.* 8.39; Germany: Tac. *Hist.* 4.61.
26 Tomlin 1993b: 121–2 (no. 2); 128 (no. 20).
27 For example, Rankin 1996: 249.
28 B. Dix (personal communication); Rynne 1974–75.
29 Crummy 1997b; Farley 1983.
30 Cart burials in Britain: Greenwell 1906: 284–94; Dent 1985; Derbyshire 2001; Keys 2001; Boyle 2004. In Europe: Pare 1992.
31 A further spindle whorl was found at King Harry Lane, in the grave of an unsexed child.
32 There is some ambiguity in the report as to the sex of this individual: on page 40, the report refers to a 'subadult/adult male', whereas in figure 33 the burial is marked as female, and in the catalogue of burials, Grave 20566 is referred to as 'probably female'.
33 Jenkins 1957; Black 1983.
34 Nutrition and health generally will be discussed in Chapter 5.

3

IDENTIFICATION IN THE ROMAN PERIOD

When we seek the women of Britain in the period of the Roman Occupation, we still have few written sources on which to draw, but the women are now not virtually anonymous. The names of some have been recorded in stone on tombstones and altars, and on metal artefacts and curse tablets; a few are mentioned in the letters found at the Roman fort at Vindolanda; and still others are known through their husbands who were Roman officials in Britain. This chapter deals with women who are known to us by name. Their rank or status can sometimes be ascertained from the inscriptions themselves, while for others it can be presumed on the basis of the position of their male relatives. For the rest of the female population, however, we are still heavily dependent on archaeological evidence, and particularly that from burials.

Roman women

It is difficult at times to differentiate Roman from Roman-British women, that is, those who were British in origin and adopted Roman names. The problem is compounded by the fact that after Caracalla's edict of 212 all free persons in the empire became citizens. This part of the analysis will, therefore, be restricted to those women who can with a reasonable amount of certainty be seen to be Roman.

The Roman women who came to Britain were from all classes, senatorial, equestrian and plebeian. They came as wives, sisters, mothers and daughters of Roman soldiers, or with the non-military part of the Roman administration, the procurator and his staff. A few were the wives of Roman civilians. For those who were the wives of senior career officers, it was part of the job to move around the empire, and it will be seen that Britain was often not the first overseas posting for many, and indeed not the last. But although they took a less active and aggressive role on behalf of Rome than did their menfolk, these women must also be seen as instruments of the Romanisation of Britain by maintaining, within the limits of their location and their status, their Roman way of life.

The ancient sources are reasonably informative about whose womenfolk could go on campaign and when this was allowed.

Tacitus (*Ann*. 3.33–4), writing at the end of the first century/beginning of the second century AD, says that 'formerly' wives were not allowed to go to the provinces or allied territories because of the provisions of the *Lex Oppia*, a sumptuary law passed during the war with Hannibal. It was repealed around 195 BC. When, two centuries later in AD 21, a conservative senator and former consul, one Severus Caecina, proposed that no magistrate could take his wife to his province, there was strong objection. Caecina had claimed that women were distractions and delayed an army's progress, played favourites with the centurions and corrupted the provincials, resulting in their own husbands' being charged with extortion. The response from the moderates was that the sternness of former times had changed, and that men and women were now much more able to share alike the vicissitudes of war. Wives would be a source of solace to their husbands after the hardships of campaign. As for corruption, was this vice not also prevalent among unmarried men? because of the weakness of one or two men, should all be cut off from their partners in good times and bad? (and the clinching argument) moreover, since women as a sex were weak, did they not need the protection and guidance of their husbands to help them preserve the marriage tie?

As the debate progressed, Drusus, son of the emperor Tiberius, reminded his audience of how often Augustus had gone on campaign accompanied by his wife, Livia, and related how he himself had taken his wife and family with him when he campaigned in Illyricum; even so, he would go on others with a less contented mind if he had 'to tear himself from a much loved wife, the mother of his many children' (It was that same devoted wife, some few years later, who encouraged the advances of and was seduced by the Praetorian Prefect, Sejanus, and poisoned her husband. So much for a husband protecting and guiding, and helping to preserve the marriage tie.) (Tac. *Ann.* 3.33; Suet. *Tib.* 62).

It is known that another member of Augustus' family, his grandson by adoption, Germanicus, took his wife and family on campaign. Tacitus (*Ann.* 1.69) relates in some detail the calming influence that the wife of Germanicus, Agrippina, had over the troops when there was threat of mutiny during the German wars. The passage in question is noteworthy also for Agrippina's introducing to the legionaries her small son, Gaius, dressed in soldier's uniform – henceforth known to the soldiers and to posterity as 'Caligula': 'little boot'.

Not all the sources are sympathetic to women on campaign. Dio Cassius (50.20.2–5) seems to blame, in part, their presence in the army train for one of the Roman army's greatest defeats, the loss of three legions led by Varus in Germany in AD 9. He says, 'They had with them ... not a few women and children and a large retinue of servants following them – one more reason for their advancing in scattered groups.'

It does appear that, by the time the province of Britannia had been established by Claudius in AD 43, the presence of women with their senior military officer husbands was commonplace. From inscriptional and archaeological evidence, it is likely that officers of equestrian rank and senior centurions were also allowed to have their wives accompany them on campaign.[1] As for the ordinary legionary soldier, it had been a law since the time of the principate that he could not be married, and if he were when he enlisted, then he must divorce his wife. It was not until AD 197 that this law was revoked and Septimius Severus allowed all soldiers to marry. That did not mean, of course, that the legionaries did not have common law wives and offspring living in the *canabae* or *vici* which attached themselves to the fortresses and forts, but such liaisons were not recognised by Roman law; and even when a soldier received an honourable discharge, while the union was recognised and the children given citizenship, the wife did not become a Roman citizen.[2]

The differing status of women from senatorial to slave is reflected in both the literary and non-literary evidence, particularly the inscriptions from Roman Britain.

At the head of the provincial administration was the governor, the *legatus Augusti pro praetore*. Britain was an 'imperial' province, and thus the governor was appointed by and directly responsible to the emperor, and for much of the Occupation there were three or more legions in Britain, if at times they were under strength. In AD 43, four legions accompanied Aulus Plautius to carry out the Conquest of Britannia on behalf of the emperor Claudius. In the early second century, with the building of Hadrian's Wall as the northern frontier, three legions came to be permanently stationed in the province: the Second Legion *Augusta* at Caerleon in south Wales, the Sixth *Victrix* at York, and the Twentieth *Valeria Victrix* at Chester. These together with associated auxiliary units remained under the control of the governor until the reforms of Diocletian at the end of the third century. Until the reign of Gallienus in the third century, the governor of Britain was normally an experienced soldier, of senatorial rank, and the position was regarded as a very senior one. Even so, the names of all the governors of Britain are not known, still less the names of their wives.[3]

The governor's wife was pre-eminent among Roman women in the province. For the first few decades of the Occupation at least, the governor and his wife were of the highest social and political rank in Rome, and seem to have come from a fairly tight pool of aristocratic families. Later appointees included some who were the first of their families to reach the senatorial ranks. The wives of several governors are known by name, but only one, Domitia Decidiana, is specifically recorded as having been in Britain as the wife of the governor of the period. Nonetheless, while only she is certain to have been in Britain, others' presence can be assumed since it was normal, as shown earlier, for these women to accompany their husbands to their provincial postings, and even to areas of conflict. By law Roman officials in the provinces were forbidden to marry local women.

The wife of the first governor was Pomponia Graecina whose husband, Aulus Plautius, led the Claudian invasion. He established the army fortress at Colchester, and for the next four years pacified much of the area formerly dominated by the Catuvellauni tribe. He returned to Rome in AD 47, when he was awarded an *ovatio*. Plautius' family had for a time been connected by marriage to Claudius through Claudius' first wife, Plautia Urgulanilla, and his brother-in-law was said to be a close friend of the emperor. Plautius himself had held the consulship in AD 29. His sister, Plautia, was the mother of P. Petronius Turpilianus, a later governor of Britain from AD 61 to 63.

According to Tacitus, Pomponia Graecina was a 'distinguished lady'. The daughter of a former consul of AD 16, C. Pomponius Graecinus, she had moved in the highest and most privileged circles of society in the capital, yet her later life at Rome was marked by suspicion and sadness. She was deeply affected by the violent death of a member of the royal family who was a friend and perhaps a distant relative – Julia, the daughter of Drusus and granddaughter of the emperor Tiberius. The murder, generally taken to have occurred in AD 43, had been engineered by the empress Messalina, third wife of Claudius. As a result, for the next 40 years Pomponia lived a life of melancholy and appeared only in mourning clothes. This apparently protected her from further treacheries during Claudius' reign and later brought honour to her memory. But perhaps her unusual behaviour attracted the attention of her detractors for in AD 57, in the reign of Nero, she was charged with having practised a foreign religion, an *externa superstitio*. In accordance with custom she then was subjected to trial by her husband in the presence of kinfolk. She was acquitted, but spent the rest of her long life, Tacitus relates, '...with a heart ever sorrowful'.[4]

More is known about another 'first lady' because her daughter married the historian, Tacitus, who wrote a biography of his father-in-law. Domitia Decidiana, daughter of T. Domitius Decidius, a *novus homo* from Narbonne,[5] was the wife of Cn. Julius Agricola, governor of Britain from 78 to 84. Agricola had previously been in the province as a young military tribune with Suetonius Paulinus in 60/61, when the Twentieth Legion earned the title of *Valeria Victrix* for its part in the invasion of Anglesey and later the suppression of the Boudiccan revolt. In 69, the 'year of the four emperors', Agricola took the side of Vespasian, which no doubt improved his prospects for promotion. He was back in Britain as Legionary Legate of the Twentieth from 71 to 73. Domitia was probably with him during that period of service because it is known that she had accompanied him to Asia some years before, around 63, when he was quaestor. It is likely that they were married in the period between his first tour of duty in Britain and his departure for Asia. She certainly accompanied him on his third appointment in Britain, when he became governor in 78 after his consulship in 77.

They appear to have had a happy marriage, despite the disappointment of the death of two sons, one born soon after the marriage, the other born in Britain. A daughter, born during the stint in Asia, survived. Tacitus says that Agricola coped with the calamity of the loss 'neither with ostentatious fortitude displayed by many brave men nor, on the other hand, with womanish tears and grief', finding solace, instead, in war. It is interesting that the historian records nothing of Domitia's grief at losing two sons. Her life in Britain must have at times been very lonely without her daughter (who had married Tacitus in 77), and often without her husband's company. It is possible that she did go with him on at least one of the seven vigorous campaigns he waged against the tribes of north Wales and Scotland. He was recalled by Domitian in 84.[6]

The wives of six other governors are known. These include Domitia Vettilla, wife of the patrician L. Neratius Marcellus, who was a friend of the Younger Pliny, and governor of Britain from *c.*101 to 103. Domitia Vettilla was well qualified for the job of governor's wife, being the daughter of L. Domitius Apollinaris, consul in 97 and a governor of Lycia-Pamphylia, and granddaughter of P. Anteius Rufus, consul in the reign of Claudius and twice a provincial governor. Domitia Vettilla was herself a member of what has been referred to as the 'power set' at Rome in the reign of

Domitian, and her husband, Neratius, became consul in 95. He evidently did not lose imperial favour when his patron was assassinated in 96, and was appointed governor of Britain *c*.101 by Trajan. It has been suggested that the appointment of Neratius was to enable a land survey of Britain in order to review tax revenues in the province.[7]

We also have some information about the wife of M. Atilius Metilius Bradua, a patrician from the Cisalpina in northern Italy. Bradua was consul in 108, and governor of Britain some time after 111. He was most likely governor of one of the German provinces before his appointment in Britain, following the footsteps of his uncle P. Metilius Nepos who had been consul in 91 and a governor of Britain in 98. His wife's name was probably Caucidia Tertulla. A son became consul before 150, and later proconsul of Africa, and their daughter married Ap. Annius Gallus, who was consul around 139. The daughter of that couple was the polyonymous Appia Annia Regilla Atilia Caucidia Tertulla, who became wife of one of the richest and most influential Greeks of the second century, T. Claudius Atticus Herodes – friend to three successive emperors, Hadrian, Antoninus Pius and Marcus Aurelius. It was to the memory of his wife, that is, the granddaughter of our Bradua and his wife, that Herodes Atticus built the famous Odeon at Athens.[8]

Bradua's likely successor was Q. Pompeius Falco (gov. *c*.118), whose wife, Sosia Polla, like Domitia Vettilla, wife of Neratius, had an impeccable lineage entirely appropriate for the consort of a provincial governor. She was the daughter of a former consul and provincial governor, Q. Sosius Senecio, and the granddaughter of the distinguished and cultivated Sex. Julius Frontinus, consul *c*.72 and also governor of Britain 73/74–77. Her husband, Falco, is known to have sought advice from Pliny the Younger when as a young man he was a Tribune of the Plebs. In time he became a highly experienced soldier and governor, having successive commands in Lycia-Pamphylia, Judaea and Moesia Inferior before reaching the consulship *c*.108. After Britain, his final posting was as proconsul of Asia. Sosia Polla's father may have been of Cilician origin, and Falco himself seems to have links with that part of the empire. Sosia Polla accompanied her husband on his last appointment. It is possible that she died in Asia, deprived of the leisured retirement enjoyed by her husband who was by this time, at least, a member of the emperor Hadrian's circle. Their son, himself a *comes* of Marcus Aurelius, became consul in 149 and later held a proconsular appointment.[9]

Novia Crispina, wife of the governor of Britain *c*.173–76, Q. Antistius Adventus Postumius Aquilinus, was also the daughter of a provincial administrator. Her father, L. Novius Crispinus Martialis Saturninus, had been legate of III *Augusta* and effectively governor in Numidia from 147 to 149. He became consul around 150. It may have been in Africa that Novia Crispina first met her future husband, a native of Thibilis. Her marriage to the *novus homo* Antistius no doubt advanced her husband's career, for he rose to be governor of Arabia *c*.164, and consul in 166 or 167. Novia Crispina accompanied him to Arabia, so she may well have gone with him then to Germany, and to Britain nine years later. Their son, L. Antistius Burrus, became consul in 181, and at some time later married into the imperial family, his wife being Vibia Aurelia Sabina, youngest child of Marcus Aurelius. This imperial favour was cut short when Burrus was assassinated by his brother-in-law, the emperor Commodus, c.189.[10]

Another governor's wife whose son suffered death possibly for his opposition to the emperor was Modestiana, wife of Caerellius Priscus who was governor c.178–80. Like other governors before him, Caerellius was an experienced general and administrator. The order of his appointments is not certain, but it is known that he had been consul around 172, governor of Thrace and Raetia, and that his appointment to Britain had been preceded by a posting to Germania Superior. Modestiana, a lady perhaps of provincial African origin, went to Germany with her husband and son; a daughter, Caerellia Germanilla, was probably born there (an assumption based on her name). The son, Caerellius Marcianus is usually identified with the Caerellius Macrinus put to death by Septimius Severus in 197 and may have been associated in some way with a plot to depose the emperor. The year before, Clodius Albinus, governor of Britain, had been saluted Augustus by the army and crossed to Gaul in the hope of raising a larger force to secure the throne. The young Caerellius was among many aristocrats murdered at this time. The fate of his parents is unknown.[11]

The wife of one further governor is known: Flavia Titiana, married to P. Helvius Pertinax, a future emperor. Pertinax himself was of lowly birth, the son of a freedman, but had risen through the ranks by way of ability and influential friends. After early military service which brought him twice to Britain, he began a procuratorial career in Italy c.168, and was adlected to the senate c.170. He rose to the consulship c.175 following some outstanding military victories in northern Italy and further east. During the reign of Commodus, around 185, he held the position of governor of Britain, putting down a mutiny in the legions and punishing offenders with great severity. He eventually asked Commodus to relieve him of his position ostensibly because of the hostility from the soldiers generated by his maintenance of discipline. On the assassination of the emperor in 193, Pertinax was proclaimed Augustus by the Praetorian Prefect. He survived for three months, only to be murdered by the same praetorians who had previously elevated him.

Flavia Titiana was not spared further plots and treachery following the death of her husband. A member of the nobility and the daughter of T. Flavius Claudius Sulpicianus, a former consul and governor of an imperial province, she now saw her father murdered on the orders of Septimius Severus and her son, also named P. Helvius Pertinax, consul in 212, assassinated by Caracalla. Flavia was said to have been a woman of culture, spending evenings with her husband and friends in literary discussions. Yet she was not, according to ancient sources, a model empress or devoted wife, and made no secret of her passion for a lyre-player at the imperial court. One might imagine that any sojourn in Britain as wife of the governor would have been among the less traumatic periods in her tumultuous life.[12]

The governor of Britain was supported from quite early in the life of the province by the *legatus iuridicus*, a man of the senatorial class with the rank of praetor. He took on many of the legal responsibilities of the governor, since the governor himself was often away on military campaign. The wife of one of these officials is known: Vitellia Rufilla, married to C. Salvius Liberalis Nonius Bassus. He was appointed *iuridicus c*.79 either by the emperor Vespasian or his son, Titus, during Agricola's term as governor. Salvius Liberalis was member of the circle of the Younger Pliny and a noted lawyer with, it has been suggested, 'a rather flexible attitude to senatorial corruption'. He may have been the first *legatus iuridicus* to have been appointed in the province; perhaps even at this early date he was based in London, as the position was a non-military one, though initially given to men with military experience. After his term in Britain he was posted as proconsul to Macedonia, and was consul around 85. He appears to have been banished by Domitian, returning to the political scene after the emperor's death. He was then appointed as proconsul of Asia, but was excused. About Vitellia Rufilla a little is known. She was the daughter of C. Vitellius who was probably a member, if not a senior member, of one of the four most powerful families of the latter half of the first century: the Petronii, Pomponii, Plautii and Vitellii. Vitellia Rufilla was *flamen* of an imperial cult at Urbs Salvia in Picenum, her husband's place of origin, where his family were great patrons of the town: an amphitheatre there was dedicated by his cousin, the cousin's wife and mother. Vitellia Rufilla and Salvius Liberalis had a son, C. Salvius Vitellianus, whose military career probably began in Macedonia under his father.[13]

Legionary legates also held the rank of a praetor. They were usually men around 35 years of age, on their first major command, and looking for the opportunity to demonstrate their talents and be promoted to senior provincial appointments. The wives of four legionary legates from Britannia of the first and second centuries are known, three of them by name.

Sergia Paulla is the earliest, the wife of one of Vespasian's officers, C. Caristanius Ser. Fronto, who may have been legate of IX *Hispania* under Frontinus and later Agricola. Fronto was an equestrian, from a Roman colonist family at Antioch in Pisidia, but was promoted to senatorial status for his support of Vespasian in 69. He was in Britain from 76 to 79, became governor of Lycia-Pamphilia *c*.81, and gained the ultimate recognition with a consulship in 90. He and his wife had two sons. Sergia Paulla came from a recently elevated senatorial family also from Antioch. Her father had been proconsul of Cyprus at the time of Claudius, and her brother was consul *c*.70.[14]

The name of the second is found on an altar at York. The inscription has been dated to around 135,[15] and reads: 'To the goddess Fortune, Sosia Iuncina (wife) of Quintus Antonius Isauricus, imperial (legionary) legate, (set this up)'. Isauricus was almost certainly a descendant of the aristocratic Servilius Vatia Isauricus (consul 79 BC) who made his name fighting against mountain bandits and pirates when proconsul of Cilicia in the late Republic. Sosia Iuncina was herself well-born, and probably connected to the Q. Sosius Senecio who married the daughter of Frontinus (governor 73/74–78), and to Sosia Polla who married Q. Pompeius Falco (governor *c*.118), discussed above. It is interesting to speculate what might have prompted this young woman to set up an altar to a goddess favoured by both the military and civilians. In all likelihood her husband was in charge of *Legio* VI *Victrix*, now based at York since the building of Hadrian's Wall. He may have been involved in some dangerous operation from which he escaped unharmed – trouble with the Brigantes provides a believable scenario, if completely unprovable as the sources for the period in Britain are inconclusive.[16] More prosaically, E. Birley suggests that the altar was a dedication at public baths in York, and that it indicates the existence there of facilities for females as well as males. Yet Fortuna, from the early days of the Republic, was also a goddess of fertility. There was a temple complex to Fortuna Primigenia at Praeneste (modern Palestrina), near Rome, where a dedication by a woman 'in gratitude for ... giving birth' has been found.[17] A desire for children or thanks for the birth of a child is thus another possibility. Whatever the purpose of the inscription, Sosia Iuncina's husband survived his term in Britain to become consul *c.*143.

Our third wife of a legionary legate is the generously named Stertina Cocceia Bassula Venecia Aeliana, wife of Q. Camurius Lem. Numisius Junior, commander of *Legio* VI *Victrix* in the mid-150s. He was from a family probably ennobled at the time of Nero. It seems clear that he had the confidence of the emperor Antoninus Pius, since this was his second legionary command, and it has been suggested that his appointment reflected the difficult military situation in Britain at the time, a situation confirmed by a 'subdued Britannia' depicted on coins issued 154–55. In view of his earlier legionary appointment, he would have been around 40 years old when he was in Britain. Numisius Junior was rewarded with the consulship in 161. Stertina, perhaps of African origin, was the granddaughter of L. Stertinius Noricus, consul in 113. The couple had one or possibly two sons, and a daughter.[18]

Tertullian, the early Christian writer, is the source of information on the (unnamed) wife of one other legate of the Sixth Legion at York some time after Numisius Junior. Claudius [Lucius] Hieronymianus had been given the command perhaps in the 170s.[19] He later became proconsul in Africa, and his final posting was as a governor of Cappadocia. In York, his devotion to Serapis, a deity interpreted as Saturn and associated with the cult of Mithras, had been apparent from a finely wrought inscription in which he dedicated to Serapis a temple which he himself had provided. He was evidently a man of wealth as well as piety. However his wife did not come to share his beliefs, and at some time converted to Christianity. (It is possible that she first came into contact with Christians in Britain: there were numbers of Christians in Gaul by this time. Conversion in Africa or Cappadocia is more likely.) Greatly angered by her conversion, Hieronymianus subjected the Christians of Cappadocia to considerable cruelty. He was soon to reap his reward, being struck down by the plague; but although he was in great agony he would not allow his plight to be made known in case the Christians should rejoice at his fate. He came to regret his actions and, apparently drawn to the religion of those whom he had previously persecuted, died 'almost a Christian' (*paene Christianus decessit*). We are told that his wife and household, presumably including his children, escaped the plague.[20]

That children accompanied their parents from the upper classes, both senatorial and equestrian, on army postings from an early period in the life of the province is certain. Among the finds from the late first/early second century site of Vindolanda in the north of Britain is children's footwear; and a child is referred to in a communication between the wives of two cohort commanders, men of equestrian rank commanding auxiliary units in the Vindolanda area prior to the construction of Hadrian's Wall. The two women are of particular interest because they are known not from inscriptions or the work of the historians, but from the intimate and very personal medium of the handwritten letter. The first, Sulpicia Lepidina, was wife of Flavius Cerialis, commander of the Ninth Cohort of Batavians, an auxiliary unit at Vindolanda. She was on good terms with Claudia Severa, wife of the commander of a cavalry unit based at Briga (perhaps Kirkbride), C. Aelius Brocchus. Severa's letter to Lepidina invites her friend to her birthday party. Another letter, which came to light in an excavation some years later, is from a centurion, apologising to Lepidina for not getting the presents from London that she has asked him to get on a recent trip there. It is very tempting to conclude that the two letters refer to the same event, Severa's birthday, and that the centurion would have received a stern rebuke from the commander's wife for failing to carry out his errand at the early second-century equivalent of Harrods![21] The presence of children at Vindolanda at the time of the first letter is confirmed by Severa's sending greetings to Lepidina from her husband and her little son.

But some children did not survive to move on to the next posting or to return to their homeland. There is a sad story related on a tombstone, probably of late second century date, from Chesters along Hadrian's Wall, in which, unlike the case of Agricola and his wife, both parents are recorded as mourning their loss. It reads, 'Sacred to the spirits of the departed (and) to Fabia Honorata: Fabius Honoratus, tribune of the First Cohort of Vangiones, and Aurelia Eglectiane made this for their most sweet daughter'. One can imagine the distress of this couple, far removed from home and the comfort of close kin. Fabius Honoratus was the commander of an equestrian cohort. The original unit had been raised in Upper Germany and had come to Britain with Cerialis in 71. Of Aurelia Eglectiane we know virtually nothing, other than that she was a mother who had lost a dearly loved child.[22]

The wife of another tribune of a cohort is known from two inscriptions. From the first, a tombstone erected by Julia Lucilla, it appears that her husband Rufinus began his career as the prefect of the First Cohort Augusta Praetoria Lusitanorum in Egypt, and then became prefect of the Second Cohort Breucorum, based in Mauretania. He went to Italy, where he held two civil positions. He was equestrian deputy to the senatorial *praefectus alimentorum* who organised public funds to give food to children of the poor, and this post also included acting as sub-curator of one of the great road systems of Rome, in this case the Via Flaminia; he also held the post of deputy to the curator of public works. At some time he married Julia Lucilla, a senator's daughter who would have lost her rank on marriage to an *eques*. Finally he was appointed Tribune of the First Cohort of Vardulli, a unit first raised in Spain, but based in Britain at High Rochester in the third century.

Rufinus' move to Britain with his household may have prompted his Greek freedman, Eutychus, to dedicate the second inscription, an altar to Silvanus Pantheus, for the welfare of the tribune and his wife in gratitude for their having arrived safely at their destination. The deity chosen was an old Roman god, given a Greek epithet. For a new arrival hoping for divine protection in the untamed countryside of northern Britain, Silvanus Πανθειος would be a good god to invoke, covering all possible deities associated with Silvanus who himself was identified with foreign (barbarian) gods found in the wilds.[23] Eutychus may have hoped to cast a wide net: other visitors to Britain had done the same.[24] Whatever the reason, the welfare of his master and mistress was preserved for at least a time. But Rufinus did not live to reach the highest rank for an equestrian officer or become a procurator since he died in Britain, still tribune, at the age of 48. Julia Lucilla probably returned to Rome. As a military widow there would be nothing to keep her at High Rochester, and if she were in her father's *patria potestas* or that of another agnate male relative, she would presumably have been restored to her senatorial status – hence her reference to her rank as *c(larissima) f(emina)*.

The army could be the means of a man's progressing to a higher census rank, by way of the centurionate. These men were the leaders of the centuries into which military cohorts were divided. The most senior was the *primus pilus*, a man of immense importance in the running of the legion, with the capacity to rise to camp prefect and, from the time of Claudius, even to procurator. The position of *primus pilus bis* (appointed twice) was highly coveted because it could advance a centurion to equestrian status. It was the ultimate prize, the attaining of which allowed a man to retire with enhanced wealth and standing, which in turn affected the status of his descendants. The appointment as *primus pilus* was also a matter of great family pride, as evidenced by a tombstone from Chesterholm to one Cornelius Victor, *singularis consularis*, whose wife in setting it up records that her husband was the son of a *primus pilus*.[25]

From early in the Imperial period, another official of equestrian rank appeared in the provinces, the procurator. He was appointed by the emperor and had military experience, but his duties were primarily non-military. The procurator was in charge of the collection of revenues in an imperial province, and he paid the soldiers in the army.[26] In Britain, he probably had the oversight of the properties of the Emperor (the so-called 'imperial estates') – mines, especially of gold, and forests and factories – and later the mint which was established for a time in London. The inscriptions from Britain suggest that the post came to include maintenance of public property, such as work on the procuratorial offices in Bath and also the rebuilding of the fort at Risingham, an establishment north of the Wall the maintenance of which may have been seen as necessary to protect nearby coal and iron mines. Most importantly this man was responsible directly to the emperor, and so at times could be seriously in conflict with the governor and could act as a kind of spy on him, reporting his actions to their imperial master. Decianus Catus, the first known procurator in Britain,[27] appointed *c.*58, was the most notorious. He is generally seen as precipitating the Boudiccan revolt when he pressed the provincials to repay the supposed 'loans' Claudius and others had given to friendly native leaders. He was no ally of the then governor, Suetonius Paulinus, but was the object of even greater hostility to the British population for his rapacity and for his part in the outrageous treatment of Boudicca and her daughters.[28]

Decianus' successor was Classicianus, who came with his wife Julia Pacata Indiana to Britain *c.*61. The pair is known from the splendid tomb in London set up by Julia to her husband (Plate II). It reads: 'To the spirits of the departed (and) of Gaius Julius Alpinus Classicianus, son of Gaius, of the Fabian voting tribe . . . procurator of the province of Britain; his wife, Julia Pacata I[ndiana], daughter of Indus, set this up.'

Plate II Tombstone of Julius Classicianus (British Museum).

Classicianus was less confrontationist than his predecessor, and it was probably on his report back to Nero that Suetonius Paulinus was recalled to Rome, to be replaced as governor by the more conciliatory P. Petronius Turpillianus. Julia Pacata was the daughter of Julius Indus, a Gallic (Treveran) aristocrat who, as a young man at odds with one of the rebel leaders, had sided with Rome in a revolt by the Treveri in AD 21. No doubt this improved his stocks with the emperor at the time, Tiberius, as he was honoured by the naming of the *ala Indiana*. Classicianus, who himself was a Treveran and a Roman citizen, died in office, probably before the death of Nero in 69. Julia Pacata would have returned to Gaul, or even gone to Rome. She would be unlikely to have met a suitable second husband in London in the first century AD, although obviously a woman of wealth and of equestrian rank.[29]

Albucia Candida, wife of C. Valerius Claudius Pansa who was procurator in Britain some time during the reign of Antoninus Pius (136–61), was also a woman of means. Her name occurs on an inscription which gives some detail of her husband's career. Pansa seems to have joined in the ranks as an equestrian, rising from centurion to *primus pilus bis*, and then to the procuratorship of Britannia. Nothing else is known of his stint in Britain but, from the inscription which was found in his home town of Novaria in Cisalpine Gaul, it seems that in the later part of his career the couple enjoyed both wealth and status. He indicates that he restored and dedicated baths (presumably in Cisalpine Gaul) which had been destroyed by fire, and that 200,000 sesterces of the cost he had contributed from a legacy which his wife had left to the state; at the beginning of the inscription Pansa proudly records his position as a *flamen* of the cult of the Divine Hadrian. Albucia Candida herself was probably descendent from C. Albucius Silus, a noted scholar and rhetor of the Augustan period.[30]

Around half a century later, one of the most flamboyant of all procurators' wives appeared on the scene: Julia Soaemias Bassiana, sister of an empress and mother of a future emperor. The daughter of C. Julius Avitus, a Syrian aristocrat, and Julia Maesa, she had been married beneath her station to the equestrian Sextus Varius Marcellus, who became procurator of Britain *c.*197. The appointment would have been due to his connection through his wife with her brother-in-law, the emperor Septimius Severus. He may have been sent to Britain to clean up after the revolt of Albinus in 196; this would include confiscation of the property of any supporters of Albinus, and it has been suggested that the imperial estates were added to at this time.[31] Varius was obviously competent and his marriage to Julia Soaemias advantageous because he was promoted to the senate some time after 204, and then to the governorship of Numidia. Julia Soaemias did not appear to have suffered greatly during her demotion to equestrian rank. She was prominent at Rome, and in the Secular Games of 204 had been honoured as chief equestrian matron. Her great purpose in life was to see her son, Elagabalus, made emperor, and to this end she claimed (falsely) that he was the son of Caracalla, the elder of the two sons of Septimius Severus who had become sole emperor after he murdered his brother and co-emperor, Geta. Julia Soaemias and her mother, Julia Maesa, schemed to have Elagabalus elevated. This was achieved in 218 with the defeat of the then emperor, Macrinus, in battle, and his subsequent execution. Their success was short-lived, however, for in 222 both Elagabalus and his mother were murdered in a palace intrigue.[32]

The governor of a province had an administrative staff, his *officium*, made up of men co-opted from the legions and the auxiliaries. The headquarters were under the control of a senior centurion (*princeps praetorii*), and the staff themselves headed by senior legionaries, the *cornicularii*. By the 60s, London seems to have become established as the commercial and financial centre of the province, and the army headquarters and provincial administration probably moved there from Colchester early in the second century. Secondment to the governor's staff would be seen as a big improvement on frontier life and keeping the peace with the fierce tribes of Wales and Scotland. These men were record keepers and archivists, secretaries and librarians, had police and escort duties, and also took on other less important but essential tasks in the administration. Some were legionaries with rank, others ordinary soldiers with particular skills.[33]

The wife of one centurion who may have been seconded to headquarters is recorded, and she herself was probably a Roman citizen, with a praenomen popular in Africa: Januaria Martina set up a tombstone in London to her husband, Vivius Marcianus, centurion of the Second Legion *Augusta*.[34] Since the Second Legion is not known to have been based in London during an undivided Roman Britain, it is likely that, if the date of the inscriptions is prior to the Severan division, Marcianus had been drafted to the governor's headquarters in some administrative capacity. The depiction on the tombstone of a soldier holding a scroll in his left hand supports this view. On the other hand, if the date is after the Severan division, he may have been part of the garrison of London formed from II *Augusta* and XX *Valeria Victrix*. Another possibility is that, on his retirement he went to London where he subsequently died. In any case, his tombstone in London would reinforce the fact that, while governors and senior officers would normally have left the province of their posting following their term of service, ordinary soldiers and even centurions rarely returned to their homeland on discharge. After 25 years of service, perhaps most of it in the one province and even (in the later empire) at the one location, their roots would have been firmly fixed where wife and family were.

The sister of a *cornicularius* based along Hadrian's Wall is identified on a tombstone found at Great Chesters: 'To the spirits of the departed (and) to Aelius Mercurialis, *cornicularius*, his sister Vacia set this up.' The stone, now lost, has a portrait of a woman above the inscription. Perhaps this is a representation of Vacia, her own spirit accompanying her brother's on his journey to the Otherworld.[35] One wonders why it was a sister who erected the stone. Did Aelius Mercurialis have no other family to mourn him? Was his sister actually with him in the wilds of northern Britain?

So far this study has examined Roman women mainly from the middle and upper classes who had an association with Britain. For the lower classes, it is difficult to be certain that the women were Roman, and not British or Romano-British. Even so, some Roman women may be presumed. Daughters of veterans would have been citizens, as, for example, Julia Sempronia, who set up a tombstone to her father, a veteran of the Sixth Legion *Victrix*, at Lincoln. This is a somewhat surprising location, since the Sixth had not been based at Lincoln, having spent the early part of its tour of duty in Britain building the Wall and then later being based at York. A possible explanation is that Gaius Julius Calenus chose not to return to his homeland in Gaul, preferring instead to settle down after discharge with other veterans in the *colonia* of Lincoln, where he raised a daughter. His marriage could have taken place during his term of military service, if the inscription dates to after the Severan reforms.[36]

A second instance of a daughter's setting up a memorial to her father occurs at Great Chesters. There, Novellia Justina dedicated a tombstone to Novellius Lanuccus, a Roman citizen, who died at the age of 70. The location of this tombstone is also curious, since it would seem unlikely that an elderly man would choose to live on the edge of civilisation in Britain, away from the creature comforts offered in a town. He may, however, have been a veteran, happy to live out his days where he had as a soldier given his service, then married and raised a family.[37]

There are three inscriptions which make it clear that the women mentioned are citizens. From Dorchester in Dorset is a Purbeck marble tombstone with the inscription, '... for Carinus, a citizen of Rome, aged 50; Rufinus and Carina and Avita, his children, and Romana, his wife, had this set up'. Avita and Carina, at least, were Romans as daughters of a citizen, though the status of his wife is unclear. York was the provenance of a stone coffin dedicated to Valerius Theodorianus by his mother, Emilia Theodora. They had come from the town of Nomentum, north-east of Rome, a town whose inhabitants had, since the early Republic, been Roman citizens. It is known that Nomentum, originally a Sabine town, was noted for its wine: perhaps here we have relics of a Roman civilian merchant class, capitalising on trade opportunities opened up by the Occupation. Roman Legionaries at York would be a ready market for Italian wine.[38] And from Lincoln is mention of Volusia Faustina, a citizen of the Roman *colonia* of Lindum (*civis Lindensis*). The fact that her husband, Aurelius Senecio, was a councillor (*decurio*), suggests that he, too, had become a Roman citizen – by way of his municipal service. Their names reinforce their commitment to the ways of Rome. The tombstone is very elaborate, with a man and woman dressed in Roman attire depicted above the inscription, and the lettering very well formed. None of the people mentioned in these inscriptions has any obvious links with the military, and the carefully inscribed stones and stone coffin give the general feeling of wealth.

One further inscription is likely to have been a dedication by a Roman woman. It was found on an altar from Carrawburgh, 'To the Goddess, Mother of the Gods', by one Tranquila Severa on behalf of herself and her family. The dedication is to Cybele, first introduced into Rome during the Second Punic War, a deity of Asiatic origins; thus Tranquila is unlikely to have been British. Her presence at Carrawburgh suggests that she had some connection with the army. The date of the inscription is unknown, but it could be Severan, since it is known that Julia Domna, herself a Syrian, wife of Septimius Severus, was identified with and popularised Cybele.[39]

For the Roman women who came to Britain, even if they were the wives of governors, life could not have been easy, particularly in the early years of the province and on the frontiers. Nevertheless it is seen that the niceties of Roman life could be observed as far as conditions or class allowed. Social intercourse and shopping, the maintenance of family life, the observance of religious ritual and of the traditional rites of marriage, birth, death and burial all helped to inject some degree of Romanisation into this far-flung part of the empire; and the women who accompanied their men folk as wives, daughters or sisters made their own individual contributions.

British and 'foreign' women

As noted earlier, there are considerable difficulties in identifying Romano-British women because it cannot be known in many cases whether the women concerned were British but given Roman names, adopted Roman names to replace their British names, or whether they were in fact Roman women. Conversely, there can be no certainty that women with 'Celtic' names are native British women, although this is likely: the study of the names on the Bath *defixiones* notes that, in provinces which were Celtic speaking, fathers with 'Celtic' names were inclined to give Roman names to their sons; presumably this would apply to daughters also.[40]

This part of the analysis will focus on those women who seem to be British (either by their status or the names they have been given) and on two other categories of women who were also in Britain – those who may be classified as 'foreign', that is, coming from a part of the world other than the major Roman centres, and those who appear to have been slaves or ex-slaves. Indeed some overlap of these categories is inevitable. Many more women cannot be identified by origin: their names appear in inscriptions as wives, mothers or daughters of soldiers, but there is insufficient information to allow classification by place of birth.

The families of the local upper classes had, from the earliest decades of the Occupation, looked to Rome for their form of local government, the Latin language, luxury goods, and loans from Roman entrepreneurs to facilitate that lifestyle. Some British women appear to have embraced Romanisation, for their names appear amongst the local aristocracy, members of which achieved status and (if before 212) progress towards full Roman citizenship as a result of service as councillors in their local *decuriones*. They included Martiola, who was the daughter of a local senator at Penrith, Flavius Martius; and Aelia Severa, wife of Caecilius Rufus, a senator at York. There was also Claudia Rufina, a 'blue Briton' who, the late first century Roman epigrammist Martial tells us, became a social success at Rome, virtually indistinguishable from Roman or Greek ladies.[41]

Many of the women in Roman Britain known to us from inscriptions and literary sources were not Roman. For some, their British or European tribal origins were proclaimed on tombstones and dedications; for others, their Roman-sounding names tended to conceal servile origins; while for a few their status as freedwomen was a matter of pride, to be declared to the world.

There are around 150 names recorded on the lead tablets from the sacred spring at Bath, about one quarter of them women. Many of these are bland Latin names, found in all parts of the empire, but there are also women's names which have a Celtic etymology. It is presumed that they, at least, were local British women, rather than Roman, seeking the assistance of the goddess Sulis-Minerva and, in one case, the god Mercury. Names recorded include Aessicunia, Brigomalla, Cunsa, Docca, Enica, Locinna, Lovernisca, Oconea, Paltucca, Senila, Trinni, Veloriga, Venibelia and Velvinna. Their role in the religion of Roman Britain will be discussed in Chapter 7. The *defixiones* from the temple to Mercury at Uley have not proved so fertile a field, but some names have been deciphered, including Cunovinna and possibly Lugula.[42]

Some British women may be identified by their names or by their tribes. A certain example is that of Verecunda Rufilia, a tribeswoman of the tribe of the Dobunni, whose tombstone was put up by her husband, Excingus, at York. This is a particularly interesting case: the Dobunni were among the tribes who had submitted to Claudius in AD 43, and their long Romanisation is reflected in the name of the woman, although her husband saw fit also to record her tribal origins. Another inscription from York records the death of Ved[.]ic[..], a tribeswoman of the Cornovii.[43] In both cases it seems the women did not travel far from their tribal lands when they married.

Other less certain examples include Sulicena from Lasborough, Glos., who died at the age of 14, and whose name resembles the native deity Sulis; also Julia Belismicus, at Caerleon, who set up an altar with her husband Cornelius Castus to the wholly Roman military gods Fortuna and Bonus Eventus, yet she appears to have a British name. Similarly, at Birrens, in Dumfriesshire, a woman named Magunna dedicated an altar to Jupiter Dolichenus. Her name is possibly a feminine form of the Irish Maguno (= 'boy', 'slave'?) so she could have been the British wife or slave of a soldier from the Greek east, making a dedication to an eastern god favoured by the military. Then there is Tancorix, 'a woman (who) lived 60 years'. Her name brings to mind many others with the Celtic suffix -rix, used, like -us, for both males and females.[44]

There is also Grata, wife of Solinus and daughter of Dagobitus, whose tombstone was found in London; Dagobitus recalls another name with the same prefix, Dagvalda, of probable German-Celtic origin, while Solinus is found in an inscription in Wales and Sulinus is known at Bath and Cirencester. Grat(us) was a common name for a slave or freedman in Gallia Nabonensis. Grata could have been a native Briton, or from some part of western Europe.[45]

European and Asian women also came to Roman Britain, and some are known from inscriptions: for example, Rusonia Aventina who was a tribeswoman of the Mediomatrici, from the Mosel region of France; Carssouna, wife of Sacer son of Bruscus, who was a citizen of the Senones tribe around the River Seine; Titullinia Pussitta, a Raetian from central Europe; and the well-known Diodora, priestess of the cult of Hercules of Tyre, in the Levant. All these inscriptions were found at sites which had a military or veterans' presence, and one can only imagine the loneliness of these women at being transported half-way across the known world to the frontiers of Britain, and the problems of language and lack of home comforts. One wonders, too, how and why Diodora came to be at Corbridge. It is understandable that auxiliary soldiers brought their cults with them to the frontiers, but a cult priestess suggests a person of some status: perhaps she was the wife of an officer from the eastern part of the empire. The Hercules altar is inscribed in Greek.[46]

Slaves and freedwomen

While is likely that there were slaves in pre-Roman Britain, it is certain that the numbers increased with the coming of Rome, whether they were foreigners brought in by the Romans, or native Britons. We know the names of a number of freedwomen, but in most cases can only guess at their origins. Many of these women were freed by and then married their former owners, some at least living out the rest of their lives in connubial happiness, if one can believe the inscriptions.

The identity of very few female slaves is as yet known. From London comes an inscription of first century date: 'To the spirits of the departed (and) to Claudia Martina, aged 19; Anencletus, slave of the province (set this up) to his most devoted wife; she lies here.' Claudia Martina must also have been slave, and the 'marriage' a common law one, as slaves were not permitted to marry.[47] Another very recent discovery at London, a deed of sale dating to the late first or early second century, reads:

> Vegetus, assistant slave of Montanus the slave of the august Emperor, and sometime assistant slave of Iucundus, has bought and received by *mancipium* the girl Fortunata, or by whatever name she is known, by nationality a Diablintian, from Albicianus[...] for six hundred denarii. And that the girl in question is transferred in good health, that she is warranted not to be liable to wander or run away, but that if anyone lays claim to the girl in question or to any share in her, [...] in the wax tablet which he has written and sworn by the *genius* of the Emperor Caesar [...].
>
> (Tomlin 2003: 45)

This document is of great interest on several counts: it shows that the slaves of the emperor could 'own' slaves, and in turn they too could 'own' slaves although, technically, Fortunata was imperial property; the price paid is very high – about twice the annual salary of a Roman soldier in the legions, which suggests that in this early period slaves were scarce, and thus attracted a high price. Fortunata (her name surely given to her when she was enslaved) came from northern Gaul; her value was probably increased because she was healthy and docile.

This last is a timely reminder, when one looks at the sentiments expressed in a couple of the inscriptions for freedwomen, that as slaves such women had been regarded as property to be bought and sold.

Inscriptions will readily identify freedwomen because it was the Roman practice for freed slaves to be given the name of their former master, who then became their patron. In a couple of instances there is at least the semblance of affection between husband and wife: for example on the tombstone set up at Carvoran by her husband Aurelius Marcus for Aurelia Aia, '... his very pure wife who lived 33 years without blemish'; and another, from Caerleon, records that the monument to Julia Veneria was set up by 'Julius Alesander, her devoted husband, and Julius Belicianus, her son'. There is also evidence of family affection on a tombstone set up by one Tadia Exuperata, a 'devoted daughter' to her mother, Tadia Vallaunius, and her brother, Tadius Exuper(a)tus. The mother was evidently the British freedwoman of the father of the siblings, as all three carried his name.[48]

But a far greater number of inscriptions involving freedwomen are silent about any such bonds: examples include Julius Valens, a veteran from Caerleon who lived to the great age of 100, and his wife, Julia Secundina, who died aged 75; Aurelius Super and Aurelia Censorina, from York; Titus Tammonius Victor and Flavia Victorina, Silchester; Aurelius Pusinnus and Aurelia Eubia, Overborough, Lancs; Publius Vitalis and Publia Vicana, Cirencester; and Titus Flavius Natalis and Flavia Veldicca, Caerleon – who, from her name, may also have been a native Briton. In these inscriptions, no sentiment is expressed. What kind of marriages these were cannot be known, but one would like to think that even here it was the ties of affection that prompted the owners to free and then to marry their slave women. In the case of Flavius Hellius (a Greek) and Flavia Ingenua, from Lincoln, they both could well have been the slaves of the one master, and had married when freed.[49]

Finally, there is an inscription which positively identifies a freedwoman who may also in fact be a native Briton. It comes from the classical-style temple of Sulis Minerva at Bath: 'To the spirits of the departed; Gaius Calpurnius Receptus, priest of the goddess Sulis, lived 75 years. Calpurnia Trifosa, his freedwoman (and) wife, had set this up'. Here is a presumed Roman citizen, priest (*sacerdos*) at the temple of Minerva-Sulis, and his ex-slave wife, given along with her freedom her former master's name (Calpurnius = Calpurnia). But Trifosa? It sounds Latin. The name, however, comes from the Greek Τρυφωσα, which has the meaning of 'delicate', 'dainty' – or more appropriate for a female slave, 'voluptuous' or 'licentious'. It is possible, therefore, that Calpurnius had come from Rome to Britain, perhaps even to 'take the waters' at Bath, and had brought his slaves or at least one slave with him. He stayed on to become a priest of the cult, and then decided to free and marry his slave. On his death, his wife erected a tombstone to her husband. But while the whole scene is very Roman, it is Sulis, not her Roman equivalent, Minerva, or even Sulis-Minerva, who is recorded by Calpurnia in the inscription. Could she have actually been a native Briton, given a Romanised Greek slave name?[50]

The role of non-Roman women in Roman Britain is difficult to assess, as is their contribution to the changes that Britain underwent during the Occupation. In recent years the term 'creolisation' has been used, rather than 'Romanisation', and while it may not fit all situations, there is no doubt that the influx of people, both men and women, from all parts of the Roman empire contributed to a mix of population, religious practices, customs and *mores* which probably best suits that term. The Britain of the third century AD, especially in the towns, would be vastly different from that of the early first century. Whether this mix will show up in the skeletal evidence in future studies, especially those involving DNA, remains to be seen. What is certain is that, where native and foreign women became part of a new Romano-British culture, that is in the towns and military centres, the women themselves contributed to the 'creolisation' if not the Romanisation of the province. Some British women kept their tribal identity, and this perhaps indicates some pride in their origins. That more adopted Roman names and were recorded on inscriptions in the Roman manner suggests they and their families *saw themselves* as Roman, and their status as defined by Rome.[51]

Notes

1 The matter of centurions' wives is not absolutely settled. See Hassall 1999, n. 5.

2 See Sherwin-White 1973: 268–9.

3 For a comprehensive study of the army in Roman Britain, see Holder 1982; for all known Roman officials in Britain during the Occupation, see Birley 1981.

4 Sen. *Apoc.* 14.2; Tac. *Ann.* 13.32; Dio 60.30.2, 60.18.4; *FOS* 640, 537.

5 *FOS* 322. Raepsaet-Charlier (1987: 284) suggests she may have married Agricola prior to her to the elevation of her father.

6 See Tacitus: *Agricola* for a full account of Agricola's term as governor of Britain.

7 SHA *Had.* 18.1; *FOS* 333, 778, 258; Jones 1992: 169, 173, 175, 177; Frere 1987: 188. Birley (1981: 89–90) sees the appointment as 'unexpected' in view of Neratius Marcellus' apparent lack of overseas experience, and evidence that Trajan did not see Britain of strategic importance at this time. Even so, Marcellus himself was evidently close to the seat of power, and his brother, Neratius Priscus, was a member of Hadrian's council. Hadrian gave Marcellus a second consulship in the 120s.

8 *FOS* 66, 118, 202; Birley 1981: 92–4. Birley does not believe Bradua had any male heirs.

9 On Falco, see Pliny *Epist.* 1.23, 4.27, 7.22, 9.15 and Birley 1981: 95–100; and on Frontinus, Birley 1981: 69–72. For Sosia Polla, *FOS* 440, 632, 723.

10 So Birley 1981: 131. Frere 1987: 147 suggests dates of 175–8. On Novia Crispina, see *FOS* 577.

11 *FOS* 168, 554; SHA *Sev.* 13.6. The identity of this governor is not absolutely certain. See Birley 1981: 132–5.

12 On Pertinax, see SHA *Pertin*; for Flavia Titiana, *FOS* 383, SHA *Pertin.* 13.

13 Pliny: *Epist.* 2.11; Jones 1992: 189–90; *FOS* 49, 818, 846; Birley (1981: 211–13) suggests three different chronologies for Liberalis' career.

14 Birley 1981: 233–4, 214; Jones 1992: 176–7; *FOS* 702, but Raepsaet-Charlier dates the brother's consulship to as late as 78. On Claudius' policy of appointing Roman citizens from the provincials see Tac. *Ann.* 11.23–5.

15 Birley 1981: 247. This date should perhaps be a few years earlier or later, since Birley (1981: 250) also gives 135–8 as the dates for P. Mummius Sisenna Rutilianus' command of *Legio* VI.

16 For Isauricus (*cos.* 79 BC) see Magie 1950: 287–90; Isauricus (*legatus legionis*), Birley 1981: 247; Sosia Iuncina *FOS* 721, *RIB* 644. A possible incident involving the Brigantes is recorded in Pausanius 8.43.4.

17 *CIL* 14.2863: 'I, Orcevia, wife of Numerius, gave a gift to Fortuna Primigenia daughter of Jupiter, in gratitude for my giving birth' (*Orcevia Numeri nationu gratia Fortuna Diovo fileia Primigenia donum dedi*; Praenestine Latin was considered 'irregular'). Fortuna might also be interpreted as the goddess Fors Fortuna, which gave her a less certain reputation as the bringer of good fortune, but rather more subject to chance, either good or bad luck. See also Billington 1996.

18 Birley 1981: 254–6; *FOS* 735, 264. Coins, for example, *RIC* 3: 930.

19 Or even as late as the 190s. See Birley 1981: 263–5.

20 *RIB* 658; Tertullian *Ad Scap.* 3.4.

21 *Tab. Vindol.* 2.291; Birley 1997, 2002.

22 *RIB* 1482; Holder 1982: 123. See Chapter 7 for a discussion of her name.

23 *RIB* 1288: for this proposed sequence of appointments and reading of the tombstone (particularly II Breucorum), see Birley 1935, cf. Collingwood in *RIB* 1271 (I Breucorum). RIB 1271: Pantheus may have been connected here with the Greek god Pan, a common association, and also appropriate for a god of the wilds.

24 For example, *RIB* 88 (To the Italian, German, Gallic and British Mother Goddesses), 201 (Genius of the Place), 1583 (To Jupiter, Cocidius and to the Genius of this place), etc.

25 On centurions and the position of the *primus pilus* see Dobson: 1974. *RIB* 1713.

26 The standard work on the position of procurator is Pflaum: 1974.

27 *RIB* 179 (Bath), 1234 (Risingham). Birley (1981: 287) suggests that P. Graecinius P.f. Pub. Laco may have been the first procurator of Britain, on the basis of Dio 60.23.3.

28 For details of Decianus Catus' actions, and of the Boudiccan Revolt, see Tac. *Ann.* 14.31–7; *Agr.* 16.1–2; Dio 62.1–12.

29 *RIB* 12 – this reading given by Collingwood in *RIB*; however, a reconstruction by the British Museum reads '... IVLIA INDI FILIA PACATA I[NFELIX] VXOR'. See also Tac. *Ann.* 3.42; Frere 1987: 74. Another reading of this inscription has recently been suggested: Grasby and Tomlin 2002.

30 *CIL* 5.6513, 5.6514; Birley 1981: 295.

31 Wacher 2000: 101. The dates for Marcellus are debated: see Frere 1987: 155; cf. Birley 1981: 296–8.

32 *FOS* 460; SHA *Elag*; Frere 1987: 155.

33 On the *officium* see Hassall 1999 and Rankov 1999.

34 *RIB* 17.

35 *RIB* 1742.

36 *RIB* 252.

37 *RIB* 1743.

38 *RIB* 188; Kajanto 1982: 51, 182; *RIB* 677; Livy 8.14.3; Martial 1.105, 10.48; *RIB* 250.

39 *RIB*1539; on Cybele, Polybius 29.10–11, 15; Livy 29.10.4–8. This devotion is illustrated by a gold aureus of 205, the obverse portraying Julia Domna, and the reverse Cybele in a quadriga drawn by four lions: coin *BMC* 47.

40 Tomlin 1988: 97. *Tab. Sul.* 94 has an example of one Uricalus (presumably a Briton) whose sons are called Docilis (also a British name) and Decentius (a Roman name). Tomlin (1988: 227) argues that, after two centuries of Roman Occupation, 'Roman' and 'Celtic' names provided an enlarged pool of names on which to draw.

41 *RIB* 933 (there is some doubt about this person's status as a civilian: see note on inscription); *RIB* 683. A possible example is *RIB* 1561, but an alternative interpretation is that this person was a military *decurion* in charge of a cavalry unity. Martial 11.53.1 (*caeruleis Britannis*).

42 Tomlin 1988: 95–7 *et passim*; *Tab. Sul.* 98, 30, 95, 34, 59, 98, 61, 60, 98, 95, 53, 53, 2 and 4; Tomlin 1993b: 128.

43 *RIB* 621; Dio 60.20. *RIB* 639.

44 *RIB* 134, 318, 2099 and *CIIC* 272, *RIB* 908.

45 *RIB* 22; Dagvalda *RIB* 1667; Solinus *CIIC* 429, *RIB* 150, 151. Kajanto 1982: 18, 73.

46 *RIB* 163, 262, 984, 1129.
47 *RIB* 21.
48 *RIB* 1828 (see Chapter 7 on Religion for further discussion on this inscription); *RIB* 375, 369.
49 *RIB* 363, 670, 87, 612, 111, 358, 251.
50 *RIB* 155. Roman priests were normally priests for life; they were citizens and free-born (Beard 1990: 22–4, n. 2), the exception being the priests or *seviri* of the Imperial Cult. Gordon (1990: 243–5) proposes that Rome, having eliminated any priestly organisation with Conquest, deliberately created local élites from which priests of acceptable cults could be drawn, in the process of Romanisation. This would, however, be unlikely for Bath, because it was not an administrative centre; moreover, the temple at Bath was in classical style, and it can probably be assumed that the ritual there would be Roman. A less likely interpretation is that the inscription dates to after the citizenship decree of Caracalla, and that Calpurnius, a Romano-Briton (despite his *tria nomina*), was automatically a citizen.

A study of the *defixiones* from the spring at Bath shows that none of the dedications is to Minerva alone, and that most are to Sulis (Watts 1998: 116–17); and Tomlin (1988: 95) reports that there are no Roman citizens' names on the tablets. It is a common misconception that a person possessing the *tria nomina* was a always citizen.
51 See especially Hill 2001.

4

NUMBERS AND STATUS IN THE ROMAN PERIOD

Numbers: the silent minority in Romano-British cemeteries[1]

An examination of the remains in Romano-British cemeteries reveals a considerable imbalance in the numbers of males and females buried. This trend is marked from an early period and continues until the end of the Roman Occupation, with a couple of notable exceptions. It is proposed here that the disparity is due to the practice of selective infanticide and that, in those parts of Britain which were Romanised, until Christianity took hold very late in the Roman period between one and six out of ten females born were not allowed to survive.

The problems of sexing skeletal material, particularly that which has been cremated, are widely recognised.[2] In respect of the Romano-British burials from Skeleton Green, Puckeridge, while the 'uncertainty of the material' was noted, and it was shown that 84 per cent of the cremations were 'well fired', the sex of 94 per cent of the adult cremations was still given. This figure does seem rather confident. By comparison, in the more recent reports from King Harry Lane, Magiovinium, London Eastern and Westhampnett Bypass, the percentage of cremated remains sexed is about half that figure or less (Table 4.1). It may be that, as suggested for the Westhampnett Iron Age cremations, the bias reflects the ease of identifying females;[3] many of the unsexed adults could well have been males. There does seem to be some justification for omitting cremations from the discussion as they constitute only 5 per cent of the sexed burials studied here; if this is done, the percentage of males and females varies only slightly.

A further problem was raised earlier regarding the possibility that the populations of some burial sites may not present a true demographic picture. This should be taken into account when interpreting the data given.

Initially, 30 cemeteries[4] from a wide area of Roman Britain were examined (Table 4.2). Many are from the fourth century, but some are earlier, and at least five extend beyond the period of Roman Occupation. They are a mix of inhumations and cremations with some cemeteries having both burial rites, and vary in size from very large to very small. A common feature is that at least a reasonable proportion, around 40 per cent, of the individuals identified as adults could be sexed.

Most were single-site cemeteries, but there were exceptions. Ashton had a formal fourth century cemetery and other burials of varying dates found in the

Table 4.1 Sexed cremations in Iron Age and Romano-British cemeteries

Cemetery	Number cremations	Number sexed	% sexed	Males	Females
Chichester, Westhampnett IA	121	26	26	4	22
Chichester, Westhampnett Roman	34	11	41	4	7
London Eastern	123	56	46	17	39
Magiovinium	44	2	5	1	?1
Puckeridge, Skeleton Green	84	79	94	49	44
Verulamium, King Harry Lane IA	472	97	35	72	25

back-yards of domestic or industrial blocks. These two sets of burials are treated separately. At Baldock, burials from the Roman period comprised three distinct organised groups in addition to a special burial (the cremation of a child with multiple grave goods), a set of four late disposals in wells, other presumably discrete adult burials within the area of settlement, and a large number of neonates or infants found near Roman buildings. These are all treated as one site. The Puckeridge data were made up of burials at Skeleton Green and at two sites on the Puckeridge Bypass. The Poundbury burials at Dorchester were separated into those in the main cemetery and those termed 'Other' in this study, including the late Roman outlying inhumations, those from Site C, and the Eastern and Northern Peripheral Burial Groups. The burials from Shepton Mallet came from three small cemeteries east of Fosse Way.

The cemetery at Guilden Morden, dating from the early first century AD to fourth century, was not included in the study, despite the fact that the number of known burials was around 125. Only 23 were examined and 21 sexed, and the results (M = 10; F = 11) recorded in the first report on the site. The second report did not give any analysis of the later skeletal material found (52 inhumations and 50 cremations). The virtually equal numbers of male and female burials recorded in the first report may well be significant, if it were possible to determine whether they were from an earlier or later part of the cemetery. It is to be regretted that this information was not given.[5]

It will be noted that, in the cemeteries analysed, the percentage of males and females overall is M = 57 per cent, F = 43 per cent. These figures do not change if small cemeteries with fewer than 30 sexed burials[6] are eliminated from the analysis; nor when cemeteries with fewer than 50 per cent of burials sexed[7] are removed. But while not 50 per cent of the total, there were still 51 burials able to be sexed at the Derby cemetery, and it is thought that this number is sufficient for the site to be included. For the following discussion, analysis of the populations of the smaller cemeteries will generally be avoided. Of the remaining cemeteries analysed in Table 4.2 if 50 per cent or more of burials are able to be sexed, and/or that figure equates to 30 or over, it is felt that the sample is sufficiently large to give some indicator of the distribution of the sexes.

Table 4.2 Sexed burials in Romano-British cemeteries

Site	Date	Approx. number dated burials	No. sexed	% of identifiable adults sexed [a]	No. of M/?M and % of sexed adults	No. of F/?F and % of sexed adults	Unsexed adults identified	Adolescents/children/infants[b] neonates identified
Ancaster[#][+]	C4	243	212	87	129/61	83/39	31	17
Ashton (backyard)[#]*	C2–late C4	106 (#105; *1)	53	87	36/68	17/32	8	A 3; C 4; I 18; N 21
Ashton (formal)[#][+]	Mid-late C4	170	117	85	81/69	36/31	20	A 3; C 21; I 5; N 4
Baldock (R)[#]*	Late C1–late C4+	95 (#74; *21)	10	48	7/70	3/30	13	I 14; N 9
Bletsoe[#][+]	Mid C4–?early C5	56	46	98	25/54	21/46	1	C 2; I/N 6
Bradley Hill[#][+]	C4–early C5	55	20	100	10/50	10/50	0	C 4; I 19; N 5
Cannington[#][+]	C4–C7	542	324	84	127/39	197/61	63	A/C 92; I 12; N 42
Chichester, Westhampnett (R)*	c.70–150	34	11	41	4/36	7/64	16	5
Chilmark, Eyewell Farm[#]	Late C4	7	6	100	3/50	3/50	—	I 1
Cirencester, Bath Gate[#]*	C3–C5	365 (#362; *3)	303	85	210/69	93/31	53	A 13; C 27; I 1; N 14
Colchester, Butt Road Period I[#]*	c.270–320/40	63 (#58; *5)	18	45	11/61	7/39	22	A 1; C 4
Colchester, Butt Road Period II[#][+]	320/40–early C5	669	310	71	170/55	140/45	129	A/C 100; I/N 6
Derby, Racecourse Road[#]*	Late C1–C3	161 (#69; *92)	50	38	31/62	19/38	82	A/C 7
Dorchester Dorset, Poundbury Main[#][+]	335–early C5	1114	672	97	326/49	346/51	24	A/C 154? I/N 77?
Dorchester, P'bury (Other) [#]*	Late C2–early C5	273 (#270; *3)	116	97	60/52	56/48	2	A/C 51; I/N 44
Dorchester, Oxon, Queensford Farm[#]	Late C4–mid C6	184	98	88	46/47	52/53	13	A 7; C 49; I 1
Dunstable[#]	C4–early C5	112	86	93	46/53	40/47	6	A 1; C 4; I 14; N 1
Icklingham[#][+]	340/50–?390	50	32	97	19/59	13/41	1	A 2; C 12; I/N 3
Leicester, Newarke Street[#][+]	Late C4	54	23	53	11/48	12/52	20	C/I 11

London Eastern#*	C1–C5 (mainly C2)	686 (#550; *136)	351	70	203/58	148/42	158	A 31; C 34; I 55
London, Watling Street#*	C2–C3	30 (#25; *5)	13	72	6/46	7/54	5	A 2; C/I 8
London Western#*	C2–C3	48 (#19; *29)	28	58	17/61	11/39	30	A ?2; C 3
Magiovinium#*	Antonine and C3–C4	83 (#39; *44)	20	61	8/40	12/60	13	C 1; I 8
Owslebury (R)#*	C2–end C4	21 (#16; *5)	15	94	13/87	2/13	1	I 4; C 2
Peterborough, Lynch Farm#	C3–C4	50	35	74	21/60	14/40	12	C 2
Puckeridge, Skeleton Green#*	Late C1–C4	102 (#5; *97)	83	93	39/47	44/53	6	C 7
Roden Downs#	C4–C5	10	10	100	4/40	6/60	—	—
Shepton Mallet, Fosse Lane#*+	C4–?C5	46 (#45; *1)	28	85	14/40	14/50	5	A 2; C 3; I/N 7
Winchester, Lankhills#*	C4	451 (#444; *7)	185	96	112/61	73/39	19	A 2; C 86; I 23; N 47
York, Trentholme Drive#*	C2–C4	395 (#342; *53)	283	98	231/82	52/18	7	A 14; I/C 10
Totals		6275 (#5773; *502)	3558	82	2020 =57%	1538 =43%	760	1254

Notes

If cemeteries with fewer than 50% of adults sexed (including Derby) are eliminated, M = 57%, F = 43%.

If cemeteries with fewer than 30 sexed burials are eliminated, M = 57%, F = 43%.

If all sexed cremations are eliminated, M = 58%, F = 42%.

* Cremation.

Inhumation.

+ Prob. Christian.

(R) Roman period burials.

a Those over about 15 yrs, and adolescents/sub-adults able to be sexed.

b 'Adolescent', 11–14 yrs; 'child', 1–10 yrs; 'infant', younger than one year but older than neonate.

No overall analysis of the distribution of males and females in Romano-British cemeteries has been published. Even the most comprehensive study of Romano-British burial practices to date by Philpott in 1991 does not look at this aspect, although some of the authors of individual reports postulate reasons for the imbalance of the sexes in their assessments.

From the table it is evident that, while overall there were more men than women, the percentage of women varies considerably, with one 'large' cemetery, Cannington (M = 39 per cent, F = 61 per cent), having appreciably more women than men. A military presence has been suggested for the imbalance at two sites. For Bath Gate cemetery (M = 69 per cent, F = 31 per cent), it was proposed that Cirencester was a place for the retirement of veterans, whose numbers would have contributed to the population imbalance. The same reason was suggested for the Trentholme Drive, York cemetery, where the figures were M = 82 per cent, F = 18 per cent. There are problems with the first site in that Cirencester is more than 80 km from the nearest Roman fortress at Caerleon, in south Wales. It is not likely that veterans would settle in such numbers in Cirencester as to skew the balance of males to females to the extent of a ratio of 7:3. The proposal for York is more convincing. It was a centre which owed its life to the army: it boasted a fortress and was also a Roman *colonia*, where veterans retired after their 25 or so years of service. Discharged soldiers would probably have settled in an area where at least some already had wives and children, the ban on marriage having been lifted by Septimius Severus at the end of the second century. Nevertheless, it will be noted that there are also very low percentages of women in the two distinct burial groups from Ashton (F = 32 per cent and 31 per cent), a town where there had never been a military presence.

The imbalance in the Lankhills cemetery (M = 61 per cent, F = 39 per cent) has been explained as an accident of preservation: the bones of males are heavier and thicker than those of females, so their survival in greater numbers is partly a result of this, in view of the acidic soils of southern Britain.

For Icklingham cemetery, it was suggested that, while the percentage of women of 42 per cent or a ratio of 3:2 was not a 'demographically normal' one, the difference was not significant because of the smallness of the sample: 50 burials in all. It is also worth keeping in mind the comment by Wells here that an imbalance between male and female burials is a 'common tendency' for Roman cemeteries, unlike Anglo-Saxons sites, where females outnumber males.

At Bletsoe, the figures were 25 male, 21 female and one unsexed adult, giving a percentage for females of 46 per cent, which was considered to be 'roughly equal' to that of males, but again the sample was small. The same kind of argument was advanced in the report on Butt Road, Colchester, a much larger cemetery: the ratio in the Period II cemetery of 1.21:1 was above the expected 1:1, although 'not statistically different (chi-square) from a normal biological population', especially when compared with Cirencester and Trentholme Drive. It should be noted, however, that a ratio of 1.21:1 gives us a percentage of 55 per cent males to 45 per cent females.

The recent publication of another large cemetery, London Eastern, also addressed the issue, but the authors do not try to justify the disparity in numbers by suggesting a military presence, burials of females elsewhere, or the effects of the taphonomic process. They merely propose that the inequality in numbers reflects a 'normal urban population' in Britain – an assessment with which this author wholeheartedly agrees.[8]

This brings us to the point of this study. Where were the females of Roman Britain? We know that almost equal numbers of males and females are born into the world (actually a slightly higher number of males); but we also know that male infants in developed countries have a higher mortality rate than female. Those facts would hold for Britain of the fourth century AD as for today. Even if the well-worn argument of high female mortality as a result of childbirth is produced, we would still expect to find roughly the same number of adult females as males in cemeteries, albeit with a lower average age.

There is nothing in the ancient literary material to suggest that there was any Roman practice which caused women to be buried separately from men, although there may have been regional traditions for such a practice in pre-Roman Britain. But there is both literary and archaeological evidence to suggest that in the Roman period selective infanticide was practised, and that this was the reason for the lower numbers of adult females in Romano-British cemeteries. The fact that the archaeological evidence is weighted to urban rather than to rural sites reinforces the view that it was as a result of Roman influence that this situation occurred.

Literary evidence for infanticide in the Roman period is considerable. The power (*patria potestas*) of the male head of the family or *paterfamilias* was, in theory, absolute over his offspring, and indeed over his wife in a *manus* marriage.[9] The *paterfamilias* had the right to order a deformed offspring to be killed (*Twelve Tab.* 4; Cic. *de Leg.* 3.8.19), or an unwanted newborn to be exposed. Even if he had previously acknowledged the child, he could still resile from this and require it to be exposed: a well-known example is that of the emperor Claudius, who ordered the exposure of the infant daughter of his wife, Urgulanilla, because he came to believe he was not the child's father (Suet. *Claud.* 27).

Exposure did not necessarily lead to death. The child might be rescued by a stranger, and reared. But exposure would often have fatal consequences, and the act might thus be regarded at best as haphazard but legal infanticide or, at worst, murder. Early Christian writers such as Tertullian (*Apol.* 9.4–11) and Minucius Felix (*Oct.* 30.2) certainly saw it as such, and spoke with abhorrence about the practice. Tertullian accuses pagans of killing babies about to be born, or of exposing them after birth to cold, starvation or dogs; and he reminds his audience that Christians are forbidden murder or abortion. The Justinian *Digest* (25.3.4), compiled in the sixth century, cites a legal opinion attributed to the third century jurist, Paulus, that those who exposed a child were, in effect, committing infanticide.

There is no mention of the sex of the child in any of these sources, and children of both sexes must have been exposed. However, records from the second and early third centuries show that public assistance for needy children (*alimenta*) was heavily in favour of males: in one instance, from Veleia in northern Italy, of 179 legitimate children given aid, 145 were boys and only 34, or 19 per cent, were girls; the return from another benefaction went to 18 boys and only one girl (*CIL* 11.1147). The discrimination in favour of boys clearly shows that they were considered more important than girls. In other words, particularly amongst the poor, male babies were reared, while the females were not.

This would appear to confirm a much older tradition in which female infants were considered expendable. A law attributed to Romulus required citizens to rear all their male children and the first daughter, which implies that subsequent daughters did not have to be reared. This seemingly contradicts the remark of Dionysius of Halicarnassus elsewhere that all children must be reared (*Ant. Rom.* 2.15.2; 9.22.2); but, in view of the above example from the imperial household, it would appear that exposure was a convenient way of getting rid of an inconvenient female infant. The unwanted female child is a frequent motif in the early Latin writers: for instance, in Terence's *Heauton Timorumenos* (626–43) a husband berates his wife for not exposing her baby daughter as he had ordered. Another example comes from Ovid's *Metamorphoses* 7.669–684, where Ligdus, a poor freeborn man, tells his pregnant wife that if she gives birth to a girl, it will have to be killed as he cannot afford to keep it.[10]

The result of the selective culling of newborns was that, by the time of Augustus, even among the nobility there were many more males than females (Dio 54.16). To redress this imbalance, a series of laws was introduced with the aim of inducing citizens, and in particular the upper classes, to marry and to raise their offspring. It has been pointed out that the fact that Augustus brought in laws to increase the population shows that he did not believe their failure to produce and raise children was due to infertility.[11]

Emperors from Nerva to Septimius Severus supported the *alimenta* schemes which helped poorer Italian families to feed their children. Doubtless imperial advisers were as much concerned with the falling numbers of Italian soldiers in the Roman army as with the plight of the citizens who would give them birth, and the scheme was probably intended to improve the numbers of potential recruits into the army (Pliny *Pan.* 26.3; 28.4–5).[12] There is, however, no evidence that the practice of exposing infants and in particular female infants was ever questioned. Certainly, in upper-class Roman circles, while *patria potestas* diminished along with *manus* marriages, one of the remnants of this power was the right to expose an unwanted child. *Patria potestas* was limited in AD 318 (*Cod. Iust.* 9.17), and exposure probably banned by the Christian emperor Valentinian in AD 374 (*Cod. Theod.* 9.14.1).

By this time Britain had been a part of the Roman Empire for more than 300 years, and the disparity between numbers of males and females observed in Rome was also reflected in cemetery populations in this part of the empire. It would appear that the practice of selective infanticide came to Britain with the Romans in the first century AD, and that it continued virtually until the end of the Occupation – with some significant exceptions.

It might be argued that this study is dealing here with Britain, not Rome, and that differing customs may have obtained in that part of the world, and even in differing parts of Britain itself. That is undoubtedly true, and there is no way of telling to what extent the concept of *patria potestas* was current in Britain or, indeed, how widespread was the adoption of Roman law. But if the sites where there is a preponderance of males are examined, it will be seen that these are found in what might be considered the most Romanised parts of the province, and in cemeteries which yielded grave goods which were indicative of long contact with Rome. For example, the late first/early second century structures 1, 3 and 4 at Derby Racecourse contained human remains accompanied by a pig, suggesting the early adoption of Roman burial practice (Cic. de Leg. 2.22.57); and Structure 1 also had a number of lamps and other Roman-type grave goods. Most of the animal bones at Derby Racecourse cemetery were from pigs, but there were also chicken bones, and the cock was an attribute of Mercury, messenger of the gods (Hom. Hymn Herm. 572), who accompanied the dead to the Otherworld.[13] Indeed, contact with Rome and Roman influence may have been well established before the Occuption: in regard to the cemetery at Verulamium, which has an atypical disproportion of males to females for the Late Iron Age, the archaeologists observe that the burials on either side of the English Channel are indistinguishable in the first century AD.

We might now look at the situation in Britain prior to the coming of Rome. In Chapter 2 the burial evidence was extrapolated from 16 sites from the late pre-Roman Iron Age (Table 2.2). It was shown that there were equal numbers of males and females in Iron Age cemeteries. When the figures are compared with those of the Roman period (M = 57 per cent, F = 43 per cent), it is obvious that there was a decline in the number of females being reared.

This premise can be supported to some extent by a study of the skeletal evidence in the cemeteries from the Roman period, and the incidence of congenital defects which are carried in families. To date only two reports have produced enough detail to allow such an examination to be made; a third may give some support. While the information from these reports differs in substance, as evidence it points in the same direction.

The first site, Icklingham, was a small cemetery of 50 identifiable bodies, with 41 per cent of the sexed adult population women and 59 per cent male. A congenital defect, gonial eversion of the mandible, seen as a family trait, was found in 68 per cent of the males in the sample, thus indicating a close relationship between them; on the other hand, the same defect was found in only 20 per cent of the females. This could suggest a certain amount of culling of female infants in the community, to the extent that the adult females in the cemetery were not as closely related to each other or to the males. The sample is very small, however, and the bone specialist concedes that the defect may be sex linked. Alternatively, it could suggest an influx of females into the settlement from outside the local gene pool.

Poundbury and Cannington cemeteries have a different type of evidence which is perhaps more conclusive. In the adult population of both there were actually more females than males. Another congenital defect, dental agenesis or hypodontia (a missing third molar), also a hereditary trait, was found in 43 per cent of females and 35 per cent of males at Poundbury,[14] and in 62 per cent of females and only 38 per cent of males at Cannington. This then suggests an *absence* of infanticide amongst females at these sites, a situation also proposed for Poundbury after an examination of the perinatal burials in the cemetery (later).

From Cannington there is also the evidence of a spinal abnormality, a cleft atlas vertebra, which was found in five men and five women, and interpreted as a congenital defect. While the sample is small, it supports the findings from the dental study.

All of these cemeteries are identified as Christian, and Christian leaders opposed infanticide. But it is, perhaps, significant that infanticide was still prevalent amongst Christians at least as late as the beginning of the fourth century: in c.305, the Council of Elvira (canons 63, 68) condemned the practice. The solution to this seeming contradiction lies, it is suggested, in the dates of the cemeteries, and the circumstances of their going out of use. The degree of Romanisation of the population might also be a factor when considering these and other sites.[15]

The cemetery at Icklingham began around mid-fourth century, over what has been interpreted as an earlier pagan site. Its use probably ceased a decade or so before the end of the century when it and a small apsidal building and associated D-shaped structure, identified as a church and baptistery, appear to have come to an abrupt end. The cemetery may have barely lasted two generations. It seems that the Christian phase at Icklingham was too short-lived to produce a change in attitude to infanticide and the killing of female infants which would effect a subsequent correction in numbers of the sexes.

On the other hand, the Christian phase at Poundbury probably began around 335, but continued to the end of the Roman Occupation and very likely well beyond: the numismatic evidence in Britain generally runs out in the first decade of the fifth century, when coinage ceased to be brought into the province; and the archaeological evidence from the burials themselves suggests that they, too, decreased in number over time with a concomitant decline in the standard of interment.[16] The cemetery probably lasted 80 or more years in its Christian phase, time enough for changed social practices to be reflected in the burial pattern.

This cemetery, like others identified as Christian, had infants buried along with adults, but in discrete graves, and given the same respect as adults. There were a number of neonates found, and these have been identified as 59 per cent male, and 41 per cent female, the kinds of figures which one would expect in a modern context and almost exactly the same percentages found in the excavation of a modern cemetery in Hungary of 59.5 per cent male infants and 40.5 per cent female. It is, therefore, very interesting to see that were more females than males in the adult population in the Poundbury cemetery: 51 per cent female to 49 per cent male. This means that more females survived to adulthood than males, and indicates that female infants had been raised to maturity. Indeed, of the very elderly, and there were quite a number at Poundbury, the greater percentage were women.[17]

It is also noteworthy that the percentage of women in the main Christian cemetery at Poundbury is greater than in the peripheral (presumably pagan) burials, many of which were contemporaneous; and at Colchester, the percentage of women in the Butt Road cemetery increases from Period I (pagan) to the later Period II (Christian). Both these sites continued into the fifth century.

It is proposed therefore, that, in those cemeteries which were in existence early in the Roman period, there is evidence that selective infanticide was practised. In the fourth century, with the expansion of Christianity, and into the fifth century with the removal of direct Roman influence in Britain, the number of female infants allowed to live increased, to the extent that a 'normal' ratio of females to males finally occurred.

But the situation at Cannington, in Somerset, is beyond what might be considered normal. The large number of women in the cemetery (61 per cent) probably reflects not only the Christian character of the population, but also the more unsettled times of the later fifth and following centuries. There may even have been some assimilation of Saxons, as a number of graves, dating to the post-Roman period, contained knives — an intrusive element in the cemetery; however the excavator believes this could as readily indicate cultural or trade links. Suggested reasons given for the imbalance of the sexes include: a higher mortality rate for male infants, despite an excess of males over females at birth; segregation of burials caused by younger males being buried away from home as the result of war; female immigration (although elsewhere in the report there is the suggestion of inbreeding); or that the bias is caused by the ease of identification of females.

It was suggested above that the degree of Romanisation might also be a factor to consider when seeking reasons for the imbalance of the sexes in Romano-British cemeteries, and that these sites are located in the most highly Romanised area of the island. Some with the lowest percentage of females, such as York and Cirencester, were also long-established towns having strong connections with Rome: both were probably provincial capitals by the fourth century. Yet there were also low numbers of females in the two burial groups at Ashton. At best Ashton could be grouped with the 'small towns' of Britain, but its early establishment in the Claudian period also points to a lengthy knowledge of Roman customs.[18]

One final problem must be addressed: the fate of the unwanted infants. Archaeologists at Romano-British sites have over many years recorded the remains of infants in buildings, wells, middens and other domestic contexts. It is clear that Roman law regarding the prohibition of intramural burial did not apply or was not applied to infants. The subject has been treated in some depth previously by the present writer.[19] Unwanted infants would have included both freeborn and slave. Freeborn children could legally be exposed until the legislation of Valentinian in the late fourth century. Slave women would certainly have taken a risk, since both they and the children they bore were the property of their master, but Dio Chrysostom (*Disc.* 15.8) tells us that many destroyed their unborn or newly born children in order to avoid adding the burdens of parenting to those of slavery. Undoubtedly slave children were among those remains found at many sites. Others were free; and a greater percentage of these would have been female. Advances in the sexing of infants will help to confirm this in future excavations.[20]

Many Roman practices were adopted by the native population of Britain, especially those in the towns and in areas in close contact with Rome. The exposure or killing of infants, particularly females, was one of the most repugnant. But it lasted only as long as the Romans in Britain, and does seem to have been in the process of being curtailed with the coming of Christianity. Had Christianity prospered in Britain, it is likely that the male to female ratios in Romano-British cemeteries might have equalised during the Roman Occupation. As it was, the failure of Christianity coincided with the withdrawal of Rome. The religions, cults and practices of pre-Roman Britain, which had co-existed and to some extent had been submerged by centuries of Occupation, resumed and even revived, the Saxons brought with them a different set of *mores*, and the disparity between the numbers of males and females largely disappeared.[21]

Status

Despite the poor prospects of survival for newly born females, when they were allowed to be reared to adulthood there is little evidence that females received worse treatment than males. The inscriptions of Roman Britain show that women could have status and respect in their own communities (see Chapter 3). We now look at them in the wider context of the Roman Empire and draw conclusions from the evidence of archaeology. It is argued that Romano-British women, while not generally equal to men were given at least the kind of status that was accorded to women at Rome and probably higher; and that, in some circumstances, particularly among the upper classes – perhaps harking back to the Iron Age when women had higher positions in society – some women were seen as having the same status as men. This was due now to the position of their husbands and fathers, rather than in their own right.

The position of women at Rome itself has been well documented: at the top end of the scale were those from the upper classes, well-born and with progressively more freedom from the end of the Republic, reaching a peak with the Severan dynasty when a few powerful women made and destroyed emperors; and at the lower end, those from the poor and the enslaved, who suffered the continued dominance of Roman men over many aspects of their endeavour. High-born women at Rome were comparatively few in number. High-born and powerful women were, of course, exceptional. Yet even one of the most influential women in all of Roman politics, the empress Livia, was reminded by her son Tiberius, when he became emperor, that she was '... a woman and must not interfere in affairs of state', a warning which she ignored and which led to their openly quarrelling (Suet. *Tib.* 50–1). The Roman world was male-dominated and, while women might have status, their potential for power was limited.[22] At no time can it be said that Roman women had equality with men.

This situation is well illustrated by Roman marriages. In the early Republic, from *c.*510 BC, control over a woman passed at marriage from her father to her husband – a *manus* marriage. The wars of expansion in Italy led to many changes, including greater freedom for women: from the last couple of centuries of the Republic, 'free' marriages became the norm, although Roman women remained in the power of their father or the nearest male relative. However, in an effort to encourage couples, particularly those of the upper classes, to have more children, the emperor Augustus (under the Papian-Poppaean Law of AD 9) granted the *ius liberorum* or 'right of three children' to free women who had given birth to three children, and to freedwomen who had had four. They had the right to apply to be relieved of the need for a male guardian or *tutor*, and thus some were able to take control of their own affairs to a large extent. The *ius liberorum* (for detailed references see Dixon 1988: 101, n. 19) could also be granted as a special honour to females who had not had the required number of children, such as the empress Livia, and to males who could thus gain accelerated progress through the *cursus honorum*.

The ancient writers and the inscriptions of the imperial period record a number of examples of upper class women who were rich and controlled large commercial interests in their own right; and while there is little evidence of similar women from the lower classes, they must have existed. It is known that Claudius offered rewards, including the *ius liberorum*, to rich freedwomen who had financial interests in the shipbuilding industry at Ostia (Suet: *Claud*. 18–19). But they would have been few. Most women of the lower classes were too busy just making a living and looking after household and family to aspire to power and influence. And even the wealthiest women, having dispensed with a guardian, did not have equality with men: they could own property,[23] make wills, and sign contracts on their own behalf, yet while they could be involved in political campaigning,[24] they could not vote or hold any political position, nor could they plead their own cases in court. In the event of divorce, they could not have custody of their own children.

It would be a simple matter to see Britannia as an extension of Rome, and to attribute to women in Britain the same place in society as those in Rome. But because of their position before the coming of Rome, it is likely that, during the Occupation, women from the old British aristocracy retained some semblance of equality with men. It seems that their rank, at least, was still recognised: there is a hint of this in Dio (77.16.5) when he reports the conversation (quoted earlier) supposedly between the wife of a Caledonian chieftain and Julia Domna, mother of the emperor Caracalla. The implication is that the native aristocracy was acknowledged even as late as the beginning of the third century AD. There is no doubt that Romano-British society was stratified and that, as shown in Chapter 3, certain women had status and at least the potential for influence, their status reflecting that of their husbands or fathers. As the Roman presence grew and consolidated, the status of Romano-British women generally came to be scarcely distinguishable from their Roman sisters.

The little that is known about women's rights prior to the Roman occupation is discussed in Chapter 2. It was seen that upper class women, at least, had considerable freedom to run their own affairs, to take positions of political authority, own property, and choose their partners in marriage; for the lower classes nothing is known. With the coming of Rome, while Roman laws would have prevailed in the *coloniae* and in the one known *municipium* of Verulamium, it likely that local law would have been maintained elsewhere in matters that did not affect the security of the state, since the administration would be largely in the hands of the local population. But it is certain that Roman law could, both then and after 212, override local law if conflict existed.[25] The situation would not necessarily reflect that in Egypt, Greece and the Hellenistic East – parts of the empire with a long tradition of civil peace, established law and strong government prior to the Roman takeover.

Despite the advances in feminist archaeology studies, the status of Romano-British women has not been scrutinised in any major study.[26] Allason-Jones (1989: 15, 190) is one of the few to suggest how status can be evaluated: one might look to Rome for evidence there, and compare with the British situation while assessing the degree of similarity and difference in the two societies. Allason-Jones believes that Romano-British women had status (a 'respected position') as wives and mothers, and because of their involvement in the production of food. On the evidence of the Bath *defixiones*, she sees it as possible that in law British women had a stronger position than their Roman counterparts. She also thinks it likely that women who came from Italy felt themselves 'superior' to the native women. This may have been so in the early decades of the province, but with the gradual blending of native and immigrant populations such differences would ultimately disappear. Upper-class Britons quickly adopted Roman ways. The numbers of the old Roman aristocracy who came to Britain in an administrative capacity declined, and they were replaced by men, some themselves provincials, whose families had only in very recent times been elevated to the senatorial class. A new Romano-British upper class thus emerged, made up of members of the old local tribal aristocracies, civic notables made important by their positions in local councils, government officials and military leaders, and perhaps even retired middle-ranking soldiers such as centurions.

We have met women from those ranks in Chapter 3. They were discussed according to their position in society, achieved by birth or marriage. A woman's name could also give a clue as to her origin, and indirectly to her status. However, for the few hundred women whose identity and position in society can be determined from literary or inscriptional evidence, there are thousands more whose status can be deduced only from the archaeological record. It is to this we now turn.

A number of criteria were established in Chapter 2 to define the status of women in pre-Roman Britain relative to men, according to the burial evidence. In general terms they included looking at burial structures or graves which involved particular expense or physical effort 'valuable', rare or numerous grave deposits, and the evidence of the bones themselves relating to the gender composition of cemetery populations. These criteria are now applied to the evidence from the period of the Occupation. Burials of importance include those which were relatively costly to build in terms of materials or energy (which might include mausolea, vaults or other structures, 'step' graves, stone- and tile-lined graves), or were isolated, or given a significant place or special treatment within a cemetery. The most visible would be mausolea, vaults or cemetery enclosures.[27] These 'status' burials are set out in Table 4.3, with data for males and females.

Mausolea and vaults are not common in Romano-British cemeteries but, where they are found, only small numbers of a cemetery population are involved. Among the most significant mausolea are the ten at Poundbury Camp in Dorset, not only because they give an indication of the wealth and status of certain groups of the population of Dorchester, but also because the fresco decorating one structure, R8, supports the interpretation of the cemetery as Christian. A reconstruction of the fragments reveals, *inter alia*, a Chi-Rho and several men and women of high status, some in purple robes and holding rods. The excavator, in a persuasive argument, sees them as members of a provincial ruling class.[28] At Butt Road Period II, Colchester, another fourth century cemetery believed to be Christian, six timber vaults were

Table 4.3 'Status' burials in Romano-British cemeteries

Cemetery	Mausolea/ vaults M/F	Lead coffins M/F	Stone coffins M/F	Step graves M/F	'Plaster' packing M/F
Ancaster	—	—	4/5	—	—
Ashton (backyard)	—	—	—	1/1	—
Chilmark, Eyewell Farm	—	—	0/1	—	—
Cirencester, Bath Gate	5/2	—	1/3	—	—
Colchester, Butt Road	—	0/1	—	—	2/4
Dorchester Dorset, Poundbury	9/6	6/10	1/4	1/0	13/12
D'chester, Oxon, Queensford Fm	2/2	—	—	—	—
Dunstable	—	—	—	—	6/5
Icklingham	—	—	2/1	—	—
London Eastern	2/3	2/0	—	1/1	25/15
London Spittalfields	—	0/1	0/1	—	—
London Watling Street	1/1	—	—	—	1/1
Roden Downs	—	0/1	—	2/5	2/2
Shepton Mallet, Fosse Lane	1/0	1/1	1/0	0/1	—
Winchester, Lankhills	—	—	—	5/4	—
Totals	20/14	9/15	6/15	10/12	49/38

identified. Eight vaults or mausolea were also found in the Eastern Cemetery of Roman London, and these buildings, like the one at Shepton Mallet, appear to have been single-burial structures; but in the Romano-British cemetery in London Watling Street, two features interpreted as 'walled cemeteries', contemporaneous with burials outside the enclosures, had multiple burials: the remains of a female and two children in one, and a male and a child in the other. The late- or sub-Roman cemetery at Queensford Farm, Dorchester, Oxon also had an enclosure, constructed towards the end of the life of the cemetery. There were two original burials, both of females, and two males were late additions.[29] Overall it appears that, where the information is available, the ratio of men to women given this preferential burial treatment (20:14) shows a bias towards males (1.6 per cent of male burials and 1.3 per cent of female burials). Of the 34 special mausoleum/vault/enclosure burials, 59 per cent were for males and 41 per cent for females.

In his study of burial practices, Philpott suggested that stone-lined cists may be an indicator of status, on the grounds that such lining would not only protect the burial from disturbance but also be seen as a mark of distinction of the dead person. The same might be believed of tile-lined inhumations, although these were found in the Roman period only. This interpretation may hold in some cases, but in others the reason was probably much more mundane: a shortage of timber but a plentiful supply of local stone or disused tiles. At Ashton there were a number of stone-lined graves, the significance of which is difficult to explain. There does not seem to be any pattern to their use, either by age or sex. The status of those so buried may even have been lower than those in coffins; in the west–east, presumably Christian, cemetery, while in numerous graves the stones are placed so as to support a plank which would act as a cover for the burial, there is actual evidence for only one grave with coffin nails or wood stain. The general impression is not one of wealth or status, but rather the contrary.[30] This is supported by the evidence at Poundbury where it was noted that the late burials were shallow, uncoffined and were stone lined – all taken as indicators of lower status in this present study.

A similar impression is gained from other sites. For example, at Cannington in Somerset, 30 graves had some form of (mostly local) stone lining but few had coffin nails or evidence for coffins at all. At Bletsoe, where almost half of the 56 inhumations had undressed limestone slabs lining or partially lining the graves, only two of these, a male and a female, also had evidence of a coffin. The cemetery at Newarke Street, Leicester contained 54 burials, 22 of which were partially stone lined, and at least two of these, both females, also had coffins. This certainly suggests that wooden coffins had higher status than stone linings or cists, but the evidence from the late period at the largest cemetery studied, Poundbury, is inconclusive, and the case not proven. It is, nevertheless, possible that stones of any kind had some significance, if not suggesting status. Of the stone cists listed by Philpott, 32 were for men and 23 for women, and of tile-lined burials, seven men and eight women. Combined, the figures are 56 per cent of all lined burials for males and 44 per cent for females, virtually the same ratio as male to females in all burials (Table 4.2), M = 57 per cent, F = 43 per cent. It will be interesting to compare these figures with those for wooden coffins (Table 4.6 later).

More important as status symbols than stone-lined cists must be stone and lead coffins or sarcophagi. These are impressive additions to a burial, and are often found together, or in association with other indicators of wealth or status. Lead lends itself to moulded decoration, and a number of the Romano-British coffins have motifs which have been seen as appropriate for a journey to the Otherworld: for example, pecten shells, Medusa or lion heads and circles, and on several examples, bead-and-reel or rope moulding in the form of an 'X' or a zigzag.[31] Even if undecorated, lead coffins required substantial resources, both financial and human, to provide such a repository for a body. It is noted that the distribution of lead coffins and ossuria in Britain corresponds with the wealthier part of the province, particularly the south-east and the 'villa belt' of the mid-south. Twenty-seven came from Poundbury. There were a further three from Butt Road Period II, and three from London Eastern. At both those sites one of the lead coffins was for a child.[32] Two came from Shepton Mallet and one each from Icklingham and Roden Downs. Included here also is the recently discovered 'Spittalfields lady', in her lead coffin set in a stone sarcophagus,[33] giving a total of M = 9, F = 15, that is, 0.4 per cent of males were in lead coffins, and 1.0 per cent of females. The figures mean that 38 per cent of lead coffins were for males and 62 per cent for females.

Stone coffins are somewhat fewer, probably because over time they have been recovered but not recorded, and recycled as garden ponds, horse troughs or similar. One from Colchester had a later life as a sink, and then a step in a High Street shop. Most coffins were finished simply, with flat-topped lids, but an example from Poundbury had a gabled lid which may have been an (even more conspicuous) indicator of wealth.

From other cemeteries analysed, the greatest number were from Ancaster, with ten, and Bath Gate, with six. The figures for sexed burials in stone coffins are the same as for lead coffins: M = 9, F = 15 (0.4 per cent of male burials, and 1.0 per cent of female) or males having 38 per cent of stone coffins, and females 62 per cent.

In view of the rich grave goods in some burials, one cemetery which is curious for its complete absence of stone or lead coffins is Lankhills. The excavator suggests that a scarcity of resources in the area might account for the absence of sarcophagi of either material, but lead, while not found in the immediate region, was readily obtainable from the Mendips area to the west. The incidence of lead poisoning in the Poundbury cemetery makes it clear that the products from the lead mines found their way to central southern Britain. For some unknown reason the wealthier residents of Winchester chose not to use lead or stone coffins as an indicator of status in burials.

On the other hand, the largest number of 'step' graves found in Romano-British cemeteries come from Lankhills. Constructed with a step on one or both sides, they are seen as indicating status[34] since they would require considerably more effort to dig than a normal straight-sided grave cut. In some cases the extra shelf was used for the placing of grave goods. This occurred in the step grave for a female cremation at Skeleton Green. In others, such as those at Lankhills, it was suggested that the ledge on both sides provided a base for crossbeams supporting a platform above the coffin, thus creating a grave chamber onto which the various grave goods were placed.

Many step burials had marks of distinction besides their depth and shape. Of the 17 at Lankhills, all but one had grave goods and all had coffins, while the Poundbury male was the sole occupant of mausoleum R6. Six of the seven step graves amongst the ten coffined burials in the small fourth-century cemetery at Roden Downs were the deepest in the cemetery, and all but two females had coins as grave deposits. Another female had a lead-lining in her timber coffin, with a layer of box leaves placed beneath the body, and a comb, a pottery vessel, coins and perhaps shoes as grave furniture; her burial was the deepest of all six females. In the two step burials at London Eastern, there was a ledge at the head end of the grave, in the first burial used as a type of pillow; the second was a 'standard' burial. There was little of significance in the Ashton graves – the male had hobnails and the female a grey-ware pot. The sum of all sites gives M = 10, F = 12, meaning that 0.5 per cent of all males and 0.8 per cent of all females had step burials.[35]

The percentages of males and females with step graves show a bias in favour of females, but this is not supported by an analysis of the depth of the graves, where, at both Roden Downs and Lankhills, the two deepest sexed step burials are for males. At both sites the shallowest is for a woman. Indeed, the excavator of Lankhills commented that, for the cemetery as a whole, male burials were deeper than women's.

This proposal and the depth of graves as a criterion for status warrant further examination. A link between the two was proposed in Chapter 2; a similar link has been suggested for Cannington by the excavator of that cemetery. All relevant information was not available from that site, but it was reported that male burials were 'consistently deeper' than those for females and that, of the eleven deepest graves, ten were for males, and one a female. The average depth of burial in Cannington overall was 0.35 m. In the present study, the depth of graves is available for only 14 cemetery groups.[36] For each of these, maximum, minimum and average depths for sexed burials have been established (Table 4.4).

It is not possible to produce meaningful figures averaging all cemeteries, since they will all have been excavated under different conditions, and the method of

Table 4.4 Depth of sexed burials in Romano-British cemeteries

Cemetery	Males				Females			
	Number (depth given)	Max. depth (m)	Min. depth (m)	Av. depth (m)	Number (depth given)	Max. depth (m)	Min. depth (m)	Av. depth (m)
Cremations								
First century								
Chichester, Westhampnett	4	0.21	0.11	0.16	6	0.90[a]	0.08	0.24
Puckeridge, Skeleton Green	6	0.35	0.15	0.27	13	0.40	0.15	0.28
Inhumations								
First century								
Derby, Racecourse Road[b] (inc. 3 'military burials')	19	2.20/ 1.00	0.00	0.65/ 0.45	9	1.00	0.26	0.53
Third century								
Cirencester, Bath Gate	67	1.98	0.17	0.91	59	1.98	0.23	0.94
Dorchester, Poundbury Other (third century)	33	1.3	0.10	0.75	31	2.00[c]	0.05	0.83
Fourth century								
Ancaster	37	1.70	0.61	1.25	29	1.57	0.74	1.19
Ashton	84	0.84	0.05	0.32	37	0.63	0.08	0.31
Bradley Hill	9	0.45	0.10	0.20	9	0.42	0.10	0.22
Chilmark, Eyewell Farm	3	0.50	0.25	0.38	3	0.40	0.17	0.29
Dorchester, Poundbury Main	305	2.67[d]	0.08	0.86	369	1.73	0.08	0.86
Dorchester, Poundbury Other (fourth century)	19	2.57[e]	0.50	1.19	19	1.57	0.15	1.00
Dunstable	20	1.01	0.12	0.65	18	1.12	1.51	0.62
Leicester, Newarke Street	8	0.48	0.10	0.35	9	0.58	0.14	0.28
Roden Downs	4	2.13	1.17	1.61	6	1.78	1.07	1.47
Winchester, Lankhills	112	1.55	0.50	0.85	72	1.50	0.33	0.83

Notes

a This maximum, for grave no. 20723, is possibly an error. If this grave is removed from the analysis, the maximum female burial is 0.14 m and the average depth of females is 0.12 m.

b This site contains three very deep inhumations burials, the remains of what appear to be Roman soldiers, quite separate from the walled cemetery. If they are removed from this analysis, the deepest male burial is 1.00 m, and the average depth of males is 0.45 m.

c The deepest female grave, at 2.00 m, held a lead-lined stone coffin, gypsum packed. It was located in the northern peripheral area of the main cemetery.

d This was by far the deepest grave in the main (Christian) cemetery, located in Mausoleum R9, and held a gypsum-packed lead coffin. The next deepest male graves were 0.73, 0.72 and 0.71 m.

e The second deepest grave at Poundbury, which contained a gypsum-packed lead coffin, and was found amongst the Late Roman burials in Site C.

recording depth of grave cut will have varied from site to site. However, from the survey, limited as it is, it is clear that although individual male graves may be deeper, it is a misconception that in general male graves are generally deeper than female. What appears to have happened is that graves of males become deeper than women's by the fourth century, although the difference is slight in most cases. The relationship between depth and status is emphasised by the presence of stone and/or lead coffins in the deepest graves at Poundbury, and the very deep graves for the Roman soldiers at Racecourse Road, Derby. There no longer appears to be the connection between status and grave goods, as occurred in the Iron Age cemeteries, and it noticeable that the incidence of grave goods decreases from the first to the fourth century.

There does appear to be some link between what have been suggested as 'status' burials and the size of the grave cut (Tables 4.3 and 4.5).

The Poundbury burials illustrate this. The largest male and female graves in the main fourth-century cemetery contained stone coffins. The female was located in mausoleum R2, while the male dominated a central space in the cemetery. Amongst the outlying late fourth-century burials ('Poundbury Other') the largest male's was located in mausoleum R6, in a stone coffin; it was also a step grave, another probable indicator of status. In the third century graves, the largest female burial had a stone coffin, gypsum packed.

Overall, for the fourth century the average size of females' graves is smaller than those of males, with the reverse of the ratio for the third century – but here there is only one set of figures. Because the number of sites is small, it is hard to generalise, but there does seem to be some correlation between these figures and the depths of graves. Over time, graves for women get shallower and smaller. This may have significance for the status of women, and will be discussed later.

Special treatment of the body can include not only the depth of the burial or the size of the grave cut, but also what is included with the body. Packing within the coffin of some substance often called by the generic term 'plaster' probably indicates status burials in Romano-British cemeteries, if only for the fact that, while the substance may not in itself have been valuable, the effort in obtaining and placing it with the body shows that the body was singled out for distinction of some kind – presumably an attempt to preserve it. Since the majority of plaster burials have been found in mausolea, or lead or stone coffins, it is reasonable to assume (at the risk of a circular argument) that its introduction into a burial was a mark of status.

In his excellent analysis of the incidence of 'plaster' burials, Philpott describes the various substances which have been found in graves, such as gypsum, lime and chalk. The rite, for which there is no known parallel in pre-Roman Britain, appears to have been predominantly an urban phenomenon and, while some examples are known from the third century, most are from the fourth. The practice has been much discussed, and has been at times taken to indicate a Christian identity for a burial, the intention being to preserve the body for the Second Coming. It is now accepted by many[37] that the practice, while adopted by Christians in various parts of the empire as well as in Britain – and particularly in Poundbury and Butt Road,

Table 4.5 Size of sexed burials in Romano-British cemeteries

Cemetery	Males			Females		
	Maximum (m²)	Minimum (m²)	Average (m²)	Maximum (m²)	Minimum (m²)	Average (m²)
Cremations						
First century						
Chichester, Westhampnett	0.60 × 0.40 = 0.24	0.13 × 0.13 = 0.02	0.17	0.60 × 0.40 = 0.24	0.35 × 0.08 = 0.03	0.11
Inhumations						
Third century						
Dorchester, Poundbury Other (third century)	3.30 × 1.30 = 4.28	1.83 × 0.53 = 0.97	1.83	3.20 × 1.80 = 5.76	1.63 × 0.51 = 0.83	2.01
Fourth century						
Ashton	2.60 × 1.30 = 3.38	0.96 × 0.67 = 0.64	1.61	2.24 × 0.95 = 2.13	0.64 × 0.50 = 0.32	1.52
Chilmark, Eyewell Farm	1.90 × 0.65 = 1.24	0.80 × 0.30 = 0.24	0.85	1.55 × 0.48 = 0.74	0.60 × 0.55 = 0.33	0.52
Dunstable	2.46 × 109 = 2.68	1.63 × 0.51 = 0.83	1.55	2.18 × 1.17 = 2.55	1.12 × 0.43 = 0.48	1.48
Dorchester, Poundbury Main	2.54 × 1.35 = 3.42	1.63 × 0.43 = 0.70	1.51	2.54 × 1.63 = 4.13	1.68 × 0.41 = 0.68	1.42
Dorchester, Poundbury Other (fourth century)	2.51 × 1.22 = 3.07	2.01 × 0.56 = 1.12	1.74	2.36 × 0.91 = 2.16	1.52 × 0.51 = 0.77	1.39
Roden Downs	3.15 × 1.47 = 4.64	2.24 × 1.04 = 2.33	3.25	2.92 × 1.35 = 3.93	1.87 × 0.96 = 1.81	2.88

Colchester – was a burial fashion also adopted by the more wealthy non-Christian members of a community and later copied by those lower down the social scale.

Figures for plaster burials from Philpott's study, and excluding his Poundbury and Colchester data, are M = 14, F = 21. Poundbury had 25 and Colchester Butt Road six of this type of special burial. All the Butt Road burials save one are from the second or west–east phase of the cemetery. To these may be added the 81 recorded in London Eastern, and a group of three, two adults and a child, in the London Watling Street cemetery, which are all aligned with Structure 2, identified as a mausoleum. But they are situated on the side of the mausoleum away from the road; perhaps this is status by association?

The identification of the 'plaster' packing is not firm: Dunstable had 14 'quick-lime' burials, and Roden Downs four graves with a substance which is interpreted as '?lime concretion'. The totals for plaster burials of sexed adults from all sites analysed are M = 49, F = 38, or 2.4 per cent of male and 2.5 per cent of female burials. Of all plaster burials, 54 per cent were for male and 46 per cent for female which, in the light of the greater ratio of males to females in all Romano-British cemeteries (57/43), shows a slight bias in favour of females – shown also in other 'prestige' burials of lead and stone coffins. The figures here do not reflect the earlier figures from Philpott's study but, as for lead and stone coffins, the numbers are small and might be quickly skewed by the addition of data from a large and well-documented cemetery.

More common than plaster in burial were grave goods – found in many guises, and in the graves of men, women and children. What has been recovered by archaeologists can be only a small percentage of the objects and substances that were originally deposited. It is a great pity that, in view of the progress of archaeological science in the field of residue analysis, the thousands of pots so scrupulously scrubbed at digs earlier in the past century had not been allowed to retain at least their inner coating of dirt, once any finds were removed. We might now have had the chance to build a much more complete picture of grave deposits of foodstuffs, liquids and the like, along with the various bracelets, pins, beads and coins more easily recorded.

Be that as it may, the archaeological record of grave deposits can still provide a wealth of detail about women, and more particularly attitudes towards the burial of women. The percentages of burials with grave goods vary from cemetery to cemetery, and from the first to the fourth century. The trend is towards fewer deposits by the end of the fourth, and this has been attributed variously to the economic situation in Roman Britain, to changes in how death and the afterlife were viewed, to the influence of Christianity, and to changes in burial practice in Britain – from inhumation to cremation with the coming of Rome, then back to inhumation by the middle of the third century. After two centuries of Roman rule and influence, Romano-British society was much more homogeneous, and the rich and conspicuous grave furniture of the pre-Roman period gave way to an almost standardised burial rite: in the towns grave goods tended to reflect only dimly the once-coveted objects of the Iron Age, now familiar and readily obtainable; in the rural cemeteries similar objects were found, but often, too, deposits of hobnailed footwear were included, perhaps harking back to a pre-Roman ritual invisible until the introduction of Roman-style shoes or boots.

In the analysis of grave furniture of the Iron Age, it was concluded that, while some items may have been sex specific (knives and swords for males, spindle whorls and probably mirrors for females), there was no apparent difference in quality or quantity in the common types of grave goods, and the overall percentages of male and female graves with any grave deposits were similar. The most prestigious items, carts or chariots and imported pottery, had been found with both sexes, although there were more male cart burials than female. Pottery and joints of pig or goat/sheep were deposited more often with women than men. The most common deposit had been the iron or copper alloy brooch, presumably used for holding the burial clothes, followed by pottery, and animal and bird remains.

The situation changed somewhat in the Roman period. The most common objects in sexed graves seem to have been hobnailed footwear, complete or incomplete pots, coins, items of personal adornment particularly in women's graves, and bird or animal remains. Other items in some quantity were knives and glass vessels, deposited in almost the same percentages in male and female graves (Table 4.6). Glass items may have constituted the only genuine 'prestige' items in burials of the Roman period. Rarely are any objects of precious metal found. The overall impression is one of tokenism rather than of any intention to impress.

It is perhaps significant that while pottery, particularly imported ware, was an important deposit in graves in the Iron Age, its quality in Romano-British graves was inferior even as early as the second century. In London Eastern cemetery, for instance, it was noted by the authors of the report that damaged pots were 'fairly frequently' chosen to accompany the deceased. It was also observed that in more than 200 burials, not one piece of samian was recorded. This suggests that any prestige which pottery, particularly imports, might have as grave goods was lost as early as mid-second century. The most common pots in London Eastern were local products which may have been made especially for holding the remains in cremation burials. They do not rank as 'fine ware'.

By percentage, hobnailed footwear was the most frequently found grave deposit in the Romano-British period, in 6.4 per cent of male and 5.6 per cent of female burials. Undoubtedly shoes were deposited in the pre-Roman period, but have left no trace because they lacked a hobnail-reinforced sole. The numbers recorded fell from 16 per cent and 13 per cent in the first century AD to 6.2 per cent and 4.5 per cent in the fourth. Hobnails seem to have been an optional extra when the boots were sold but, in view of the numbers found in graves it does appear that many people chose to have this form of reinforcement. The effect would have been similar to that of golf spikes, giving the wearer a grip on certain surfaces. They were not used for shoes worn in the house, and this might account for there being fewer in the graves of females than males. The more elegant soft leather shoes worn indoors would normally leave no trace in the ground unless in a watery context.[38] A possible exception is from Roden Downs, where the report includes '?shoes' in a high status female grave. In this same cemetery, one or more burials had evidence for a pouch containing coins as a grave deposit, indicated by 'scraps of material' identified as leather; so the interpretation of leather 'shoes' (without hobnails) in the woman's grave is probably a correct one.

With regard to the other types of grave goods, overall the remains of birds or animals were recovered more often from the graves of women than men, with no difference at all by the fourth century; but the types of deposits had changed considerably from the pre-Roman period, with the most common now being remains of domestic fowl, usually chicken. This compares with the pig and sheep remains frequently found in Late Iron Age burials, and reflects the Roman influence. It may also reflect the increasingly urbanised nature of settlements with the coming of Rome.

Unlike the figures for deposits of birds and animals, there is a major disparity in the numbers of items of personal adornment found in male and female graves. In the Iron Age various objects were found in 33 per cent of male and 33 per cent of female burials, mainly in the form of iron or copper alloy brooches. The East Yorkshire brooches range in length from $c.25$ to 114 mm, and would have been used for outer wear such as cloaks as well as for garments which would have been pinned on both shoulders. For the Roman period overall the figures were $M = 1.8$ per cent, $F = 4.8$ per cent, but by the fourth century the percentages were down to 1.2 per cent and 3.9 per cent. A breakdown of the Romano-British deposits has jewellery and, to a lesser extent, dress pins, as the preferred items of adornment for female burials, whereas brooches and finger rings were favoured for males.[39] It is possible that the difference in figures reflects a cultural change, with the Roman tunic, often unbelted, being more widely adopted by men of all classes, and perhaps the British hooded cape used instead of a cloak which would require a fastening.

Very few items of personal adornment were of any great value. The most valuable came from London Eastern: one young woman in a burial dating 300–400 with beads of jet, emerald and glass, bracelets of silver and jet, as well as numerous other grave goods; another with two unworn gold-in-glass bead necklaces; an adult woman, possibly a 'foreigner', with a pair of Germanic silver brooches; and a child of 5–12 years, with gold earrings. It would be reasonable to assume that the child, who was buried in a lead-lined wooden coffin, was female. Other valuable jewellery included a gold ring with a blue glass insert from Poundbury and a silver brooch from Butt Road. At Lankhills, there were necklaces of rare imported material, coral and carnelian, found in the graves of women or children, as well rings of silver. In none of the male graves studied were there items of similar intrinsic value.

Most grave goods were deposited in coffins, where coffins existed, although some were found in the grave fill. Wooden coffins were ubiquitous in Romano-British burials, and might easily be dismissed as possible indicators of status. Virtually all burials at Poundbury were coffined, as were those at Butt Road and Lankhills – three of the largest Romano-British cemeteries. Cannington, which continued well beyond the Roman period, has less evidence for their use. Some cemeteries, such as the formal west–east burial ground at Ashton, had almost none: there, in a remarkable uniformity of burial rite, the bodies were laid in the ground and a wooden cover, presumably the bier on which they were conveyed to the cemetery, placed over them.

Table 4.6 Main grave goods for sexed burials in Romano-British cemeteries

Cemetery	Pottery M/F	Hobnails M/F	Coins M/F	Bird and animal M/F	Personal ornament M/F	Glass M/F	Knives M/F
First century							
Chichester, Westhampnett	3/3	—	—	0/1	—	—	—
Derby, Racecourse Road	4/3	8/4	4/1	—	2/1	1/1	—
Puckeridge, Skeleton Green	16/21	4/5	3/0	—	0/1	0/3	—
Numbers	23/27	12/9	7/1	0/1	2/3	1/4	—
Percentages M/F	31.1/38.6	16.0/13.0	9.5/1.4	0/1.4	2.7/4.3	1.4/5.7	—
Second century							
Baldock	1/0	1/0	—	—	1/0	—	—
London Eastern	19/9	10/5	9/4	8/5	7/14[b]	6/5	—
London, Watling Street	1/1	1/2	—	—	—	4/0	—
London Western	0/2	1/0	—	—	0/1	—	—
Owslebury	1/0	—	—	—	—	—	—
York, Trentholme Drive[a]	20/9	—	—	—	—	—	—
Numbers	42/21	12/7	9/4	8/5	8/15	10/5	—
Percentages M/F	8.8/9.4	4.9/4.1	3.7/2.3	3.3/2.9	3.3/8.8	4.1/2.9	—
Third century							
Cirencester, Bath Gate	—	2/3	4/2	—	6/2	0/2	3/0
Colchester, Butt Road Period I	3/3	1/1	—	—	0/4	0/1	—
Dorchester Dorset, P'bury (Other)	0/1	14/14	1/0	1/5	1/4	—	0/2
Peterborough, Lynch Farm	—	—	—	—	0/1	—	—
Numbers	3/4	17/18	5/2	1/5	7/11	0/3	3/2
Percentages M/F	1.1/2.7	6.2/12.2	1.8/1.3	0.4/3.4	2.5/6.8	0/2.0	1.1/1.4

Fourth century

Ancaster	—	—	2/1	1/1	1/4	—
Ashton (Formal)	—	1/1	—	—	4/0	1/0
Bletsoe	—	2/0	1/0	1/1	—	—
Bradley Hill	—	—	4/1	—	1/7	8/6
Cannington	—	1/1	0/1	—	—	—
Chilmark, Eyewell Farm	2/3	1/1	1/0	—	2/4	—
Colchester, Butt Road Period II	—	17/14	8/11	—	2/14	—
Dorchester Dorset, Poundbury Main	2/0	1/2	0/4	1/1	1/1	—
Dorchester Dorset, Poundbury (Other)	1/2	2/1	0/1	—	0/5	0/2
Dunstable	—	—	1/0	—	—	0/1
Icklingham	—	—	0/3	—	—	—
Leicester, Newarke Street	0/1	—	4/3	0/1	—	—
Roden Downs	—	—	3/2	0/1	—	—
Shepton Mallet, Fosse Lane	—	—	—	—	—	—
Winchester, Lankhills	18/10	45/27	8/2	3/2	3/6	5/0
Numbers	23/16	70/47	32/29	6/7	14/41	14/8
Percentages M/F	2.0/1.5	6.2/4.5	2.8/2.8	0.5/0.7	1.2/3.9	1.2/0.8
Totals (1–4 centuries)	91/71	111/81	53/36	15/18	31/70	17/10
Percentages M/F	4.6/4.7	6.4/5.6	3.0/2.5	0.9/1.2	1.8/4.8	1.0/0.7
% Objects in M/F graves	56/44	58/42	63/37	45/55	30/70	63/37

Notes

a Trentholme Drive is included in pottery figures, but excluded for all other grave goods.

b In the London Eastern report, one burial, listed as ?M had as grave goods a mirror and jewellery. This is the only instance I have found in either Iron Age or Roman burials where a male identification has been suggested for a burial with a mirror and jewellery. I prefer to believe that this is a female grave.

Identification of coffins rests mainly on the presence of coffin nails, since the timber has almost always long disappeared, and often not even a wood stain remains. The timber used was generally oak, but other trees were used, such as willow, poplar or yew. Of recent times two wooden coffins were found virtually intact in a water-logged context at the Western Cemetery site in London, and this has allowed a study of the construction, including the use of iron nails. But not all coffins used nails, as it was quite possible to build one using wooden pegs, so not all coffins in cemeteries even recently excavated can have been recorded. In this analysis, one can only assume that, by the law of averages, the vanished coffins were used more or less equally for male and female burials. Cremations have been excluded, with the exception of the 'casket' burials from the cemeteries collectively named Skeleton Green. Those burials are clearly of high status, made of wood and with elaborate bronze ornamentation, including medallions depicting a lion's head, which probably had funerary significance. The accompanying grave goods are of a much higher standard than others from Skeleton Green, and the caskets themselves appear to have been set apart from the general burial area. In the discussion of the caskets, it was suggested that the people cremated were members of the local wealthy class, living in Braughing or in nearby villas. Six caskets were found, five from the first century Skeleton Green site and one from Puckeridge, dating to the late-second century.[40] The distribution by sex was M = 2, F = 3.

Twenty-two of the cemeteries studied have details of male/female coffin use (Table 4.7).[41] There does not seem to be a firm trend in coffin use by male or female, particularly amongst the smaller sites. What is probably more significant is that, in the three large, late cemeteries of Butt Road, Poundbury and Lankhills, the percentage use by males and females varies only slightly. The use of coffins increases from the first to the fourth century, although in the very last years of the fourth and into the early fifth century there is evidence of burials without coffins, or burials in logs, indicating a decline in the general wealth of Britain by this period.[42] Any such decline affected both men and women, but from the figures above, it seems there is a bias towards women in the use of coffins in Romano-British burials. They were found in the graves of 63 per cent of males and 69 per cent of females. Overall, 66 per cent of sexed burials were coffined; 53 per cent of these were males and 47 per cent females (cf. total cemetery population 57/43 per cent).

The greater part of this study has dealt with members of the upper classes. There is one further aspect of status which might be examined through the archaeological evidence: the incidence of slavery. The evidence is slight, but in the Icklingham report the bone specialist proposed that the lesions on three skeletons in the fourth-century cemetery indicated that they had been fitted with shackles on the wrists and ankles. The damage caused by these fittings would have caused inflammation, thickening and changes to the leg bones. He concludes that the three people, two males and one female, were slaves. It was not possible to carry out a more detailed examination of the bones, owing to damage caused since the bodies were first buried.[43]

Table 4.7 Coffins for sexed burials in Romano-British cemeteries

Cemetery	Males		Females		% use M/F burials
	No. coffins and M	% M in coffins	No. coffins and F	% F in coffins	
First century					
Derby, Racecourse Road	10/31	32	8/19	42	43/57
Puckeridge, Skeleton Green (Caskets)	1/37	3	2/43	5	33/67
Totals first century	11/68	16	10/62	16	50/50
Second century					
Bletsoe	3/25	12	1/21	8	75/25
London, Eastern	138/186	73	89/109	82	53/47
London, Watling Street	1/5	20	2/6	33	33/67
London, Western	2/9	22	0/5	0	100/0
Owslebury	4/13	31	0/5	0	100/0
Totals second century	145/213	68	91/125	73	61/39
Third century					
Cirencester, Bath Gate	72/210	34	37/93	40	67/33
Colchester, Butt Road Period I	6/10	60	5/6	83	55/45
Dorchester, Poundbury Other (third century)	28/37	76	28/34	82	48/52
Totals third century	106/257	41	70/133	53	60/40
Fourth century					
Ancaster	21/129	16	12/83	14	64/36
Chilmark, Eyewell Farm	2/3	67	1/3	33	67/33
Colchester, Butt Road Period II	159/170	94	138/146	95	55/45
Dorchester, Poundbury Main	297/319	93	354/378	94	46/54
Dorchester, Poundbury Other (fourth century)	19/19	100	19/20	95	50/50
Dorchester, Oxon, Queensford Farm	16/46	36	20/52	38	44/56
Dunstable	8/46	17	4/40	10	67/33
Leicester, Newarke Street	4/11	36	3/12	25	57/43
Peterborough, Lynch Farm	6/21	29	6/14	43	50/50
Roden Downs	4/10	100	6/10	100	40/60
Shepton Mallet, Fosse Lane	10/14	71	8/14	57	56/44
Winchester, Lankhills	105/112	94	69/73	94	60/40
Totals fourth century	651/900	72	640/857	76	50/50
Totals	913/1438	63	811/1177	69	53/47

Having looked at the evidence, epigraphical, literary and archaeological, we may now assess the status of women in Roman Britain. The inscriptions and limited literary material indicated that a woman could have status, but this seemed to be dependent on her relationship with a male member of her immediate family circle – usually husband or father. This is in contrast to the pre-Roman period when women could have status in their own right. The shift in the balance was not immediate, but over the centuries of Roman occupation British women seemed to lose any equality with men – or even, at times, their pre-eminence. Only in special circumstances do women appear to have had higher status than men in numerical/material terms, and it is suggested that these women belonged to what constituted the upper classes in Britain.

This is more clearly shown by the archaeological evidence, especially if the data from the Iron Age are taken as a starting point. The size and depth of graves were examined for both periods, and it was shown that in most sites in the Iron Age females had larger and deeper graves than men. The graves with the largest dimensions were in fact for women from the earliest cemeteries studied – the Arras burials in East Yorkshire, dating from the third to the early first century BC. Women still generally had the largest and deepest graves in the first/second century AD, but by the fourth century their graves were in a couple of cases the same size as men's or, in more cases, smaller.

With regard to grave goods, it has already been noted that there was a marked decrease in the quantity and quality over the centuries of the Occupation, and also in the percentage of males and females with grave goods. This was to the detriment of females in some important cases. The point may be illustrated by reference to the figures for pottery in Table 4.5. In the Iron Age, pottery had been found in 15 per cent of male and 34 per cent of female burials, but this increased in the early Roman period, with imported ware now appearing consistently in male graves as well as in female. By the first/second century the figures had risen to 31 per cent and 39 per cent, but from then on there was a marked decline in the number as well as the quality and even completeness of the vessels deposited. By the fourth century, only 1.5 per cent of females had pottery, compared with 2.0 per cent of males. The decline is even the more curious when it is considered that females would be much more likely to have used the pots which were later to find their way into graves.

A similar steep decline occurs in the deposits of glass: in this current work found in only 15 male and 16 female graves for the whole period. In the first century the percentages were 1.4 and 5.7, and by the fourth century they were 0.4 and 0.3 in a period when presumably glass products were more easily obtainable, although glass would have to be considered a luxury product at all times. It is difficult to draw conclusions on any decline in status of women with such a small sample, and the figures from Philpott's study where the dates of grave deposits can be determined actually show an increase in the number of glass objects in women's graves over men's from the second to the fourth century.

Even more conspicuous than luxury grave goods as status symbols were structures for burials, and the lead and stone coffins which on occasion were found there.

The statistics present some problems of interpretation. For instance, in the second century mausolea held the burials of three males (0.6 per cent) and four females (1.8 per cent), and for the fourth century there were 17 males (1.5 per cent) and only 10 females (1.0 per cent); but other figures show a different picture, with women's burials having most of those features which have been suggested in this study as indicators of status.

For example, the number of step burials in the first and second centuries was M = 2, F = 1 (0.2 per cent, 0.7 per cent), and in the fourth it was M = 9, F = 10 (0.8 per cent, 0.9 per cent); stone coffins in the third century totalled M = 1, F = 3 (0.4 per cent, 1.0 per cent), and in the fourth century M = 8, F = 11 (0.7 per cent, 1.0 per cent); in the second century there were two males (0.4 per cent) with lead coffins or coffin linings, and no females, but in the fourth the figures were seven males and 13 females (0.6 per cent, 1.2 per cent); and coffins were packed with 'plaster' in the burials of 26 men and 17 women (3.4 per cent, 4.4 per cent) in the second/third century but, while the practice became less popular over time, in the fourth century the percentage of men with plaster burials was still smaller than for women: 2.4 per cent and 2.8 per cent (M = 28, F = 30).

It then must be asked why women were singled out for status burials, and why was there not also a preponderance of women in mausolea. The first question is probably the easier to answer. It is suggested that all these types of burials were the prerogative of the wealthy and the important in society, and that the women were representative of the upper class in Britain, either descendent from the pre-Roman tribal leaders, or members of the new élite which coalesced over the centuries of Occupation, made up of native and Roman leaders in their various capacities. It is further suggested that, for some at least, the leading role which women had taken in the pre-Roman period had not been completely lost, that the composition of the population in these status burials reflected that role in some small way and that, within the family, these women did have an important position. Given that these status symbols would been seen by the public for only a short period before being covered by the earth, we can assume that any ostentatious display was for the benefit of family, retainers, and the close community for a short period.

The sexed burials in mausolea, vaults and enclosures are male dominated and it is proposed that, even more than the stone and lead coffins, these structures were the means for the head of the household to demonstrate to the outside world his Romanisation, his position and the position of his family, and this for a much longer period. Burial structures replaced tombstones, which had by the late Roman period fallen out of fashion perhaps because the élite were so few they did not have to compete for status. Such ostentation was not the prerogative of the British only – and the self-display of woad-painted, limed-haired, gold-torc-wearing Late Iron Age warriors is recalled – but it was also a trait demonstrated by many Romans from the noble Augustus, buried in his grand mausoleum on the banks of the Tiber, to those vulgar little Trimalchios whose greatest wish, when they were interred in their equally vulgar tombs, was to bedazzle passers-by on the roads to Rome.

This chapter has focused on the numbers and status of women in Roman Britain. Their position does appear to have changed from the first century to the fourth, and much of the change was the blending of cultures, native and Roman. This is illustrated by the decline in the numbers of women as compared with men. From the burial evidence, certain women retained some semblance of status, even by the fourth century, and this was probably due to their native heritage, and/or the position of their husbands or fathers; but it is concluded that by and large there would be little to differentiate the 'ordinary' Romano-British woman from her Roman sisters.

Notes

1 This section on numbers in women's burials in Roman Britain is a revised and expanded version of a paper published previously (Watts 2001).

I am most grateful to Northamptonshire Archaeology and to Mr David Wilson for access to unpublished material on Ashton and Ancaster cemeteries, respectively, and for permission to use it here.

2 See, for example, Buchet 1993 in relation to burials in Gaul, and Welinder 1988–89 on burials in Norway.

3 Fitzpatrick 1997: 65. See also Barber and Bowsher 2000: 266 for comments on Eastern London, Baldock and St Stephen's cremation burials.

4 Published accounts are as follows: Ancaster (Wilson 1968; Watts 1991); Ashton (Frere 1983, 1984; Watts 1991); Baldock (Stead and Rigby 1986); Bletsoe (Dawson 1994); Bradley Hill (Leech 1981); Cannington (Rahtz 1977; Rahtz *et al.* 2000); Chichester, Westhampnett (Fitzpatrick 1997); Chilmark (Fitzpatrick and Crockett 1998); Cirencester, Bath Gate (McWhirr *et al.* 1993); Colchester, Butt Road (Crummy *et al.* 1993); Derby, Racecourse Road (Wheeler 1985); Dorchester Dorset, Poundbury (Farwell and Molleson 1993); Dorchester, Oxon, Queensford Farm (Chambers 1987); Dunstable (Matthews 1981); Icklingham (West 1976); Leicester, Newarke Street (Cooper 1996); London Eastern (Barber and Bowsher 2000); London Watling Street (Mackinder 2000); London Western (Watson 2003); Magiovinium (Neal 1987); Owslebury (Collis 1968, 1970, 1977); Peterborough, Lynch Farm (Jones 1975); Puckeridge, Skelton Green (Partridge 1978, 1981); Roden Downs (Hood and Walton 1948); Shepton Mallet (Leach and Evans 2001); Winchester, Lankhills (Clarke 1979); York, Trentholme Drive (Wenham 1968).

5 Fox and Lethbridge 1926; Lethbridge 1936.

6 That is, Baldock, Bradley Hill, Chichester Westhampnett, Chilmark Eyewell Farm, Colchester Butt Road I, Leicester Newarke Street, London Western and Watling Street, Magiovinium, Shepton Mallet and Owslebury (Roman period).

7 That is, Baldock (Roman period), Chichester Westhampnett, Colchester Butt Road I and Derby Racecourse Road.

8 Bath Gate: Wells 1982: 135; Trentholme Drive: Warwick 1968: 147; Lankhills: Clarke 1979: 123, 137, and table 9; Icklingham: Wells 1976: 103; Bletsoe: Dawson 1994: 30; Butt Road: Pinter-Bellows 1993: 62; London Eastern: Barber and Bowsher 2000: 311.

9 For a comprehensive coverage of this topic, see Boswell 1989: 3–180.

10 Also a papyrus from Oxyrhynchus, which has an apocryphal letter from one Hilarion of Alexandria to his wife, telling her to raise their child if it is a boy, but to expose it if it is a girl (*Oxy. P.* 744).

11 Wiedemann 1989: 38.

12 See Patterson 1987; cf. Woolf 1990.

13 That is not to say, however, that grave offerings of pigs or fowls were unknown in the Iron Age. There were a pig and two fowls in the Late Iron Age cemetery at Mill Hill, Deal. Pig joints were also found in high status burials of the Arras culture in Yorkshire.

14 Farwell and Molleson 1993: table 169.

15 Christian identification: see Watts 1991. Women and religion in Roman Britain will be dealt with in more depth in Chapter 7.

16 Farwell and Molleson 1993, table 5; 128; Watts 1998, 114.

17 See Chapter 5.

18 Burnham and Wacher 1990: 279

19 Watts 1989.

20 For example, Schutkowski 1993.

21 Watts 1998: chapter 7.

22 For details on the rights of women in the Republic and Imperial periods, the standard work is by Balsdon: 1962. The question of the status of women in Roman Britain has been discussed obliquely by Keegan 2002: 27–8, 106–7.

23 *Contra* Allason-Jones 2004: 273

24 On their role in canvassing for votes, see Savunen 1995.

25 Modern debate on the adoption of Roman law after this date is not resolved. See Sherwin-White 1973: 392–3. On the administration of empire, see Richardson 1976; Hanson 1988.

26 A fact noted by Hill 2001: 15.

27 The use of tombstones to indicate status in Roman Britain is not proven, and I am inclined to the views expressed by Millett 1990: 81–3 and Hope 1997 that the real élite in Roman Britain had no need for such displays as they had little competition for status. Hope expands on this, suggesting that tombstones were more a means for those who lacked status (in the form of Roman citizenship for auxiliaries, marriage for common-law 'wives' of soldiers, free birth for freedmen) to 'communicate a message' regarding their aspirations to achieving status.

28 See Sparey Green 1993.

29 At the Derby Racecourse Road site there were five stone structures identified as mausolea, three of which contained some cremated human remains, but sexing the individuals here was not possible. Similarly, at Kelvedon in Essex, nine vaults were suggested by the archaeologist, but little information on the cemetery population was possible as all skeletal remains had dissolved in the acid soil (Rodwell 1988: 26, 37–41).

30 The presence of stones in the graves at Ashton has parallels in other Romano-British cemeteries, such as Ancaster, and one excavated the grounds of Girton College, Cambridge, dating from late Roman to early Anglo-Saxon (Liversidge 1959). The closest parallel is to a site at Raunds, Northants., where the overall placement of stone, while not as frequent, is similar to that at Ashton (Boddington 1986).

31 Toynbee 1964: 337. See Toller 1977 on lead coffins in Roman Britain.

32 In the text of the report on London Eastern (Barber and Bowsher 2000: 95), only one male with lead coffin is mentioned – for burial B255; however, in the Inhumation Burial Summary Table (table 7), burial B98 is also listed with a container type of 'wood and lead'.

33 As yet unpublished, but widely seen on BBC television. Internet sites: 'Princess of the city' http://www.bbc.co.uk/history/archaeology/princess_1.shtml (24/02/04); 'Noble Roman discovered in London' http://www.britannia.com/history/londonhistory/spitbod.html (24/05/04).

34 For example, Philpott 1991: 69–70.

35 A further step burial occurred at Kelvedon but, owing to the acid soils all human remains had disappeared.

36 If the Poundbury cemeteries are taken as three groupings, divided by date.

37 For example, Philpott 1991: 95, 223; Watts 1991: 60; Barber and Bowsher 2000: 321.

38 On Roman clothing, see Croom 2000. Clothing is dealt with Chapter 5.
39 The assumption here is that the selection of burial clothing was a matter for the relatives of the deceased.
40 Borrill 1981: 318.
41 The incidence of coffins was not covered in detail by Philpott 1991 – a reasonable decision in view of the thousands that have been reported.
42 See Watts 1998: 113–14.
43 Wells 1976: 112–13.

5

LIVING AND DYING

Life in early Britain was not easy. Being born was hard enough; survival was even more difficult. But if girls managed to get through the dangerous years from birth to five, they were likely to reach maturity. Their next hurdle was to survive the childbearing years, to live in good health to what might be considered a reasonably old age. The final achievement was, at death, to be honoured and mourned by those left behind.

Birth and childhood

One of the common features of Late Iron Age and Romano-British communities was the high incidence of neonatal and infant mortality. Because it was not the practice during the pre-Roman period to bury the very young or, indeed, any children in the same burial grounds as adults, very few of their remains have been recovered. In the Roman period, it became more usual to find infants in cemeteries, particularly by the fourth century, but the numbers were far smaller than might be expected in a normal demographic sample. Thus it is difficult to estimate with any degree of certainty the actual rate of infant mortality for this period. A possible parallel might be sixteenth century York, where the death rate for infants was somewhere between 25 and 33 per cent. However even this figure might be too low for early Britain, and the percentage could be as high as 40–50 per cent. These rates might be compared with a figure of around 4.7 per cent for a mid-twentieth century American population.[1]

Only one site studied here, Poundbury, has yielded significant numbers of infant burials dated to the pre-Roman Iron Age period. Eleven foetal/neonates and a further four infants to one year old were identified among 22 babies and one adult found in a discrete burial area. They made up 26 per cent of all the Iron Age burials at the site, a percentage similar to that quoted for York, above. At Mill Hill in Kent, no children at all under the age of one year were recovered, and in the East Yorkshire cemeteries there was one neonatal burial.[2]

In the Roman period, the percentage of infant burials in cemeteries varied considerably. Foetal or neonatal burials at Poundbury for the Roman period were 3.8 per cent, and all infants to one year old 11.3 per cent; for Lankhills, neonatals made up 10.4 per cent and all infants to one year, 15.5 per cent; and for Bath Gate the figures were 3.9 per cent and 4.1 per cent. In London Eastern 2.2 per cent of burials were under one year old, while for Period II at Butt Road the figure was only 0.1 per cent; there was no distinction made between newborn and infants in these reports. In rural cemeteries percentages are higher: the neonates at Cannington comprised 10.7 per cent of the cemetery population and all infants to one year, 13.7 per cent; at Ashton, foetals and neonates were 10.6 per cent and all infants 14.5 per cent; at Ancaster, neonates were 9.6 per cent, and all infants 12 per cent; and at Baldock, the figures were 10.7 per cent and 27 per cent. The rate was even higher at Bradley Hill, where infants to one year made up 44 per cent of the burials and at Owslebury, where the percentage of neonates and infants under one year was a staggering 58 per cent of the overall burial population. At these two sites it was proposed that a birth rate of five or six per family unit would have been necessary for survival. A small country farmstead was a difficult environment in which to have and rear children.

From the mortality rates for infants at the major burial sites in Roman Britain, it is clear that most were being buried in places other than formal cemeteries. This aspect of Romano-British burial practice has been dealt with at length in earlier publications by the present writer[3] so will be only briefly summarised here. It was shown that, in accordance with Roman practice, infants up to one year or 18 months were not normally given the burial accorded to adults and interred in cemeteries outside the city bounds, as required by Roman law, but were permitted to be buried within the city walls, most commonly around domestic properties, in back yards, under floors, etc. It was also argued that, with the coming of Christianity, infants came to be recognised as worthy of burial, and were given the same burial rites as adults. It was one of the defining criteria for the identification of Christian cemeteries. We should, therefore, expect more infants – given equal respect as adults – in cemeteries of the late fourth century and beyond in those which have on other criteria been seen as Christian.

Not all babies went to full term, and others were stillborn. It has been estimated that 20 per cent of all foetuses were spontaneously aborted,[4] and it is unlikely that any of those would be found in a formal cemetery, if early in the pregnancy. Five burials were identified as miscarriages at five to six months of development at Poundbury, and there were a further 11 stillbirths. In the same cemetery a full-term foetus was surgically dismembered and removed from its mother, and the remains carefully collected, coffined and buried; the fate of the mother is not known. At Cannington, there were three possible instances of the burial of a woman with a foetus *in utero* and another at Poundbury. A pre-Roman example came from Kirkburn. There are other cases of a woman being buried with a neonate, the deaths of both presumably occurring at the same time: Kirkburn, Ancaster, Dorchester (Oxon), Dunstable, Lynch Farm, and London Watling Street are among the sites having examples.

Mortality rates continued to be high in the months after birth. In the Poundbury report, it was noted that infants beyond the first couple of months were small for their age and their bones actually less robust than those of neonates. This was attributed to malnutrition and the attendant susceptibility to disease, probably brought about by premature weaning. It was also suggested that some infant deaths may have been caused by lead poisoning. This is a feature of the skeletal remains at Poundbury for the Roman period, and evidence for lead intake was shown in 50 per cent of the children's bones examined. High levels of lead were also found in the bones at Bath Gate, and lead poisoning is believed to have contributed to the deaths of children there. In some places deficiencies in a pregnant or nursing mother's diet, such as lack of iron as found in meat and green vegetables or deficiency in folic acid, might contribute to sickly or disabled children: for example, cribra orbitalia found in two infants, probably newborn, from the Roman burials in King Harry Lane; and spina bifida in its severe form – rare, though known (e.g. at Poundbury), resulting in handicap and premature death. In others a certain amount of inbreeding, as suggested for Mill Hill, Bradley Hill, Lynch Farm, Cannington and possibly Shepton Mallet, may have produced birth defects contributing to death. From the figures above it is seen that the numbers of children who survived the first year of life were at best about 70 per cent of those born, and probably fewer.

The years from one to five were also fraught with danger, and the mortality rates were still very high. From six to ten years the death rate was lower, but children still struggled to make up for the slow rate of development in infancy. At Poundbury, evidence has been found of parasitic infections which would have contributed to malnutrition; and deficiencies in diet and susceptibility to disease, rather than lack of food, were probably even more the cause of death in these years. The incidence of cribra orbitalia or orbital osteoporosis, a pitting around the eye socket, could indicate anaemia which had occurred in the formative period; it could also be an indicator of gastro-intestinal disorders caused by poor hygiene. It is found in the skeletal remains of both children and adults in most cemeteries to varying degrees. Shepton Mallet has an adolescent with cribra orbitalia and other indicators of probable scurvy: while it is tempting to see this case as a teenager who refused to 'eat her greens', death was probably due to long-term general malnutrition, including deficiencies in vitamin C. Dental enamel hypoplasia is a similar indicator of malnutrition or perhaps ongoing gastro-enteric problems in childhood, and can appear on permanent teeth from the age of one year to about seven.[5]

Clearly malnutrition in childhood was widespread and, even if it did not always cause the death of children, it was a factor contributing to their slower development. If, as has been suggested for Poundbury, children were often not weaned until three or four years old, then the consequent deficiencies in diet would become obvious, not just on the teeth or orbits, but in the overall size of the child. It does seem that children, both girls and boys, did not develop at the same rate as modern children and that, on comparing dental with long bone development, they were found to be about two years behind their modern counterparts. This was noted for the children at Ancaster and also at Poundbury, and it is something which seems to have been common in early cemetery populations. Women never made up for this retarded development, and this contributed to their smaller size generally, as compared with those of today.

It is believed that adolescents of 10 to14 years should have been the healthiest in the population, and it is certainly true that there are fewer from this age group in the cemeteries of early Britain than from younger groups. The percentages for the Iron Age are difficult to explain, but for the Roman period we might be getting closer to the demographic norm. In the East Yorkshire burials, those aged 12 to 16 were only 1.2 per cent of the total, but at Danebury 10–14s made up 9.4 per cent. In the

Roman period, burials in this age group at Cirencester accounted for 3.2 per cent, at Cannington 5.3 per cent and at Ancaster 5.8 per cent of all burials; and the 10–15 years age group represented 4.7 per cent at Colchester, 4.8 per cent at Trentholme Drive, and 4.0 per cent at Poundbury.

Because of the difficulties in sexing prepubescent girls, this discussion has so far centred on children, rather than girls, although some girls in the 10–15 years age group have been identified (e.g. Poundbury: M = 9, F = 31). Others are known from the inscriptions of Roman Britain.

As would be expected, baby girls under one year were very rarely given the distinction of a separate burial and an inscribed stone coffin or tombstone: one was Simplicia Florentina, aged ten months, daughter of Felicius Simplex of the Sixth Legion which was based at York. His affection for her is obvious as he refers to her as *anima innocentissima*, 'a most innocent soul'. Another from York was buried with her mother and honoured on the same tombstone; perhaps they died about the same time. Se(m)pronia Martina was only six months when she died, and her mother 31 years of age. From Carrawburgh another infant, her name and age now lost, is recorded on a stone along with her father, mother and two brothers. She may have lived for less than a month, as her age had been given only in days.[6]

That little girls did not take long to win the hearts of their parents or carers is shown by the sentiments expressed in the inscriptions. Two examples come from Corbridge: a dedication to his 'very dear daughter' Julia Materna, aged six, by Julius Marcellinus; and one to Vellibia, pet-named Ertola, who was mourned by Sudrenus (presumably her father) after she had 'lived happily' for only four years.[7] This latter dedication was inscribed on a reused tombstone. The names here are not Roman, and this suggests the adoption by a local Briton of the Roman practice of erecting tombstones. Other examples include a dedication at Risingham by Blescius Diovicus to his one-year-old daughter, another at Corbridge by Nobilis to five-year-old Ahteha (Plate III), and, at Old Penrith, an inscription, set up by Limisius to his wife and to their daughter, Lattio, who died at the age of 12.[8]

Inscriptions such as these are from the military areas, and many of those who set them up were Roman soldiers, or were associated with the army. From the *colonia* of Gloucester (*Glevum*), a place where many Roman veterans were to be found, comes a dedication to a young girl, Successa Petronia, from the parents who lost their 'dearest daughter' at the age of three. There is also an interesting inscription, provided by Magnus to his 'freedwoman and fosterdaughter' Mercatilla, who lived for a year and a half. The likely situation here is that this infant had been the child of a slave woman and, instead of emancipating the woman, marrying her, and acknowledging Mercatilla as his, Magnus merely freed the child and kept her in his household as his daughter without any formal adoption procedure before a magistrate. Indeed, the mother may have died. That the little girl was afforded an inscribed stone coffin suggests that her father had a close attachment to his daughter.[9]

Sometimes the pain of the loss of a child can only be imagined, for the inscription reveals no sentiment. There is a brief dedication from Chester by the parents of two little sisters: Restita died when seven years old, and Martia was only three. Even more

Plate III Tombstone of Ahteha, daughter of Nobilis (Corbridge Museum).

terse was the dedication at Carlisle reading, 'To the gods of the departed: Vacia, an infant, aged three'. Who set up the elaborate tombstone or mourned this small child will never be known.[10]

In other cases, the grief of parents was palpable and their classical learning obvious. Two tombstones had some evidence of erudition on the part of the parents, with inscriptions in Latin verse: at Lincoln, the dedication for a girl aged nine (her name now missing) reads:

> ...she lived a most sweet [child, torn away no less suddenly] than the partner of Dis;...after she was carried away suddenly...I have mourned thy fate...
>
> (*RIB* 265)

A similar sentiment and classical background is shown in another from York:

> ...Ye mysterious spirits who dwell in Pluto's Acherusian realms, and whom the meagre ashes and the shade, empty semblance of the body, seek, following the brief light of life; sire of an innocent daughter, I, a pitiable victim of unfair hope, bewail her final end...

> (*RIB* 684)

The elegant tombstone was set up by Quintus Corellius Fortis to Corellia Optata, aged 13 years.

From this last inscription it is clear that, even when girls approached or reached maturity, their ties with family were still close. From the military site of Risingham are two inscriptions: one for Aurelia Quartilla aged 13, the stone set up by her father; and the other by a parent for Juliona, who was a fortnight short of her seventeenth birthday. A young woman of a similar age is commemorated at Caerleon, by the girl's mother: Julia Ibernia lived to the age of sixteen years and eleven months, the stone having been provided by Flavia Flavina.[11]

In Chapter 4, it was demonstrated that female infanticide was practised in the Roman period, although this was not so in the pre-Roman Late Iron Age. Having survived this culling, girls do not seem to have suffered any further discrimination, at least insofar as burial rites are concerned, and the evidence from the inscriptions shows that they were loved in life and mourned at death. Indeed, the burials of girls and young women were often singled out for rich grave deposits, usually items of jewellery. Even in cemeteries proposed as Christian this distinction continued (although with less ostentation) beyond the period of Roman occupation. It has been proposed that those buried were offered to the gods of the Otherworld, and the jewellery was a form of dowry.[12]

This seems to be a development of the Roman period. As early as the first/second century young children were given items of jewellery as grave goods.[13] Two in the Racecourse Road cemetery at Derby, one aged three or four and the other nine, were the only individuals with items of personal adornment in the walled cemetery. These objects, one ring and two bracelets, may at this stage have been of little significance. In the London cemeteries, which were mainly second century, while there is little evidence that girls and young women were as yet singled out for multiple deposits of jewellery, an important exception was the burial in London Eastern of one young woman aged between 19 and 25; the grave yielded a large variety of objects, including bracelets, beads (one an emerald), stone and glass seals, silver coins and pottery. A small cemetery at Linton, in Cambridgeshire, dating to about this same time had a child buried with a number of bracelets and a part of a glass bottle.[14] It is only in the third/fourth century, with the re-emergence of inhumation and the more common incidence of large urban cemeteries that the practice appears to have become widespread.

At some sites, the number of items deposited with young women is remarkable: for example at Dunstable, a teenage girl had three bronze bracelets on her left wrist, two bronze and one iron ring on her left hand, and a necklace comprising 61 small glass beads around her neck; an 18-year old also had a pile of jewellery in her coffin. Of children, one 8-year old was very generously endowed,[15] and another significant burial was of an infant with a small bronze and blue enamel bracelet placed on its head. At Lankhills, a young women aged 17–20 had, besides a spindle whorl and hobnailed footwear, seven bracelets, two rings and some beads; another of the same age had bracelets, beads and pins. Two children also had multiple deposits of jewellery.[16] Even those cemeteries which are believed to be Christian, such as Butt Road Period II, Icklingham, Poundbury and Ancaster, reported one or more items of jewellery in the graves of girls or young women. The proposed association with marriage and dowry is one which is hard to dismiss.

Adulthood and relationships

After about the age of 15 girls might, in accordance with Roman practice, expect to be married – although there is no literary or inscriptional evidence for wives as young as this in Britain, and it is likely that the average age at marriage was higher. The youngest recorded may have been around 17 or 18 years old: from Gloucester comes an inscription for a young man aged 20, set up by his wife, Ingenuina, who would probably have been a couple of years younger than he; marriage could be quickly followed by widowhood. Equally distressing may have been the circumstances surrounding the erection of a tombstone from Colchester which reads, '...Macri...us, Roman knight, lived 20 years; Valeria Frontina, his wife, and Florius Cogitatus and Florius Fidelis set this up'. Here is a young woman, also widowed at a very early age if her husband (Florius?) was only 20 years old at his death, left in a foreign land with his freed slaves perhaps her only support.[17]

But women in this age group also died, and in much greater numbers than men. They had entered child-bearing age and lived at a time when childbirth presented as many dangers to the mother giving birth as it did to the child being born. The information from the major cemeteries confirms that numerous deaths occurred at this age (Table 5.1).

All large cemeteries but one have a markedly higher proportion of females than males in the age bracket which might be loosely termed 'young adult', that is, in the early part of a female's child-bearing years. The exception, which is quite remarkable, is London Eastern, with 14.8 per cent of males to 12.8 per cent of females. These figures are very difficult to explain satisfactorily. It is possible that there is some connection between them and the high nutritional standard in London, as shown in the figures for dental hypoplasia in cemetery populations (Table 5.4). London seems to have been atypical in a number of respects.

From the reports where such information was provided, it is also of note that the mortality rates for females in the age group 25–35, which constituted the second half of the major child-bearing years, are as high as, if not higher than those for the years 15–25. Death in childbirth was not restricted to youthful brides.

Table 5.1 Young adults in Iron Age and Romano-British cemeteries

Cemetery	Range (years)	Male		Female	
		No.	% sexed	No.	% sexed
Pre-Roman Late Iron Age					
Deal, Mill Hill	16–25	2	15.4	4	25.0
Dorchester, Dorset, Poundbury Iron Age	17–25	4	36.4	4	33.3
East Yorkshire	17–25	32	33.7	47	43.9
Romano-British					
Ancaster	17–25	8	6.2	11	13.3
Ashton	15–25	12	10.7	15	31.6
Bletsoe	17–25	1	4.0	6	28.6
Bradley Hill	17–25	1	10.0	4	40.0
Cannington	15–24	25	19.6	47	23.9
Cirencester, Bath Gate	18–28	24	11.6	15	16.1
Colchester, Butt Road, Period II	15–30	32	18.8	38	27.0
Derby, Racecourse Road	17–25	8	25.8	6	31.6
Dorchester, Dorset, Poundbury (all Roman)	16–24	49	12.7	56	13.9
Dorchester, Oxon, Queensford Farm	17–25	7	15.2	16	30.8
Dunstable	16–25	10	21.7	12	30.0
Leicester, Newarke Street	17–15	0	0.0	4	40.0
London Eastern	19–25	30	14.8	19	12.8
London, Watling Street	17–25	2	28.6	2	28.6
Winchester, Lankhills	17–25	30	26.8	35	47.9
York, Trentholme Drive	15–25	49	21.2	21	40.3

The inscriptions from Roman Britain record women such as these who died in early adulthood. In view of the low mortality rates for adolescents, their deaths were most likely the result of complications during pregnancy or parturition. As newborn infants were not regarded as proper people until they had been acknowledged and named by their father, usually eight or nine days after birth, any inscription recording the death of a young mother would not also include the death of her newborn child.

Some inscriptions give more information than others. All that can be gleaned from two is the name of the woman and her age: from Gloucestershire, Julia Ingenuilla, aged 20, and Fesonia Severiana, aged 25, from Chester. Julia Ingenuilla's name is a diminutive of Ingenua, frequently taken to mean 'freeborn' – although there are examples of the use of this name by freed slaves in Britain. Little can be deduced from the second name, other than that it indicates a date of at least the third century. One which has a little more detail is on a tombstone from Chesterholm, and is for Aurelia [...], who died at the age of 20. Her memory was celebrated by her father, Aurelius Luc[...], probably a soldier or former soldier. There is also a dedication to Ulpia

Felicissima, who died at York at the age of 23, and whose inscription was set up on what was probably a cremation canister by her parents, Ulpia Felix and [...] Andronica. The interest here is in the name of Ulpia's mother. Andronica is Greek, so it is likely that she was of servile origins.[18]

More can be said about two young women who were members of the provincial upper class. The first, Volusia Faustina, was the 'well-deserving' wife of a local councillor, Aurelius Senecio of Lincoln (*Lindum*). Her tombstone proclaims that she, like her husband, was a citizen. Another inscription, on a stone coffin, commemorates Aelia Severa whose husband, Caecilius Rufus, was a senator at York. Both women were aged 27 and, in view of their husbands' rank, were probably considerably younger than they. One wonders how many children the women produced to claim Roman citizenship before they, too, succumbed to the rigours of birth, illness or disease.[19]

A further example comes from Risingham, a military base north of Hadrian's Wall, and was dedicated by the woman's husband, a soldier (*singularis consularis*) with a cavalry regiment seconded to the governor's guard. Aelia Matrona lived to the age of 28. The inscription is of particular interest because it includes other members of her family. Such tantalising but fragmentary detail provides a small vignette of a Roman army family unit living in the wilds away from the sort of medical care that would help to preserve the lives of women and children. In view of her age, Aelia Matrona could well have lost her life in childbirth.[20]

It is interesting to see that, of the seven inscriptions presented here, for only two is it certain that they were dedicated by the woman's husband. For two others the name of the dedicator is missing or was not given initially. That it was the parents or father, rather than a husband, who set up the inscriptions for Ulpia Felicissima and Aurelia could mean either that the husband was dead or that, in accordance with Roman marriage tradition since the late Republic, the power of the father over a daughter (*patria potestas*) was still recognised, even if the woman were married. It may also mean that the parents of these young women lived in Britain and probably somewhere near to their daughters. The coffin and its inscription for Aelia Severa, on the other hand, were provided by her husband's freedman, one Caecilius Musicus, and it might be asked why the husband, Caecilius Rufus, did not dedicate it himself. Perhaps he had died, and this prior instruction had been given to a trusted freedman in the event of his predeceasing his young wife. But another scenario, less flattering to Caecilius Rufus, presents itself. Perhaps, rather overcome with his elevated status as a local senator (one whose wealth is demonstrated by the use of a stone coffin) Caecilius himself worded the inscription to advertise to the world his position and that of his wife in the local hierarchy, and the fact that he had slaves, or in this case ex-slaves, to do his bidding. It does all have the hallmarks of provincial snobbery. Often is one reminded of Tacitus' biting criticism of the local nobility – that they wanted very much to be Roman, and that their 'civilisation' was actually servitude (*Agric.* 21).

Some women who survived the early stresses of marriage and childbirth might look to a reasonably old age. The figures from Poundbury, for instance, indicate that 40 per cent died before they reached 35, and 60 per cent before reaching 45. But 16 women died after the age of 55 and of those, eight lived beyond 65. The Lankhills figures are more drastic: only one person, a male, is estimated to have lived beyond the age of 45. Obviously the percentages varied from place to place, and there is the added difficulty in closely estimating the age of the skeletal remains of adults over the age of 25. Figures for mature adults from the major sites are set out in Table 5.2.

It does seem that, in the 25–45 year age group, more often than not there are more male than female deaths, and so the balance has been redressed from the previous age group, 15–25 years, when more females died (Table 5.1). With the notable

Table 5.2 Mature adults in Iron Age and Romano-British cemeteries

Cemetery	Range (years)	Males		Females		Range (years)	Males		Females	
		No.	%[a]	No.	%[b]		No.	%[a]	No.	%[b]
Pre-Roman Late Iron Age										
Deal, Mill Hill	25–45	9	69.3	8	50.1	45+	1	7.7	4	25.0
Dorchester, Dorset Poundbury IA	25–45	1	9.1	4	33.3	45+	5	45.5	4	33.3
East Yorkshire	25–45	52	54.7	51	47.6	45+	10	10.5	7	6.5
Romano-British										
Ancaster	25–45	75	58.0	35	42.2	45+	13	10.1	14	16.8
Ashton	25–45	60	53.6	16	32.7	45+	8	7.1	4	8.1
Bletsoe	25–45	18	72.0	10	47.6	45+	3	12.0	2	9.5
Bradley Hill	25–45	3	30.0	4	40.0	45+	6	60.0	2	20.0
Cannington	25–45	52	40.9	79	40.1	45+	15	11.8	9	4.6
Cirencester, Bath Gate	29–43	64	30.9	29	31.2	44+	77	37.2	26	28.0
Colchester, Butt Road Period II	30–50	88	51.8	54	38.6	50+	20	11.8	13	9.2
Derby, Racecourse Road	25–45	8	25.8	7	36.8	45+	6	19.4	0	0.0
Dorchester, Dorset, Poundbury (Roman)	25–45	178	46.1	150	37.3	45+	95	24.6	129	32.1
Dorchester, Oxon, Queensford Farm	25–45	18	39.1	23	44.2	45+	16	34.8	5	9.6
Dunstable	25–45	30	65.2	15	37.5	45+	0	0.0	0	0.0
Leicester, Newarke Street	25–45	3	33.3	5	50.0	45+	5	55.6	1	10.0
London Eastern	25–45	99	48.8	67	45.3	45+	32	15.8	21	14.2
London, Watling Street	25-45	2	28.6	1	14.3	45+	0	0.0	0	0.0
Winchester, Lankhills	25–45	62	55.4	24	32.9	45+	1	0.9	0	0.0
York, Trentholme Drive	25–40	160	69.3	21	40.4	40+	55	23.8	8	15.4

Notes
a Percentage of sexed males.
b Percentage of sexed females.

exception of Poundbury, and to a lesser extent, Ancaster and Ashton, in the large cemeteries the percentage of women past child-bearing age including those who may be termed 'elderly' (the 45+ group) is less than that for males of the same age bracket. This point will be discussed further below. In summary it would appear that, unlike in modern populations, women did not live as long as their husbands although there are instances of women who lived to an exceptionally old age.

Marriages in ancient times were hardly made in heaven. The arranged marriage was the norm (e.g. Pliny *Epit.* 1.14). If the parties were wealthy, unions would be organised to maximise advantage to the families of both. If from the ruling classes, political advantage would be a primary motivation for a suitable match. Caesar (*B.G.* 1.2–3) gives testimony to this in his discussion on the proposed migration and land seizure by the tribe of the Helvetii, in which a member of its nobility, Orgetorix, offered his daughter as wife to the chief of the Aedui in the hope of inducing him to join the campaign and to assist Orgetorix to become king. For pre-Roman Britain, there is little literary material available, but it can be confidently assumed that Boudicca, wife of Prasutagus the king of the Iceni, was herself of aristocratic extraction. Similarly Cartumandua, queen of the Brigantes in her own right as daughter of the previous king, would not have been married to a man below her station. Her shedding of her husband in favour of his groom scandalised her tribes people, and contributed to the civil war the tribe endured before the conflict was smothered by Rome.

The only other evidence for marriage in early Britain is from the inscriptions from the Roman period, but there is, naturally, a bias in favour of highly Romanised civilian centres such as London, the military areas in the north and bases like York, Chester and Caerleon. While the inscriptions themselves mention 'wives' and 'husbands', it is a moot point whether these describe actual legally recognised marriages. Until the reforms of Septimius Severus at the end of the second century, the ordinary legionary soldier was not permitted to marry. That did not prevent liaisons with local women, and there is no reason to believe that the relationships so formed were not as close or as binding as any legal Roman marriage.[21] So while the inscriptions may or may not indicate a legal tie, they might be taken at face value when looking for evidence of duty, love and fidelity within 'marriage'.

Examples are few, and an examination of epitaphs from elsewhere in the empire show that they are standard formulas – that does not, of course, negate the expression of real feeling. Wives are 'most devoted' (*pientissima*), 'well-deserving' (*merita*), 'most chaste and pure' (*castissima et sanctissima*), 'faithful' (*fida*), and 'very beloved' (*carissima*); husbands are 'most devoted' and 'peerless' (*incomparabilis*). A number of examples come from military areas, such as the dedication to Aelia Matrona who was the 'incomparable wife' of Julius Maximus, a cavalry officer. But others were put up by civilians. One woman, Aelia Comindus, was the wife of Nobilianus, a local councillor somewhere near Carrawburgh.[22] Her elaborate tombstone with its well-formed lettering is testament to the status of her husband in the community, and to his commitment to Roman ways. Another, from London, also suggests a native origin: 'To Grata, daughter of Dagobitus, aged 40; Solinus had this erected to his dearest wife.' But perhaps the most touching and the best known of all such inscriptions is that to

Regina, the freedwoman and wife of Barates from Palmyra. The inscription records in Latin that Regina was a member of the Catuvellauni tribe, and ends in Palmyrene script with the simple phrase: 'Regina, the freedwoman of Barates, alas!'[23]

Ties of matrimonial affection are not the only relationships inscribed on stone. Other familial connections are recorded: an uncle who set up a tombstone to his niece; a sister who mourned the death of her teenage sibling and another whose sister was 'very much missed'; and a 'steadfast' (*tenacissima*) mother-in-law, interred along with her daughter and grandson by her soldier son-in-law – a reminder that for many families in Britain, especially army families, grandparents were a luxury. Moreover, the low average age at death in Roman Britain would mean that many children would never know their grandparents, and that the extended family would be a relative rarity.[24]

There are two or three inscriptions which resonate of duty, rather than parental or spousal affection. These refer to heirs or heiresses. There is not even any certainty that there was a family connection in the first case: from Bath a tombstone erected to Rusonia Aventina, aged 58, whose origins were the Mosel region, by one Lucius Ulpius Sestius, designated 'her heir'. It is interesting to speculate on why this woman, a foreigner, was buried at Bath, and also why her heir was not, as far as can be ascertained, a member of her own family.[25] Fortune hunters were a favourite target of the satirists:

> She longs for me to 'have and hold' her
> In marriage. I've no mind to.
> She's old. If she were even older,
> I might be half inclined to.
> (Martial 10.8)[26]

It may be that Rusonia Aventina was recovering at Bath from some illness when she met her Ulpius Sestius. If so, Martial again assesses the situation:

> He sighs, pleads, pesters, sends a daily present.
> Gemellus wants to marry Maronilla,
> Is she a beauty? No, a hideous peasant.
> What's the attraction, then? That cough will kill her.
> (Martial 1.10)[27]

But perhaps it would be more charitable to assume that Ulpius Sestius had a legitimate claim to the woman's estate.

Another inscription refers to the wife as heiress to a man clearly a citizen. Julia Similina set up a tombstone to her husband, a *beneficiarus* of the commanding officer of the Twentieth Legion *Valeria Victrix*. By Roman law a couple would normally only inherit from each other's estate a portion equal to that of a child, but achieved testamentary freedom if they were granted the *ius liberorum* (the right of three or four children, according to whether free or freed) or if the man were over 60 and the woman over 50 years of age. The inscription records the age of Titinius Felix as 45, so it must be assumed that, while there were or had been children from the marriage, Julia Similina was the main beneficiary in her husband's will. This is in contrast to the situation represented in two other inscriptions, one where a [...] berius was honoured with a tombstone by his heir, Tiberia, presumably his daughter,[28] and another in which a daughter and heiress, Martiola, sets up a monument to her father, Flavius Martius. Here the relationship is clear.[29]

One further inscription involves a testamentary instruction and appears on the stone coffin for Valerius Theodorianus, provided by his mother and heir, Emilia Theodora. That she was her son's heir suggests that he had no offspring, no wife (although he was aged 35), and probably no will. It had been a law of the Twelve Tables that a mother could not inherit from a son who died intestate, but this was changed under the emperor Hadrian and, provided she possessed the *ius liberorum*, she could then be the heir. The impression one gains from this inscription[30] is that the pair were civilians, and not far removed from slavery. It is likely that Emilia was the freedwoman of Valerius' father, who himself may have had a servile background, as Theodorianus is a Greek name. It was also suggested earlier that they may have been involved in commerce – a well-inscribed stone coffin is an indicator of wealth. They came from Nomentum in Italy, and so were Roman citizens. It is also interesting to note in these few inscriptions relating to heirs that they are very impersonal, and that there is no sign of affection between the parties.[31]

To complete this discussion on relationships, we cannot omit Tretia Maria, whose life, mind and organs are cursed on a *defixio* found in London. The name Tretia is probably a misspelling of the common Roman name, Tertia, and the mistake the handiwork of a poorly educated scribe:

> I curse Tretia Maria, and her life and mind and memory and liver and lungs mixed up together, and her words, thoughts, and memory; thus may she be unable to speak what things that are concealed, nor be able ... nor ....
>
> (*RIB* 7)

This curse on liver and lungs may be a blight on a woman whose affections have been, in the eyes of the instigator, misdirected to another. According to Horace (*Ep.* 1.18.72), the liver was believed to be the seat of the emotions – affection, passion etc. – and we could take the lungs as the means of forming words and thus expressing feelings. Perhaps Tretia had given her affection to another man, and the one cursing was a rejected lover? Or the curser may have been a woman, whose lover had been stolen by Tretia? Either way, we seem to have here a romantic triangle![32]

Release from an unhappy marriage was by divorce. From the classical sources, it seems this was readily obtainable in both the Late Iron Age and the Roman period, although it is likely that it was not a particularly frequent occurrence in Britain in either period. Cartimandua's divorce of her husband to marry his squire outraged the Brigantians – not because of the divorce itself, but that she took as consort a man of lower rank, and her husband, Venutius, seems to have been a favourite of the tribe. Instances of divorce for Romano-British women are not recorded but, given the accessibility to divorce by women at Rome, it can be fairly safely assumed that this was also the situation in Britain. Only in the fourth century would this change, as Christianity was adopted by successive emperors and the power of the Church increased. Divorce became, for Christians, more difficult to obtain, and for women acting on their own behalf, extremely so.[33]

Appearance and health

Dio Cassius has given the world one of the most famous descriptions of a woman from ancient times:

> In stature she was very tall, in appearance most terrifying, in the glance of her eye most fierce, and her voice was harsh; a great mass of the tawniest hair fell to her hips; around her neck was a large golden necklace; and she wore a tunic of divers colours over which a thick mantle was fastened with a brooch.
>
> (*Epit.* 62.2.4)

This description of Boudicca has inspired sculpture and painting but, by its very vividness has led many to question it as a veristic portrait of the queen, or indeed of women in early Britain. We must look to archaeology to try to discover what the women of this period really looked like, and whether there is any truth in Dio's dramatic picture.

The emphasis on her height might seem to indicate that British women were tall, perhaps as tall as their sisters across the Channel. Certainly Ammianus Marcellinus (15.12.1) described the women of Gaul as 'taller than their husbands, and stronger by far', and Diodorus (5.27.32), probably drawing on Posidonius, also comments on their size ('as large as their husbands') and beauty. But there is no reason to believe that British women were generally exceptionally large. The evidence of archaeology throughout all sites examined in this present study in no way gives rise to the belief that British women, either in the pre-Roman Iron Age or during the Occupation, were 'taller than their husbands' – although there are instances of very tall women amongst the various cemetery populations (Table 5.3).

In this analysis of the heights of the adult populations of early British cemeteries, it is quite clear that the average for females was well below that for males. In the Iron Age, the tallest woman in the few cemeteries with this detail was, at 1.71 m, 0.09 m shorter than the tallest male (1.80 m). Both of those came from the Arras burials in East Yorkshire. The average height of females in the Iron Age burials was 1.58 m, as compared with 1.69 m for males. A 'Boudicca' at 1.71 m would tower over the average female, some 0.13 m below her. An eye-witness account would understandably depict the queen of the Iceni as 'very tall' – and Dio would not need to embroider that statement. The average British woman, however, was of small stature.

If a Boudicca-type had lived in the later Romano-British period, she might have come from the central-south of the island, perhaps Somerset or Dorset, because it is there that the tallest women were found. Cannington, in Somerset, had the tallest female (1.76 m),

Table 5.3 Heights of adults in Iron Age and Romano-British cemeteries

Cemetery	Male			Female		
	Maximum	*Minimum*	*Average*	*Maximum*	*Minimum*	*Average*
Pre-Roman Late Iron Age						
Deal, Mill Hill	1.79	1.61	1.70	1.61	1.50	1.58
Dorchester, Dorset Poundbury IA	1.71	1.63	1.66	1.69	1.55	1.63
East Yorkshire	1.80	1.59	1.71	1.71	1.50	1.58
Maiden Castle	1.75	1.57	1.64	1.60	1.50	1.56
Romano-British						
Ancaster	1.80	1.57	1.69	1.60	1.45	1.57
Ashton*	—	—	—	1.71	1.49	1.56
Baldock	1.77	1.68	1.73	1.62	1.50	1.56
Bletsoe	1.83	1.63	1.71	1.70	1.45	1.57
Bradley Hill	1.80	1.60	1.69	1.68	1.50	1.59
Cannington	1.80	1.57	1.68	1.76	1.54	1.64
Cirencester, Bath Gate	1.81	1.60	1.69	1.70	1.48	1.58
Colchester, Butt Road	1.90	1.55	1.68	1.71	1.41	1.56
Derby, Racecourse Road	1.79	1.61	1.70	1.70	1.52	1.59
Dorchester, Dorset, Poundbury	1.85	1.48	1.66	1.71	1.51	1.61
Dorchester, Oxon, Queensford Farm	1.82	1.56	1.66	1.70	1.48	1.57
Dunstable	1.85	1.56	1.68	1.69	1.52	1.59
Icklingham	1.75	1.55	1.65	1.68	1.51	1.60
Leicester, Newarke Street	1.77	1.61	1.71	1.70	1.51	1.59
London Eastern	1.80	1.58	1.69	1.72	1.45	1.58
London Western	1.73	1.69	1.72	1.61	1.55	1.58
Shepton Mallet, Fosse Lane	1.78	1.62	1.72	1.68	1.57	1.62
York, Trentholme Drive	1.80	1.59	1.71	1.68	1.44	1.54

Notes

* Heights of males in the population at Ashton were not extracted from the original site records when they were first studied by the author some years ago. The heights of 'females' were, but since that time the bones have been studied and sexed, and a few discrepancies have been detected. It is believed that such discrepancies do not affect the average height initially calculated.

and also the largest mean for females (1.64 m), followed by Shepton Mallet (1.62 m). The next highest average was from Poundbury, in Dorset (1.61 m), a site which also had the highest average for Iron Age women. The norm for Romano-British females was 1.59 m, and for males 1.68 m.[34]

The 'fierce glance' of Dio's Boudicca cannot be confirmed, but the very limited evidence of the physiognomy of women suggests that some, at least, may have had strong features, which could have contributed to a 'terrifying appearance'. The Poundbury report describes the cemetery population as having 'distinctly larger jaws' in comparison with later peoples, and thus would seem 'heavy jowled'. Similarly at London Eastern, it was noted that some females had a jaw line which resembled the male. At Cannington, it was suggested that the heads of the population tended towards 'longheadedness'. It must be admitted that these features are not a clear indication of a terrifying visage, but her streaming hair does recall the priestesses at Anglesey, whose dreadful appearance ('black attire like the Furies, and hair dishevelled') put paralysing fear into the hearts of Suetonius Paulinus' soldiers only a short time before (Tac. *Ann.* 14.30.1).

Dio's description of Boudicca's long and 'tawny' or chestnut hair is easier to verify. Strabo, when writing of the European Celts (4.4.2), notes that those living either side of the Rhine 'resemble each other in their nature and their societal institutions (and) they are also kindred to one another', and Tacitus (*Germ.* 4), in describing the tribes who live across the Rhine, refers to their 'fierce blue eyes (and) red hair'. British archaeology supports the description at least as far as the hair is concerned. The fourth century remains of a young woman at York was found complete with a head of hair of reddish colour (Plate IV);[35] and at Poundbury, seven burials with human hair were found, two males, four females aged 20–45 years, and a child, probably female, aged about eight. The hair colour ranged from dark blonde to various shades of brown.

From this rare evidence it is possible to have an idea of the colour of some women's hair, and to see how they wore their hair in the late Roman period. As at York, the Poundbury hair was long but coiled or plaited, and pinned at the back of the neck or on top of the head. It has been suggested that one intricate style would have necessitated the woman's having a maid to create the five- and six-strand braids. One braid was probably coiled in a bun at the back of the head, the other encircling the head. The effect would have been simple but attractive, and reflected the hair fashions seen on tombstones and other sculptures, such as those of the Matres on a relief now in Cirencester Museum (Plate V). The arrangement for the young girl was more difficult to recreate because of the condition of the hair, but it was probably much the same as an adult's without the oiling and elaborate finger crimping. It is also difficult to verify this arrangement of the hair in sculpture, because children are often depicted on memorials as little adults, wearing the same clothes and hairstyle. A typical example is the tombstone at York for Flavia Augustina, and her infant son and daughter who lived one year, three days and one year, nine months and five days respectively. The clothing and hairstyles of the two children, who themselves were depicted as much older than one year, reflect those of their parents (Plate VI).[36]

Plate IV Hair from woman's grave (Yorkshire Museum).

Plate V Three mother goddesses (*Matres*) (Corinium Museum, Cirencester).

Plate VI Tombstone of Flavia Augustina (Yorkshire Museum).

There is good evidence for Dio's description of Boudicca's jewellery and clothing from both archaeological and other literary sources. The 'gold necklace' was undoubtedly a neck ring or torc, worn by both males and females in many parts of the Celtic world as a symbol of status. Gold was the preferred metal, although examples in silver and bronze are also known. The finest torcs from the Late Iron Age in Britain were found at Snettisham, in Norfolk – in Boudiccan country. Now in the British Museum, they form an outstanding collection representing late La Tène art styles and brilliant craftsmanship. A continental European example was found at Mont Lassoix, France, in the burial of the 'Lady of Vix'; it is an exquisite piece of metalwork with strong classical Greek influence. Others come from Ireland, and are displayed in the Irish National Museum in Dublin. Torcs were obviously status symbols but, as both Diodorus (5.27) and Strabo (4.4.5) tell us, armlets and bracelets were also favoured, and these are occasionally found in graves which appear to be of the ordinary people. Other items of personal adornment included pendants and amulets, ear-, finger- and toe-rings, anklets and bead necklaces. Materials favoured, often in association with gold, silver, copper alloy or iron, were enamel, amber, coral, jet and glass. Amber and coral may have been deliberate prestige imports, but a female burial at Kirkburn yielded one of the few indisputable continental imports in the cemetery: a distinctive hollow copper alloy ring, found near the skull. The most common item of personal adornment, however, was the brooch, which served a decorative as well as a practical function.[37]

It is this dress brooch to which the ancient sources refer in descriptions of Celtic clothing. It was used to hold the cloak worn by Boudicca over her multi-coloured dress. Dio's description of a 'tunic of divers colours over which a thick mantle was fastened with a brooch' matches that by Diodorus Siculus (5.30): 'clothing...dyed and embroidered...; and...striped cloaks, fastened by a brooch on the shoulder...in which are set checks, close together and of varied hues'. It is augmented by Strabo (4.4.5): '...those having an honourable rank wear garments that are brightly coloured and shot with gold'.[38] The brooch worn by men was used, as Diodorus says, to fasten a cloak, and was worn on the shoulder; women might also use a single brooch usually fastening a cloak at the chest, but on occasion two pins connected by a chain or chains were chosen. A pair of brooches, with part of the chain attached to each, was found in a woman's cremation burial in the Westhampnett Late Iron Age cemetery. Brooches were made of copper alloy or, particularly in the East Yorkshire burials, of iron. A number in both female and male burials here were embellished with an enamel-like material. The frequency of brooches in burials suggests that they were worn with other garments besides the cloak.[39]

The garments worn by Boudicca and those described by Dio and his fellow historians warrant attention, especially as the fabric appears to resemble modern tartans. The wearing of this material seems to have been an indicator of status, the more so when gold thread was applied as decoration. It is extremely fortunate that an actual piece of embroidered textile, now mineralised, has been found at the Iron Age site of Kirkburn. It was probably part of a cloak, the edges hand embroidered in contrasting colour giving a checkered effect; it came from a prestige male burial. Gold thread for embellishment of garments was also favoured by the wealthy over succeeding centuries in Britain – a small quantity was found in a mausoleum burial at Poundbury, dating to the fourth century AD, and a fragment of gold-embroidered silk in the burial of the 'Spittalfields lady' in London.[40]

While this discussion of appearance and clothing has dealt with women of the upper class, it is reasonable to assume that the ordinary Late Iron Age or Romano-British woman would, in her own way, emulate the fashions and styles of her social superiors. Brooches occurred in many Iron Age graves, not just those of the wealthy; items of jewellery, while not the gold torcs of the rich and powerful, were still deposited in graves and were probably representative of the items of value in the lives of those women; and even if our lower status woman did not have a gold-embroidered checkered tunic and cloak, she at least could have garments made of wool or linen, woven in distinctive patterns.[41]

With the coming of Rome, both women and men adopted Roman style of dress, if this is a correct assessment of the depictions on tombstones and the evidence of the graves. Materials were still wool and linen, and examples of these have been found as imprints on metal objects found with burials, or the actual textile has been preserved in gypsum burials or in watery contexts. A luxury addition was silk, a fragment of which was found at Butt Road.[42] Identified as a Chinese import, the fabric was made of raw, rather than spun thread. (It was not until the sixth century AD that silkworms were introduced into Europe.) Silk damask probably came from Syria – a recent find being that in the burial of the Spittalfields woman (above). Such imports were the prerogative of the rich, and were the target of periodic, unsuccessful, sumptuary laws at Rome from as early as the first century BC.[43]

It has been suggested that errors in the depictions on tombstones indicate that the wearing of the toga by Romano-British males was not common, and was perhaps limited to the upper classes; but if the presence or absence of the brooch is any indication, a change in dress fashion (or more particularly the method of dressing a body for burial) did occur with the advent of the Romans. So common in the burials of pre-Roman males and females, the brooch now largely disappears from the corpus of grave goods. In the cemeteries analysed here, for the second to late fourth/early fifth century Roman period only 13 brooches were found in 12 sexed burials (M = 8, F = 4), and another five with unsexed adults. Of the deposits with females, two came from one grave in London Eastern cemetery. Probably a linked pair, these brooches together with a comb also found with the remains were of Germanic origin, and the burial may have been of a foreign woman. It is very late in the cemetery sequence, c.350–410. A third brooch was found with a female at Poundbury, in the grave fill; and the fourth, a trumpet brooch in almost perfect condition, came from an early excavation at Trentholme Drive. The example from Butt Road Period II was with a burial identified as possibly female. The position of the brooch, on the right shoulder, is unusual for a female, and this burial may have been male. Generally the evidence points to the abandonment of pre-Roman burial practices fairly early in the Occupation. Items of personal adornment now came to be mainly jewellery – necklaces, bangles, rings and hairpins (see Chapter 4). Few pieces have a high intrinsic value. What was found in graves did not necessarily reflect what women actually wore in life.

The jewellery a woman wears is a personal decision, and was probably so in Roman times and earlier. Gold was an obvious choice, but only of the rich. In the Roman Republic, the Oppian sumptuary law had limited the weight of gold jewellery a woman could wear to half an ounce. That law lasted but 20 years. Gold jewellery could form part of a girl's dowry; so too could precious stones, and particularly pearls, which seem to have been the most desirable of all jewels. Pliny the Younger (*Epist.* 5.16.1–7) writes of the death of the daughter of one of his friends on the eve of her marriage. The dowry included her 'wedding clothes, pearls and jewellery'. Pearls were worn on the hands, around the neck, in ear lobes and in the hair. Long teardrop pearls were very popular. Pliny the Elder (*N.H.* 9.121) relates a story that Cleopatra not only dissolved a pearl earring worth ten million sesterces in wine, but that she then drank the liquid. The story may be apocryphal.

But pearls did dissolve in the acid British soil, and it is most disappointing that some of the most beautiful pieces of jewellery found in Britain have gaps where pearls must have been. Very few pearls have ever been found from the Roman period, yet the bluish-coloured British pearls must have been used in jewellery. They were known to Tacitus (*Agric.* 12), who lists them along with gold and silver as prizes of Conquest from Britain.

Other valuable gems and items of jewellery worn by the wealthy of Roman Britain have been found of recent times as part of hoards at the fourth/fifth century sites of Thetford and Hoxne. These treasures include rings, bracelets and necklaces of gold, precious and semi-precious stones.[44] A unique piece was a gold body-chain from Hoxne decorated with two medallions, one enclosing a gold coin of the emperor Gratian, the other a setting for nine stones. It is thought to be the size to fit an adolescent girl or a slender woman (Plate VII). Such items never found their way into Romano-British burials, and this confirms the view voiced previously that many grave goods were, by the later Roman period, merely token or symbolic.[45]

British women very quickly adopted Roman-style footwear. Hobnailed footwear is found in burials as early as the first century at Jordon Hill, Dorset, and in graves of both sexes in the second century cemeteries at London Eastern and Derby studied here. Not all footwear was hobnailed, and some soft soled shoes have been recovered from watery contexts. A lovely openwork pair, now in the British Museum, came from a sarcophagus at Southfleet in Kent (Plate VIII). Similar shoes have now been found at

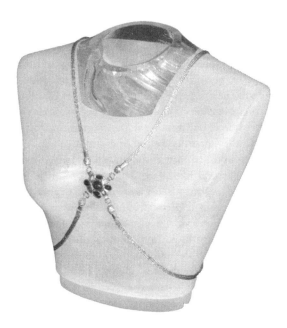

Plate VII Hoxne body chain (British Museum).

Plate VIII Woman's shoes from Southfleet (British Museum).

Vindolanda, which may even have belonged to Sulpicia Lepidina, the wife of the Prefect of the Ninth Cohort of Batavians, Flavius Cerialis. Another pair of what has been seen as a style common in the northern provinces, and dating to the late third/fourth century, was found on the body of a woman in a bog near Amcotts, Lincolnshire. If she had the resources, the Romano-British woman could be very well attired.[46]

While a fine appearance might be important, good health was essential. Earlier we looked at the mortality rate of women in their child-bearing years, and it was concluded that many who died in the age group 18–35 years did so as a result of complications with or the repercussions of childbirth. Their overall health might now be considered, as far as can be determined from the skeletal remains.[47]

It is difficult to make a general assessment, as the health of the population seemed to vary considerably, but an analysis of the incidence of dental enamel hypoplasia goes some way to making the picture clearer for some sites (Table 5.4).

If the presence of enamel hypoplasia, manifested as a horizontal groove across permanent teeth formed in childhood, usually between four and ten years, is taken as a sign of ill health or particularly poor nutrition, and if the small number of sites can be representative of the whole country, then in the pre-Roman period the people of Britain were relatively healthy and well-fed; furthermore, there is virtually no difference in the number of males and females showing signs of malnutrition.

The results from the Roman period are more complex. First of all it should be noted that the percentages for males and females have little to separate them; there is nothing to suggest that very young male children were given better food than female, as sometimes occurred in more primitive societies. The good nutrition rate for York does not seem

Table 5.4 Hypoplasia in Iron Age and Romano-British cemeteries

Cemetery	% of all inhumations	Male		Female	
		No.	% sexed	No.	% sexed
Pre-Roman Late Iron Age					
Deal, Mill Hill	4.8	1	7.1	1	6.3
East Yorkshire	1.9	1	1.1	3	2.8
Verulamium, King Harry Lane	17.6	0?	0.0	1	33.3
Romano-British					
Ashton	19.4	*c.*29	25.9	*c.*13	26.5
Bletsoe	47.8	13	52.0	9	45.6
Cannington	15.9[a]	26	20.4	43	21.8
Cirencester, Bath Gate	13.0	30	14.3	13	14.0
Colchester, Butt Road Period II	9.6	25	14.7	24	17.1
Dorchester, Dorset Poundbury (all periods)	11.2	—	—	—	—
Icklingham	16.0	4	21.0	4	13.0
Leicester, Newarke Street	'rare'	—	—	—	—
London Eastern	11.9[b]	—	8.5	—	11.0
London Western	—	0	0.0	0	0.0
Shepton Mallet	11.1	2	14.3	2	14.3
York, Trentholme Drive	1.5	—	—	—	—

Notes

a There is discrepancy in the figures given in the Cannington report (Rahtz *et al.* 2000: 253). The percentage above is based on 26 males, 43 females, 8 adolescents and 8 juveniles (total 85) out of a cemetery population of 542.

b The figures for London Eastern are approximate only, and based on numbers of the teeth affected, rather than burials.

to be accidental, since the figures for the earlier Iron Age East Yorkshire burials are also low. Perhaps the same might be said for London and Colchester – that in those regions food was plentiful and there was sufficient variety for people to avoid the conditions which would lead to anaemia or similar disorders revealed on the bones. The report for London Western commented on the apparently 'well balanced, healthy diet' enjoyed in life by the inhabitants. It might also be that, because of the heavy Roman influence, a fresh, clean water supply and a more positive attitude to hygiene and waste disposal would have contributed to the health of the population. Cirencester, too, is situated in a prosperous farming area, and while the cemetery at Bath Gate has few pointers to wealth, the nutrition of its population was better than in other areas, especially later in the Roman period.

This, in fact, may be a factor determining the higher figures above: a number of the cemeteries with a higher hypoplasia record are relatively late. This might suggest that health standards were dropping by the fourth century. It would be interesting to see if the evidence for hypoplasia could be narrowed down to burials dated to the later part of the fourth century, to support this hypothesis.

Care of teeth was a hit-or-miss affair in most ancient societies, and the remains from early British cemeteries confirm this. It is not possible to say definitively that females took less care of their teeth than did males, because it is a well-known fact that the teeth of women deteriorate during their child-bearing/lactating years. Nor can it be said that in the pre-Roman period dental health was better than during the Occupation. There are few data for the Iron Age, and they are inconclusive: for the East Yorkshire burials, tooth loss was M = 2.4 per cent, F = 1.3 per cent, and caries M = 1.4 per cent, F = 3.9 per cent; however for Mill Hill the figures are much higher, and are closer to those of a late Roman cemetery such as Cannington: tooth loss of M = 6.7 per cent, F = 17.7 per cent; caries M = 13.7 per cent, F = 11.2 per cent (cf. Cannington M = 15.3 per cent, F = 17.6 per cent and M = 8.4 per cent, F = 5.4 per cent). It may be that being in a high fluoride area contributed to a better dental record, but such information is not available. It is likely, however, that overall both males and females suffered fewer tooth losses and had fewer caries in the Late Iron Age than in the Roman period. This can be attributed to the absence in the diet of substances which were later brought to Britain by the Romans, such as dried fruits, wine, and foods heavy with carbohydrates which clung to the teeth. Tooth loss was not reported for many sites, but ranged from an average of 1.9 per cent for the East Yorkshire burials to 16.6 per cent for Cannington, with no clear bias towards males or females. The incidence of caries was mostly in the range 2–10 per cent, with no clear gender bias. The rate for Poundbury was very high at 15.8 per cent.

Evidence of nutritional deficiency shows up in bones as well as teeth, and cribra orbitalia has been mentioned above. Rickets, a disease usually resulting in bowed legs, is caused by a deficiency in vitamin D. In our period of study it affected males and females, but not in the large numbers found in the Middle Ages and later. One female was reported with rickets at Ancaster, one child in London Watling Street cemetery, two infants at Poundbury, and there was a group of males who apparently had the condition at Ashton – a surprising find, explicable as men who in their youth spent much of their daylight hours inside stoking the iron furnaces and kilns which were a feature of that small town.[48]

Bones thus reveal information about the lives of the community – work, accidents, illness, even the actual society. The development of Schmorl's nodes on the lower spine is evidence of the carrying of heavy loads, or of heavy work, particularly in adolescence/early adulthood. They are found in males more frequently than females. For the Iron Age there is little information available, but at Mill Hill the only instances of Schmorl's nodes were of two females. In the Roman cemeteries, all sites had more males than females affected. Mostly the examples come from rural centres, but two do not, and the figures are somewhat surprising: at Bath Gate the percentages are M = 7.7 per cent and F = 5.6 per cent of vertebrae, this latter figure considered high. The cemetery was not a well-organised one and would not be the burial ground of most of the wealthier inhabitants of Roman Cirencester, which was one of the most prosperous towns in Britain and probably a provincial capital late in its life. The cemetery might best be interpreted as 'working class', and this is reflected in lack of grave goods and the wear and tear on the bones. London Eastern also produced evidence for males and females with Schmorl's nodes, and again it is the incidence among females that is surprising. Despite the low mortality rate for young women and the relatively high nutrition levels, people in Cirencester and London worked hard for their living. Other sites recording women with the condition include Ancaster, Butt Road, Leicester Newarke Street and Shepton Mallet.

'Squatting facets' found on the lower tibiae are also a possible social indicator. They are believed to be formed from prolonged squatting, activities such as preparing skins, picking over grain, grinding flour, etc., and are more common in rural than urban communities.[49] In this study they were usually found more frequently among women, whose tasks these were, than men. The figures for Iron Age sites are again few, but fairly conclusive: Mill Hill and Danebury both have $M = 3$, $F = 5$. Roman sites have much the same result, and the same kinds of figures, with Bradley Hill, Icklingham, Lynch Farm, and Trentholme Drive all having more females than males affected. But at Ashton, one-third of females and one half of males had the condition.

In a similar societal class were injuries on the bones of three people, two male and one female, from Icklingham. They all had lesions on their wrists and shins which were consistent with the damage to tissue and ultimately to bones caused by shackles, and the group has been tentatively identified as slaves. The palaeopathologist commented that he had 'never before seen a group (of injuries on bones) like these' and, if his interpretation is correct, they will be the only slaves ever identified physically in Britain, although some slave and freed women have been identified by name in this present study (see Chapter 3), and slave chains have been found in Britain.[50]

Evidence of accidental trauma was found in burials of both sexes, but less frequently with females. Fractures of the ulna, termed 'parry' fractures, and usually interpreted as indicating some degree of hostility as a person raises his or her arm to ward off a blow, are not very common, although they do occur in women's bones: Bath Gate (one), Butt Road (four), Dunstable (one) and Poundbury (four). At Leicester, one woman had a broken ulna, and another suffered not only a similar injury but also a broken nose. There were also four males with broken ulnae. The author of the report was perhaps understating the situation when he wrote that there was little evidence of violence in this small cemetery of 54 burials.

Fractures of the ribs, particularly at the front on the left hand side, may also indicate domestic or community violence: this is the part of the rib cage which would be in line from a blow delivered by a right-handed aggressor.[51] Two women from Bath Gate have broken ribs on the left side. Here three quarters of all rib fractures, both male and female, were on the left side, suggesting a community far from peaceful.

Women suffered fractures to other bones, but overall such injuries were not common, and fractures and wounds generally healed well and without infection. Rudimentary splinting would have served simple breaks. But poor healing could cause inconvenience and probably pain: at Ancaster a female had broken both bones of her lower left leg, and when they healed the subsequent shortening of the bone would have resulted in her walking with a limp.

However some interventions were fatal. One of the most remarkable finds at any site was that of a skull which had quite clear evidence of trephination. The man did not survive, as there is no evidence of healing of the skull. One can imagine his desperation even to contemplate the risk and the pain of such an operation. Yet it may be that he had some medicinal help: among the mineralised plant remains found at the site were opium poppy seeds (*Papaver somniferum*). Perhaps the unfortunate patient just did not wake up from a drug-induced sleep. This case was discovered at in the cemetery at Newarke Street, Leicester. There was another possible trephination – of a female – at Poundbury (Burial 625), and one at Trentholme Drive, but no further details are available.

Other painful complaints suffered by women did not cause death, but made life miserable. Several cases of maxillary sinusitis were reported. This affliction, brought about by the physical conditions endured by the sufferer, such as central hearths and lack of ventilation, smoke, dust and cold, on occasion resulted in chronic infection of the sinuses which ultimately affected the bone. Women, because they spent more time indoors than men, were possibly more susceptible. Examples are found in the skeletal remains at Bath Gate (M = 4, F = 3), Shepton Mallet (F = 3), and Leicester Newarke Street (F = 1). The cold dampness of a British winter also increased the difficulties of those suffering with degenerative bone disorders, particularly arthritis. It is by far the most common affliction found in British cemeteries, affecting adults from a quite early age, and many of the mature and elderly. The disease does not appear to discriminate between males and females.

Less easy to discern on the skeletal remains were infectious diseases which were probably the cause of death. The incidence of tuberculosis may have been quite high, but a large percentage of cases, such as those of the lungs, will not show up on the bones. In some of the earlier reports, probably because it was seen for the first time, tuberculosis was identified only tentatively, the bone specialists suggesting brucellosis as an alternative. However, more cases have now been confirmed. It might have been thought that the greater percentage of them would have been women who spent more time inside a house than in the fresh air and sunshine, but this does not show up in the data, for example, Ancaster M = 2, F = 1, Ashton M = 2, F = 1, Cannington M = 2, Leicester Newarke Street F = 1, Poundbury M = 1, F = 2.

It was once widely believed that leprosy, the scourge of the Middle Ages, did not come to Britain before the Dark Ages, but it has been found at the Cannington cemetery, perhaps introduced from the Middle East towards the end of the Roman period. Three or more cases have been identified, including one woman so afflicted that her right hand was virtually useless, and her foot 'boat-shaped', its arch flattened, insensitive to pain and infection on the soles. She was about 22 years old.

A further infectious disease, so far rarely reported in early British archaeology, is poliomyelitis. This affliction is difficult to diagnose from bones, as there might be other reasons for atrophy of the limbs. However, four cases have been proposed at Bath Gate, two females and two males, and one male from the Iron Age site of Burton Fleming in East Yorkshire.

Not all afflictions showed up on skeletal remains, but would still have caused discomfort or worse. A number of oculists' stamps which marked the maker's name have been found in various parts, showing that eye complaints were widespread. The wording of the stamps gives some idea of the symptoms: running eyes, cloudy vision, inflammation, soreness and 'white scars'.[52] Fear of blindness would have been very real, with little understanding of the physiology of the body, or the eye.

The curse tablets from Bath and Lydney give us an idea of what types of illness or condition were particularly feared. Romano-Britons may not have been able to define the actual complaint, but certainly knew the symptoms. Among the conditions wished upon enemies – which ranged from vague 'ill health' to death – were loss of sight or speech, loss of teeth, insomnia, infertility, insanity, tremulousness (Parkinson's disease?), gout, and possibly cancer ('intestines eaten away'). Curses invoking the gods did not differentiate between men and women. The names of both sexes are recorded on these tablets.

Finally in our examination of the health of women we might look at evidence for the well-fed and well-to-do. One of the very interesting discussions in the recent publication of London Eastern was on osteological indicators of status. The presence of worn teeth (coarse, perhaps poor, diet = lower classes), evidence on bones and teeth of nutritional deficiencies, and signs of environmental stress all indicate the lower strata of society, whereas evidence of less wear and tear and of 'an excessively rich or ample diet' pointed to those higher up the social scale. From the Iron Age, the warrior burial at Mill Hill was of considerable interest in this regard, and the examination of the skeletal remains confirmed that a person of the élite class would have shown little evidence of a strenuous life. There is no female burial similar to that of the warrior with which to compare, but the presence of a condition known as DISH (Diffuse Idiopathic Skeletal Hyperostosis) or Forestier's disease is seen as an indicator of a very rich, not necessarily healthy, diet to which the upper classes would be accustomed. DISH causes a fusion and calcification of the spine, resulting in stiffness and pain. The condition is not widely recorded, and is usually found in elderly males. A number of affected males in Romano-British graves have other indicators of status and wealth. However one woman with the affliction has been found in London Watling Street; she was in a grave packed with chalk, and this is also seen as a status burial (see Chapter 4). Yet her age, in the range 26–45, is hardly 'elderly' even by Roman standards.

Old age and death

In an ideal society, having survived the childbearing years and menopause, women might have looked forward to an old age surrounded by loving children and grand-children, retaining their good health by keeping active, and being honoured for their age and their wisdom. But that ideal is not necessarily close to the mark.

In the first place, it is clear that most people in early Britain did not reach their forty-fifth birthday (Table. 5.2 earlier); so if a woman survived to become 'elderly' it is very likely that she would be a widow, and that her own children and even many of her grandchildren would have predeceased her. An examination of the maximum ages of females and males in Iron Age and Romano-British cemeteries (Table. 5.5) shows that some women would have outlived their husbands but, as has already been indicated, there were fewer females than males who survived beyond 45.

Table.5.5 Maximum age at death in Iron Age and Romano-British cemeteries

Cemetery	Males	Females
	Age or range	Age or range
Pre-Roman Late Iron Age		
Chichester, Westhampnett By-Pass	26–45+	45+
Danebury	40+	25–35
Deal, Mill Hill	45–55	50–60
Dorchester, Dorset, Poundbury (IA)	70	75
East Yorkshire	45+	45+
Owslebury IA	40–50	35–45
Verulamium, King Harry Lane (inh.)	17–25	40+
Romano-British		
Ancaster	55+	45+
Ashton	45+	44–54 (45+)
Baldock (Roman)	30–35	52–59
Bletsoe	50+	50+
Bradley Hill	50	45+
Cannington	58	60+
Chilmark, Eyewell Farm	35	18–25
Cirencester, Bath Gate	50–65	50–65
Colchester, Butt Road	50+	50+
Derby, Racecourse Road	45+	40–45
Dorchester, Dorset, Poundbury	75	80
Dorchester, Oxon, Queensford Farm	45+	45+
Dunstable	40+	40+
Icklingham	'elderly'	50
Leicester, Newarke Street	45+	45+
London Eastern	45+	45+
London Watling Street	45+	26–45
Owslebury (Roman)	40–50	45–60
Roden Downs	50–60	65–70
Winchester, Lankhills	45+	35–40
York, Trentholme Drive	50+	45–50

It is to be regretted that a closer comparison cannot be made between burial populations because the method of recording ages differs from report to report, and in a number of cases no maximum age is given. It would, for instance, be interesting to know if the supposed higher nutritional levels in the London and York cemeteries translated into longer lives. There does appear to be some correlation.

The inscriptions from the Roman period illustrate the longevity of some women, although the ages stated should be used with some care. For example, the oldest woman recorded in Roman Britain was one Claudia Crysis, who died at Lincoln at the age of 90. This woman was probably a freed slave; her name is Greek (Crysis = 'gold'), and her age is given in years only, not in the Roman fashion of years, months and days – although this is not a certain indicator. If a former slave, she may not even have known the actual year of her birth.

There are fewer than ten other women recorded on the inscriptions aged 45 or more: one was 48, four were in their fifties, two in their sixties, and one aged 75.[53] The oldest of this group was Julia Secundina, for whom a tombstone was set up by her son, Gaius Julius Martinus. An earlier tombstone had been provided by this same Julia Secundina to her husband, Julius Valens, who himself lived to be 100.[54] Like Claudia Crysis, Secundina was probably a freedwoman, taking the name of her master when she was freed, and then becoming his wife when he retired from *Legio II Augusta* around 45 years of age. If she had been a young woman 20–25 years old when they married, then the couple could have been together for over 40 years, a very long time for a marriage in Roman times. Perhaps, too, Julia Secundina might have been one of those rare Romano-British women who lived long enough to have the pleasure of seeing grandchildren grow up.

Even so, it is unlikely that she also enjoyed good health. From the cemetery evidence, the elderly were beset with a number of conditions and afflictions including tooth loss and debilitating arthropathies. Since dental hygiene was not a priority in the health care of ancient societies, those who lived to their forties and beyond could expect to have lost teeth, as well as having others which were carious and perhaps painful. There was the added inconvenience of trying to eat with at best an unbalanced bite, with subsequent excessive wear on remaining teeth. Food was not highly refined, and if eating was one of the simple pleasures of life in early Britain, for those who had lost their teeth this was one pleasure diminished. Examples of women who experienced heavy tooth loss included one at Shepton Mallet, referred to as 'old', who had lost 21 of her teeth, and another at Lynch Farm also termed 'old', and described as 'almost edentureless'. At Poundbury, 62 people had lost all their teeth; at least two of these were very old, a male and a female both aged *c*.80.[55] This cemetery is noteworthy for the high percentage of males and females over the age of 45.

Of arthropathies, by far the most common were vertebral osteophytoses affecting the spine and sometimes fusing vertebrae, and osteoarthritis which caused degeneration of the cartilage at joints. Both conditions can be caused by life style, but there may also be a genetic link in osteoarthritis. In the cemeteries of early Britain the incidence of arthritis in its different forms was widespread but varied: about 40 per cent of the Iron Age burials in the East Yorkshire cemeteries; at Bath Gate about 80 per cent of the population; at London Eastern, 70 per cent of those in the 19–25 year age bracket and 83 per cent of those over 45 years; on the other hand, at Cannington the figure was only 29.8 per cent of the population for any form of joint disease. Both sexes were affected, and this probably indicates that women as well as men performed heavy manual tasks such as carrying water, hoeing, digging and other farm tasks. From the Racecourse Road, Derby burials, it seems that women suffered from spinal arthritis earlier than men.

While osteoarthritis was more common in males than females, the reverse should be the case for osteoporosis, if modern populations are a guide. However, since only a small percentage of the population lived beyond 45, the condition is not often reported. At Poundbury almost three times as many females as males were affected (M = 8, F = 23): all but two were over 40 years old, and most were more than 60.

At Cannington, however, only four or possibly five males and two females had osteoporotic indications other than orbital, and these were mainly of the skull or femoral head (hip). Those affected were between 20 and 35 years of age.

One of the results of osteoporosis is that fractures occur more readily. But osteoarthritis can also affect mobility, and accidents were hard to avoid. At Icklingham an elderly woman aged 55–70 was found to have spinal arthritis to the extent that her lower discs had fused giving her a condition known as 'poker spine'. She also had extensive osteoarthritis in her shoulders, knees and feet, and had suffered from fractures of the right collarbone and the left fibula. To add to her misery she had bunions, probably from wearing tight, ill-fitting shoes. She may have been sickly all her life, and yet she survived, had children,[56] and died at what was then an advanced age. She was given a status burial in a dressed limestone coffin.

Julia Secundina, dying at the age of 75, was accorded similar distinction. She was honoured by her son with a tombstone. Other inscriptions for older women were typical of the dedications in Roman Britain. Some were utterly bland, some legalistic or dutiful rather than personal, and others expressed something resembling regret or regard: a devoted daughter dedicated a stone to her mother and brother; a husband and sons remembered their wife and mother; and a son wished his mother and father eternal calm in their afterlife. There are also the stones set up by heirs noted earlier, obviously carrying out testamentary instructions. These inscriptions lack the warmth of the others but recall duty and obligation, in best Roman tradition.[57]

This then begs the question of whether old age was respected in early Britain, and in particular whether older women were deferred to or given especial treatment. It has been proposed that, at Rome, while the elderly were marginalised generally, some older women were involved in occupations such as midwives, and if widows, may have controlled the family wealth to some extent – in practice if not in law – and thus retained some status.[58] This opinion is based on a reading of the classical material. However nothing survives from the literary sources for Britain. The only way that the question can be resolved is, as previously, through archaeology, which gives us only an indication of how they were treated at death.

In Chapters 2 and 4, various criteria were proposed to determine status, including type, size and depth of burials, and types of coffins and grave goods. The information for the pre-Roman period was limited to just three cemeteries where the ages of the burials and the dimensions of the graves had been published: the East Yorkshire group, Mill Hill and Poundbury Iron Age. With regard to the depth of burials, nine females over the age of 45 out of 135, or 6.6 per cent, were in graves beyond the average depth; and six out of 135 or 4.4 per cent had larger than average grave cuts. These figures do not compare particularly well with those in Table 5.2 giving the percentage of females over the age of 45 for all burials (range 6.5–33.3 per cent), but when broken down it is clear that elderly women were, in fact, given status in death. For example, at Poundbury, of the four women in that age group, three had graves both deeper and larger than the average. In the East Yorkshire burials, there were seven women 45 years or more, and five of these had graves deeper than the average, and two also had larger cuts. In Mill Hill, there were four women, of whom one had a grave both deeper and larger than the mean.

Grave goods were also examined, and compared with those deposited in the graves of younger women. This might have been a subjective analysis, because it is impossible to compare or to know the significance of a deposit of the joint of a pig or sheep, an iron brooch or a spindle whorl, so a numerical basis was employed. In the East Yorkshire burials there was virtually no difference in the grave goods for older or younger women, either in quantity or type of deposit. At Mill Hill, on the other hand, the one burial which was both the largest and deepest of the elderly females had an iron knife – the only knife in a woman's grave. None of the other three had any grave goods at all, and there were only four other females of any age with deposits. Of the four Poundbury burials, two had no grave goods, one had a copper alloy brooch, and one a copper alloy ring and animal bones. No female burials from any other age group had grave goods.

The general impression from the Iron Age cemeteries is that elderly women received at least the same respect as younger women, and possibly were given a little more status. Certainly there is no evidence that they were interred without due care and attention. There were a couple of quite shallow burials, but this is balanced by the fact that nine out of the 15 females in this study were in deeper, and seven in larger graves than the average.

For the Roman period, an examination was made of special or 'status' burials – mausolea, vaults, enclosures, step and 'plaster' burials, stone and lead coffins – as well as very deep and large graves (Table 5.6). The data came from those cemeteries analysed in Chapter 4, but excluded those where the ages of burials were not given.

Although the numbers are again low, the percentages here fit comfortably with those of Table 5.2, where the range of females over 45 years as a percentage of all sexed females is 0–32 per cent. In other words, in burials which required consider-able extra effort or expense there is no discrimination against elderly women and, as for the earlier period, they were given at death at least the same respect as those who were younger, and possibly more.

When it came to grave goods, however, there is a reversal. Most grave goods in female burials were found with children and young adults. This helps to confirm

Table 5.6 'Status' burials for females aged 45 years and over

Type of burial	Total females	No. females aged 45+	Percentage
Mausolea/vaults/enclosure	12	3	25
Step burials	12	5	42
'Plaster' burials	38	3	8
Stone and lead coffins	23	4	17
Very deep grave cuts	539[a]	77[b]	14[c]
Very large grave cuts	463[a]	63[b]	14[c]

Notes

a Total females in cemeteries where depth/area given.

b Number of females 45 yrs and over in graves deeper/larger than the mean.

c Percentage of female graves where ages of females and depth/area given.

that, by the Roman time at least, grave goods were not seen as status items; the high incidence of jewellery and items of personal adornment in the graves of these younger women supports the belief that their presence indicated some ritual, perhaps associated with marriage and dowry.

What can be said of these data is that in early Britain women did not lose their status in the community as they got older, and possibly received more deference or honour because of their age: the elderly woman at Icklingham who, arthritis-ridden, hobbled around on bunion-afflicted feet, was buried in an expensive stone coffin; tombstones were erected for some; others were interred in special burial structures or enclosures. The fact that so many actually survived until a very great age at a time when few might expect to live beyond their forties means that their families must have cared for them. It would be nice to believe that this was done with warmth and regard, rather than merely duty.

For a woman in early Britain, if she survived the traumas of birth and the illnesses of early childhood, there was every likelihood that she would grow to adulthood. Marriage brought companionship and perhaps affection, but it also brought children, and the risks associated with childbirth. Even if the mother survived, she might lose her child; the infant mortality rate was very high. She most likely would die before her fortieth birthday. If lucky – and luck probably had more to do with it than a careful health regimen – she avoided life-threatening diseases to go on to an old age in which she might hope for family support for any frailty. Her life was not necessarily one of unrelenting hardship, although she may as a child have suffered from malnutrition. Her diet was coarse, though generally adequate, and probably had little variety if she lived outside one of the bigger towns. She carried out heavy work which later showed in the onset of arthritic diseases. In many ways, her life is replicated in numerous third world countries today.

Notes

1 Figures from Farwell and Molleson 1993: 174; Rahtz et al. 2000: 143–4.
2 At Danebury, children 0–2 made up 19.2 per cent of the bodies found, but few newborn remains were discovered. Cunliffe (1984a: 64) believes that half or more of the infant population would have died before two years old.
3 Watts 1989, 1991.
4 Wells 1982: 192.
5 On bones and disease in archaeology, see Roberts and Manchester 1995; Mays 1998; Roberts and Cox 2003.
6 RIB 690, 686, 1558.
7 RIB 1181. The name Vellibia is similar to Vilbia, found on a lead curse tablet at Bath (RIB 154), which bears both Celtic and Roman names.
8 RIB 1180 (possibly a stonemason's error for Athene); 936.
9 RIB 164, 162; Gaius Instit. 1.97–100.
10 RIB 566, 961. An inscription similarly brief is RIB 750: 'To the gods of the departed: Salvia Donata lived eight years one month.'
11 RIB 1251; 1252 (the name of the dedicator is lost): in the commentary on this inscription it is suggested that her name may be of Gaulish origin; RIB 377.

12 For a full discussion on the significance of jewellery in graves, see Puttock 2002.

13 Individual items of jewellery and personal adornment will be discussed later in this chapter.

14 This fragment of a dolphin-handled glass bottle was worked to remove the sharp edges. Perhaps the object had been a 'treasure' of the little girl in her short life, or alternatively it, too, formed part of a symbolic dowry, in which glass would have been seen as of considerable value (Lethbridge 1937). My thanks to Dr Sonia Puttock for the reference.

15 With items apparently originally contained in a box or bag: two glass bead necklaces strung on bronze wire, another 200-odd more glass beads, seven bracelets, one finger- or ear-ring, four jet beads and two pins.

16 One was buried with four bracelets, beads, a necklace and a pewter bowl, and another, aged around six, with five bracelets.

17 *RIB* 202. The inscription records one of the very few Roman civilian *equites* known from Britain.

18 *RIB* 133, 563, 1715, 691.

19 *RIB* 250, 683.

20 *RIB* 594.

21 Examples include *RIB* 20, 858.

22 Alternatively, he may have held an army position as a *decurio*.

23 *RIB* 594, 1561, 22, 1065.

24 *RIB* 1830, 1745, 1829, 594.

25 *RIB* 163. Lucius Ulpius Sestius has an obviously Roman name, but we must not be tempted to assume that he was a citizen. Examples of non-Romans having the *tria nomina* are known.

26 Trans. J. Michie.

27 Trans. J. Michie. See also Juvenal 2.6.38–40.

28 Rather than a freedwoman, because if freed she would have had two names, her own and that of her former master.

29 *RIB* 505, 554, 933.

30 Also discussed in Chapter 3.

31 *RIB* 677. See also *RIB* 688.

32 A similar situation is probably the reason for the curse on a lead tablet from Bath (*RIB* 154).

33 For example, *Cod. Theod.* 3.16.1–2. See Clark 1993: 21–7.

34 Cf. the figures given by Roberts and Cox 2004, in which they give Roman females 1.59 m and males 1.69 m. The cemeteries analysed for these data are not given. Their Iron Age figures were also not given.

35 RCHM 1962: 83; Allason-Jones 1989: plate IV. The hair was coiled and secured with two jet pins. It is now displayed in the Yorkshire Museum.

36 Displayed in the Yorkshire Museum.

37 On jewellery and adornment, see Champion 1995.

38 It is most likely that all three descriptions come from the one original source, Posidonius. See Tierney 1960.

39 On the dress of British women and placement of fibulae, see Wild 2004.

40 On appearance and clothing, see Lloyd-Morgan 1995.

41 Fine wool was considered superior to linen (Croom 2000: 21).

42 Silk was extraordinarily expensive – in the third century AD, a pound of gold for a pound of silk (Balsdon 1962: 253–4). See also Dio Cassius 43.24.2.

43 For example, Julius Caesar, in his reforms on becoming dictator in 45 BC, limited the wearing of scarlet robes or pearls to those who were entitled to do so by virtue of position or age, and then only on set days (Suet. *Caes.* 43.) The best purple dyes came from the murex shellfish off the coast of Phoenicia, in the eastern Mediterranean, but vegetable dyes could produce the same result. (See Croom 2000: 24–7 on dyes in the Roman world.)

44 Johns and Potter 1983; Bland and Johns 1993. Included were silver spoons, strainers and various table items. The Hoxne hoard also contained some 14,780 coins of gold, silver and bronze. See Johns 1996 for a comprehensive coverage of jewellery in Roman Britain.

45 See Chapter 4; Watts 1991: 191–2.

46 Jordon Hill: Warne 1872; Vindolanda: Birley 2002: 141, figure 100; Amcotts: Turner and Rhodes 1992.

47 See Roberts and Cox 2003: 107–63 for an analysis of health and disease in Roman Britain, using a different set of data from those in this present study.

48 Unpublished information provided by Mr Brian Dix, formerly of Northants. Archaeology.

49 There is, however, some debate as to whether this condition is actually caused by squatting (Leach and Evans 2001: 269).

50 Wells 1976: 113. See also Thompson 1993. Slave chains are displayed in the Museum of London.

51 Wells 1982: 161; Arnold 1995.

52 Found at Sandy, Kenchester, Cirencester, Lydney Park, Verulamium and London (*RIB* II. 4.2446: 2, 3, 21, 4, 9, 11and 27).

53 *RIB* 163, 263, 369, 371, 374, 612, 688, 958.

54 *RIB* 373, 363.

55 The sex of the others was not given in the main report.

56 Wells (1976: 110, 116) suggests that she may have had 4–6 children, a calculation based on an examination of her pelvic bones and evidence for tearing of the pelvic ligaments and muscle attachments. The problem of determining the number of children a woman has had by examining the bones is still a matter of debate, so the question of fertility will not be dealt with in this study.

57 *RIB* 163, 263, 688.

58 Parkin 2003: 246.

6

DAILY ACTIVITY

The lifestyle of women in early Britain depended to a large degree on their wealth and status and, in the Roman period, the extent to which they had absorbed Roman customs. This survey looks at aspects of the daily life of women from both the richer and poorer classes. It is found that the coming of Rome had a considerable impact on the living conditions and lives of the women of early Britain in those areas where such influence had extended, and even in the less Romanised parts the impact was not completely negative. Moreover, the gap, which may have not been so great between the leaders and the led, and between rich and poor, widened during the Occupation.[1]

Housing

By the Late Iron Age, and probably before the invasions by Julius Caesar, most of the countryside had developed settlement patterns which remained the same until the coming of Rome.[2] The hill fort had largely disappeared, to be replaced by groupings of tribespeople linked by some commonality of purpose and probably kinship. The focus of this was an enclosed cluster of buildings which in some cases formed the beginnings of a basic administrative unit. Some of these proto-towns, or *oppida*, developed more formal layouts, with roads separating rows of buildings. Besides houses, the enclosures incorporated storage buildings, pits and grain drying racks.

The typical Iron Age house was a circular structure, sometimes large enough to hold an extended family. Size was probably the indicator of social standing, otherwise status would have been hard to identify externally. The house was made of timber, wattle and daub or even dry-stone, with a thatched roof and a clearly defined entrance usually marked with some kind of porch. It probably reflected the description by Strabo (4.4.3): 'They have houses made from beams and wicker, big and with a conical roof, over which they throw a lot of thatch.' The roof could, on occasion, be covered with turf instead of thatch. The houses would have been dark, smoky and probably uncomfortable.

Archaeology has left little evidence for interiors and furnishings; but from the ancient writers it appears that hides and skins on piles of leaves on the floor made acceptable seats and beds, and a central hearth, constantly stoked, provided warmth. Low tables may have been provided for meals. Water was obtained from the nearest spring, presumably brought to the house in buckets by the women or, for the upper classes, by slaves. Cooking of food was done on a spit or in cauldrons suspended over the fire. Fine examples of kitchen implements were discovered in a rich Late Iron Age (La Tène III) cremation burial at Baldock, Herts: a large bronze cauldron with iron handles along with a pair of iron firedogs, a bronze-bound wooden bucket (possibly two), two bronze bowls and an Italian amphora. Such finds confirm various descriptions by the ancient writers.[3]

Women would certainly not be much concerned about 'housework' in a small house.[4] But if they lived in a building such as the 'Great Roundhouse' constructed at Butser Ancient (experimental) Farm, some attention to detail would be needed. This particular building, constructed on the basis of the layout of an Iron Age house at Longbridge Deverell, Wiltshire, was 15.4 m in diameter, with a floor space of around 176 m². The double ring construction allowed for the formation of a series of small rooms to be used as storerooms or possibly bedrooms. In such a house some organisation and control over the space would be necessary, and if it were for an extended family, then no doubt it would be the senior women of the household who supervised this. Such a large house, it was noted, would have belonged to a person of substance and status.[5]

The round house had a long history extending back to the Bronze Age, and continuing into the Roman period, sometimes with Roman touches. At Magiovinium, the interior of a house of likely pre-Antonine date was given a quasi-Roman appearance with the application of plaster to the walls. In the Iron Age such refinements were unknown. Round houses continued to be built for centuries, particularly in the country: at Ewe Close, Cumbria, they grew up along the Roman road, and at Odell, Bedfordshire, it was only in the fourth century that circular houses were replaced by rectangular structures. The Cornish village of Chysauster has some of the best-preserved examples of this style of house. It was an Iron Age foundation and extended well into the Roman period, but showed virtually no Roman influence.[6]

With the coming of Rome the Romano-British town arose, and with it the gradual evolution of a more Roman-style house although adapted to suit the local climate. But, as shown above, this did not happen immediately. Strabo (4.3.3) notes that, even in his day (first century BC–first century AD) 'many' of the Belgae still kept their Iron Age style houses, and slept on the ground. This was at least two generations after the Conquest of Gaul.

Initially the Romano-British house comprised merely a row of single-story interconnecting rooms, then a series of rooms tied together externally by a veranda or corridor along the length of the house. In time this developed into a house with a wing at one or both ends; a story could be added. Its final form was the grand, though limited, winged Romano-British villa, found in the countryside by the end of the second century, and coming into its own in the third and early fourth. The true Roman courtyard house did not appear until around mid-second century, but was never widely adopted, undoubtedly because of the unsuitability of the design for the British weather, and the need to catch what little sunlight might appear during short winter days.[7]

The first Romano-British houses were simple constructions of wattle and daub with timber framing. Later, stone might be used for foundations, and even for walls, and the archaeological evidence shows that they were frequently plastered and whitewashed, and the interiors painted in bright colours. The roof, initially of thatch, came to be covered by slates or terracotta tiles if the owner could afford them, while window glass let in the light and kept out the weather. The Romano-British woman was presented with much more easily maintained floors with the introduction of *opus signinum* – a flooring made of crushed tile, brick or pottery shards mixed with mortar and tamped hard to form an attractive, hard-wearing and relatively inexpensive surface. For the wealthy, mosaics were the ultimate floor covering, although it is doubtful that this was the most appropriate surface for the British weather. Under-floor heating by way of a hypocaust system would have improved conditions somewhat. It has been suggested that mosaics as a floor covering would have had many drawbacks in Roman Britain, and that their popularity was the result of a desire by the provincial élite to 'satisfy their aspirations to grandeur' and, presumably, display their Romanisation.[8] By the fourth century, Britain had a number of major mosaic workshops, providing the wealthy with designs and themes which might be found in any Roman province throughout the empire, although the quality of the workmanship is not as high as those found in, say, North Africa or at Rome.[9]

More easily produced than mosaics were frescos. Walls, and sometimes ceilings, could be covered with plaster painted to resemble marble panelling, or with geometric patterns or depictions of plants, flowers and the like. Like mosaics, frescos were an entirely new addition to British houses, and were found in town and country alike, in the houses of those who had adopted or aspired to a Roman way of life. Early examples of fine painting, but now fragmentary, were found in the first century Fishbourne 'palace', and others come from villas such as Kingscote (Gloucestershire), Tarrant Hinton (Dorset), Lullingstone (Kent) and from the major towns, including Colchester, Lincoln, London, Verulamium, Wroxeter and York.[10]

Furniture also reflected the adoption of Roman styles, and houses went from having virtually no furniture at all to displaying a variety of pieces which, if not actually Roman imports, were at least Roman in inspiration. Folding metal stools with leather or textile seats were a common item of Roman furniture, and at least two have been uncovered in Britain, one on the Cambridgeshire-Essex border and another in Kent. Major items were chairs and couches or beds. Those known include a folding chair which came from the cemetery at King Harry Lane, Verulamium and couches from Verulamium and Colchester. The couch from Folly Lane, Verulamium was found with the remains of a cremation. Pieces of ivory inlay were a clear indication of prestige furniture, since ivory is a rare find in Britain. Colchester has produced two couches or beds. Of the first, excavated in 1866, little is known. The second was reported quite recently. Both may have been partially destroyed in the Boudiccan fire of *c*.AD 60.[11]

Parts of other beds and chairs have been found, as have fragments of small tables with carved legs made of Kimmeridge shale. This material has, fortuitously, withstood the test of time whereas any furniture made of wood has long since disappeared.

Plate IX Tombstone of Julia Velva (Yorkshire Museum).

A number of table legs from Dorset, carved from the locally obtained material into the shape of an animal's head with pointed ears and a lolling tongue, clearly copy the style of the classical Roman marble furniture found at Pompeii.[12] Cushions and mattresses were used: the folding stool from Kent appears to have had a cushion filled with chaff, and one of the Colchester beds had a mattress covered with a twill fabric and was stuffed with wool.

There are several representations of chairs, couches and tables on Romano-British tombstones. Two from Chester, one for Curatia Dinysia, the other for Fesiona Severiana, are very similar: they depict the draped figure of a woman reclining against the curved back of a couch, and holding a wine cup in the right hand. A three-legged table stands in front of the couch. The tombstone of Julia Velva at York is more elaborate: it depicts various family members or attendants as well as a couch, table and a wicker chair (Plate IX).[13]

The transformation of living quarters from the dark, almost featureless and primitive Iron Age houses to the relative sophistication of even a modest Roman-style house must have been quite dramatic, and it is interesting to speculate to what extent our Romano-British woman was involved in the choice. If the Roman historical sources are any indication, it is more than likely that only in the highest ranks of British aristocracy would women be involved in the decision making – and then because they had their own independent source of wealth. It is known, for instance, that the Empress Livia, wife of Augustus, had a house in Rome on the Palatine and a splendid villa at Prima Porta with a beautifully painted dining room.[14] For lesser beings, it seems to have been the husband who made the decisions regarding the house and its construction, if not also its interior. In a letter to a friend, Pliny the Younger describes one of his smaller villas:

> At the head of the terrace and the gallery is a garden apartment, my favourite, really my favourite, for I had it constructed myself. It contains a sun parlour... opposite the centre wall is my retreat, very neatly recessed, which... can be joined to or shut off from the bedroom. It contains a couch and two chairs.
>
> (*Epist.* 2.17)

There is no mention at all in the letter about a wife's involvement in the building or decorating of the extension to the villa, although Pliny was married three times. This state of affairs probably reflects the fact that, in Roman marriages, a husband's and wife's possessions remained separate. In Britain, with Roman influence on many aspects of life including law and marriage, it is likely that any pooling of resources which may have been customary practice in the pre-Roman period (Caes. *B.G.* 6.19.1) no longer applied. A wife may thus have had little right to 'redecorate' her husband's house. Indeed, it may be that the Roman (and presumably the Romano-British) woman had little interest in such projects, preferring to spend money on jewellery, rather than on costly household items, and that expensive furniture was a male indulgence (e.g. Pliny *N.H.* 13.29.92; 9.58.117–18).[15]

Any restriction on house decoration or furnishing would not affect her enjoyment of Roman domestic innovations, such as running water, reticulated through wooden, terracotta or even lead pipes. Aqueducts brought water to towns, and to various points in the town. One such distribution point has been found at Wroxeter, located on the street outside the public baths complex; it is evidence of the kind of improvement to the standard of living brought by Rome to the new towns.[16] This running water also flushed out sewers, which in turn helped to preserve public health. From the tables produced in Chapter 5, the overall standard of health of Britons did not appear to have deteriorated during the Occupation, despite higher density living. Community leaders paid for such amenities, but they must have felt they received value for money.

Availability of a good dependable water supply, provided either by aqueduct or by natural springs, made possible the provision of public baths and, in the villas of the rich, private bath suites. The earliest of these was most likely that established at Fishbourne, and many others have been uncovered, especially in Gloucestershire. The best known is probably that at Chedworth. In other words, private baths suites are found in villas throughout Roman Britain, and represented wealth as well as Romanisation. They are not common in the towns, which had their own public baths. A late Roman example was found at Billingsgate, in London. In a town where public baths had been provided as early as AD 70–80, private baths would have been the ultimate status symbol.[17]

Despite these advances brought about by the influence of Rome, some areas failed to develop along the same lines – the 'non-villa settlements' which formed a considerable proportion of the population. This does not mean that they did not benefit from the presence of Rome, and this applied particularly to those settlements which may be seen as associated with or ancillary to Romano-British villas. Further down the scale were the small farm owners isolated from the villas and towns, who were probably much less affected by the arrival of Roman law, Roman commerce and perceptions of personal wealth.[18]

Food service and food

During the Occupation, in those areas heavily influenced by Rome, household objects which had been seen only as the prerogative of the rich and powerful in the Late Iron Age came to be commonplace. Fine wheel-thrown imported pottery replaced the rougher hand-made native product of earlier times.[19] Most popular were the imports from Gaul and southern Germany, attractive red, glossy pots known collectively as Samian ware. Mass production had resulted in their wide distribution throughout the empire, and Samian vessels had been brought to Britain as prestige goods well before the Conquest. The popularity of the style never waned for, when in the third century disturbances on the Continent disrupted trade to Britain and production was cut off, local copies were produced and came to be almost as popular as the real thing – less refined, but probably less expensive. Oxfordshire and Nene Valley wares continued to be made until the end of the Occupation.

Even more highly prized than imported pottery were vessels made of glass. Glass itself was not unknown in the pre-Roman period. In native contexts, it was found in the form of beads, bangles and other small solid objects, and as 'enamel' on brooches and on large objects such as the Battersea shield and the Kirkburn sword. To date, archaeologists have not discovered any evidence in Iron Age Britain for the manufacture of raw glass, which has led them to suggest that the material was imported in this form. Hengistbury Head, a major entrepôt for southern Britain in the first century BC, has yielded just such evidence: blocks of yellow and purple glass ready to be melted and reworked. Fragments and finished beads suggest that this was also a centre for the manufacture of these objects from the imported raw material. The scarcity of production centres reinforces the belief that glass was a luxury item in the pre-Roman Iron Age. Roman glass vessels were deposited in Late Iron Age high status burials at King Harry Lane in Verulamium. Beads were also found – rarely in numbers, as in a necklace, but rather as single items perhaps threaded on a thong to be worn around the neck or wrist, as personal adornment or having a talismanic purpose. An example of this, but with the large glass bead threaded onto a bronze bracelet, was found in the Iron Age burial of a child at Owslebury.[20]

Glass continued to be a prestige item in the Roman period, but was now found not only as beads in necklaces but more often in the form of vessels – from tiny unguentaria and elegant cosmetic jars to relatively large and stocky storage jars. Because of the fragility of the material, vessels are not normally found complete other than in a funerary context, and even then they are rare.[21] However fragments on the sites of houses and villas give testimony to their presence in the Romano-British house, where doubtless they were treasured household items. Roman glass vessels abound in British museums, the finer pieces being imports particularly from the Levant, although glassblowing may have been carried out in London by the Flavian period.[22] Important pieces from female burials published in recent times include: a complete two-handled barrel jug found at Butt Road, Colchester; from London Eastern a second century bottle also moulded in the shape of a barrel, a type which was rare in Britain but more common on the Continent where it was manufactured; and a tall cylindrical bottle with handles in the form of dolphins. There was also a rare clear glass Rhenish beaker decorated with applied blue blobs in the grave of an unsexed adult.[23] All these vessels had a household use, and their being deposited in graves suggests families who possessed considerable portable wealth. Glass, like Samian ware, represented a continuity from the Late Iron Age in what were perceived as luxury or status goods.

Luxury utensils, on the other hand, appeared with the Romans. Fine silver jugs, cups, platters, spoons, ladles, strainers and other objects adorned the tables of the wealthy. Spoons had been found in the Late Iron Age in Britain, Ireland and Scotland, but it is doubtful whether these had a table use. They were usually found in pairs, one having a hole piercing the bowl near the rim. They may have had a ritual use.[24] The silver spoons in Romano-British hoards were very different in style, and probably of Roman manufacture. There were two main types, the *cochlear* or *cochlearium* with long handle, and the *ligula* or *cignus* with curved handle. Both types were found in the treasure from Thetford. Spoons were found as part of hoards from Mildenhall, Water Newton, Canterbury and, most recently, Hoxne.[25] The Hoxne silver included a matching table setting of spoons, ladles and strainers. Some of these finds, it has been proposed, were used in a (Christian) religious context.

A number of remarkable pieces of table silver have been uncovered. Among the most unusual and beautiful items from Hoxne is a set of four gilded silver objects. One is a small bust possibly representing a Late Roman empress; it was made hollow and with plates attached to the bottom was designed to be used as a pepper pot. Another is in the guise of Hercules, and two more are modelled as animals. The 'Great Dish' from Mildenhall is, however, the most spectacular piece so far found in Britain. It measures 605 mm in diameter, and weighs 8.256 kg. It is elaborately decorated in classical style and was, with the other pieces, undoubtedly a Roman import. The sumptuary law of the Roman Republic limiting the silverware to be displayed at dinner parties to a total of 100 pounds' weight was evidently long forgotten.[26]

It is not hard to imagine the tables of the owners, their boards glowing with silver, glass and glossy terracotta – a scene replicated across the empire in the homes of the rich and powerful. That there were women in these rich British households is without doubt: among the finds from Hoxne was a collection of gold bracelets and armlets, one of which carries, in pierced work, the inscription VTERE FELIX DOMINA IVLIANE (*sic*), 'Use this happily, Mistress Juliana'. This suggests that not only was the lady in question rich, but that she was also probably aristocratic. The names of other wealthy women are known from the Thetford, Mildenhall and Water Newton treasures: Persevera, Silviola, Pascentia, Innocentia, Viventia and Ianicilla. Their names were inscribed on silver vessels or on spoons. We shall meet these ladies again, in Chapter 7.

Few Roman spoons of bone or base metal have been found intact. Their presence, whether whole or fragmentary, in many archaeological sites indicates that the lower classes adopted this implement – but to what extent spoons were used at table by the *hoi polloi* cannot be known. Several spoons dating from the early second to the fourth century were excavated at Shepton Mallet. One of these had evidence of tinning: the impression given is that the poor aspired to the silver tableware of the rich. Knives had always been used at meals (e.g. Athen. 4.36), and this continued. Forks were unknown until the Middle Ages.

The types of food and drink served in these vessels and eaten with these utensils in Roman times showed continuity from the Iron Age, with the addition of comestibles which had rarely, if ever, been available prior to the Occupation. As in the later period, the food consumed in the Iron Age varied according to the status of the consumer and, to a lesser extent, his or her geographical location.

Evidence of the food eaten by pre-Roman Britons is very scarce in the literary sources, and what information is given must be seen in the light of the bias of classical writers with regard to barbarians. It is, for instance, widely recognised that primitive peoples are routinely depicted as meat-eaters and milk-drinkers: a well-known example is the Cyclops in Homer's *Odyssey* (9.296–7). Even so, the provision of great feasts by the tribal leaders in the Celtic lands of Europe, similar to those which supposedly took place in heroic times, is well attested, and was probably a means of political control. Posidonius recorded a feast which lasted several days, given by one Lovernius, a Gaul, in order to win the favour of his people; and Phylarchus had a similar story of another Gaul, Ariamnes, and notes the consumption of 'all kinds of meat' and large quantities of wine and bread.[27] Confirmation of this practice in Britain is found at the Iron Age site of Ferrybridge in West Yorkshire: on top of a cart (or chariot) burial were the bones of at least 250 animals, mostly cattle. Presumably these were the remains of a huge funerary feast which took place soon after the burial.[28]

But while feasts did not happen every day, the normal diet of the Iron Age Briton appears to have been quite nutritious and not lacking in essential vitamins and minerals. Strabo (4.3.3), himself guilty of the milk-and-meat topos, mentions various meat sources, and he also notes that surplus pickled pork was exported to Italy. Besides the bread and wine noted above, there was also fish: Posidonius says (Athen. 4.152a) that the Gauls took fish from the sea or rivers and cooked them with salt, vinegar and cumin. He also says that olive oil was not favoured because the taste was unpleasant to the Celtic palate. Cheese and butter would have been preferred. Aversion to olive oil may have been the case in some areas of Britain, but there is no doubt that it was, in fact, imported in amphorae to sites in Bedfordshire, Dorset, Essex, Hampshire, Hertfordshire and Wiltshire in the years before the Claudian invasion.[29]

Archaeological records show that there was a good supply of meat, in the form of pig, goat, sheep, cow, horse and fowl. Surprisingly, in Britain sheep and cattle bones usually rank above pig in numbers found, and this situation may be compared with that on the Continent, where pig bones were the most numerous. It has also been noted that wild species such as deer formed only a very small proportion of the animal remains recorded,[30] so game may not have been popular; and Caesar may have been correct in claiming that the Britons of his day did not eat the meat of hares (B.G. 5.12), although they were certainly eaten in Roman times.

The diet of Iron Age Britons was varied: fish were supplemented by shellfish; cereals included various types of wheat (emmer, spelt and to a lesser extent bread- and club-wheat), rye, oats and barley; peas and the Celtic bean were cultivated, as well as various vegetables of the turnip and cabbage families; hazelnuts and fruits, including wild apples and various berries were harvested; honey was readily available. Most of these foods were probably grown or obtained within a few kilometres of where they were eventually consumed. An exception would be figs, the remains of which were found at Hengistbury Head, but which would have been imported from the Continent or Africa. There is little evidence of other imported foods excepting wine, taken neat by the upper class, rather than mixed with water as was done in Greece and Rome. Beer was the drink of the ordinary folk (Athen. 4.152c).

Rome's contribution to the diet of Britons ranged from the improving to the exotic and the bizarre. The staples from the pre-Roman period remained, but were improved by better management or stocking techniques: for example, selective cattle breeding and the introduction of new strains from the Continent increased the overall production of beef, and there may have been some hand-feeding in the winter to avoid the heaviest culling. Sheep/goat continued to be the predominant meat eaten in the least Romanised areas, with progressively more cattle and pig eaten in the areas which showed strong Roman influence.[31] An introduced animal was the fallow deer, its meat and that of the native red deer being consumed in areas where sufficient woodland remained uncleared in order for the animal to survive. Wild birds and other game were probably more popular now than in the Iron Age, and fish were transported to inland centres, many miles beyond their previous Iron Age destinations. Some fish seem to have been extraordinarily expensive: at the time of Tiberius, mullet at Rome had been for sale at 100 gold pieces each (Suet. Tib. 34). Fish breeding at villa sites is likely, and the practice of salting fish was introduced by the Romans, providing a welcome addition to the winter diet when fresh supplies were not available. Improved strains of native vegetables and some new ones were introduced, and imported varieties of apples were grafted onto native stock.

A noteworthy addition to the table of the upper classes of Roman Britain was that of garum, a fermented fish sauce made particularly in Spain and Italy, and used in cooking and to enhance the flavours of a meal. The distinctive amphorae used to transport this product have been found in major centres such as London, Colchester, York, Gloucester and Chester. These were places which had large numbers of Roman soldiers, veterans or citizens, and it may be that a taste for garum was never acquired by the ordinary Romano-Britons.[32]

Vegetables introduced included lettuce, radishes, beets, parsnips and broad beans; and nettles, a native plant, were now cooked and eaten. Fruits new to British taste included plums and damsons, peaches, cherries and pears. Pomegranate seeds were found in London. Figs and dates were imported, as were walnuts, almonds and olives. Introduced edible novelties included dormice, the bones of one being found at York; frogs (edible varieties found at Sheffield and York); and snails (Silchester, and Dorchester in Dorset).

The effects of these improvements on the availability of food varieties would be noticeable in urban centres such as London – the source of much of the evidence. Undoubtedly ambitious Romano-British hostesses of the upper classes would rush to embrace the new and the unusual. It is debatable, however, whether the diet of the ordinary Romano-Briton would have changed drastically. Certainly there was greater choice, breaking the monotony of the simple meals which the countrywoman would have prepared day in and day out. But many were on subsistence farms, they had little need to go to the markets of the large towns, and their conservatism and self-reliance probably meant that these Romano-Britons were little touched by the introduction of new or exotic foodstuffs.[33]

Occupations and activities

Although there is a considerable amount known about the foods eaten by the people of early Britain, virtually nothing is known directly about the occupations of the women who prepared or ate them. The inscriptions and graffiti give us only a priestess, a slave and an actress,[34] while the *defixiones* from Bath and Uley are silent on the matter. Beyond these, all that can be done is to offer suggestions as to likely occupations, based on the archaeological evidence available, and analogies with Rome.

Since the Late Iron Age was mainly an age of subsistence farming,[35] the production of items for sale or exchange might not have been widespread. One area involving women may have been in the manufacture of glass beads, perhaps as a husband-and-wife industry with the man carrying on metalworking, and the woman's dexterity utilised in the creation of these tiny objects. Such an occupation could be a sideline to the manufacture of copper alloy and iron brooches, which also needed a furnace; and glass 'enamel' is found on some high-class brooches. An inscription on a curse tablet from Roman Athens indicates that such family businesses operated there: Dionysius, a helmet maker, and Artemis, his wife, who worked as a gilder in their workshop.[36] Women may also have been involved in the creation of pottery for sale – hand-moulded, as the potters' wheel was a very late introduction to Britain. This is, of course, speculation only. It simply cannot be determined who did what in the pre-Roman period, as no literary sources exist. Science might assist such identification in the future.

Activities within the home, rather than involvement in some organised, if small, 'industry', would have been the real basis for women's employment, although on farms they would also have a role to play in the production and harvesting of crops.

Preparing food, carrying water, creating thread and fabric for clothes, tending children and caring for the elderly or weak, including new-born animals, were daily activities. (The quality of maternal care given by Belgic women to their children was noted by Strabo (4.4.3).) To these would be added external chores, such as scraping and cleaning skins for leather and picking over grain to remove the seeds of weeds and other foreign material prior to grinding in querns.

In the field, it was probably the task of the women to remove weeds from standing cereal crops before harvesting. That such a task was performed at all was shown by an analysis of the material at Westhampnett, West Sussex, where the grain remains on what had probably been an earlier farming site had fewer weed seeds than did those of the cremation pyres: this suggested that grain and weeds on the periphery of a field were used as fuel, and that the wheat in the field itself had been kept relatively free of weed. This would most likely have been something done by the woman or women of the household, as would tending the family's vegetable patch cultivating cabbage, cauliflower, broccoli, kohlrabi, turnips, swedes and black mustard. They may even have been involved in guiding the draught animals used in ploughing, working alongside the menfolk in the field.[37]

Women of the native aristocracy avoided many of these tasks by virtue of their position and wealth. Their place was taken by slaves. That does not mean that these women were not engaged in meaningful employment. It would be drawing a very long bow indeed to suggest that upper class women in Iron Age Britain led the leisured lives of their Roman contemporaries. But life would have been easier, and slaves and servants allowed time for tending to one's personal appearance, and producing (and wearing) textiles which were more elaborate than those worn by the lower classes − functional but attractive garments of colour and skilful patterns.[38] The presence of jewellery and bronze or iron mirrors in status burials gives at least the impression of some luxury. The mirrors date from as early as the fourth century BC in Yorkshire to the early first century AD in Verulamium. A couple of very recent finds came from Colchester. One was found in a *bustum* or cremation pit of early Roman date. It and another very similar mirror, as yet unpublished, are smaller than the pre-Roman examples, but their deposition follows a well-established pre-Roman custom of mirrors with female burials.[39]

It is doubtful whether, with the arrival of Rome, the lives of women living in simple style in rural settlements or farms changed appreciably, although access to markets and shops in nearby towns was possible, and they had the opportunity to buy, rather than to make, items for home use. The types of shops were many and varied in major centres,[40] and have been identified by archaeologists. Some were quite obviously male-oriented: blacksmith, cobbler, coppersmith, pewterer, tanner, stonemason and wineseller; women would perhaps be more interested in the shops of the fuller-launderer, dye worker, potter, glass worker and gold- and silversmith. Evidence of shops for foodstuffs are more difficult to find, owing to the organic nature of any remains, but it is clear that 'the shop' was a major departure from the old exchange economy of the pre-Roman Iron Age. Its impact, however, is impossible to assess.

The social aspect of 'going to market' should not be dismissed as unimportant, although it must be conceded that the extent to which pre-Roman or Romano-British women were involved in such activity is unknown; it may have been limited.[41] Gatherings where women could meet other women must have been very restricted in the Iron Age, perhaps to religious festivals and their associated fairs, but year-round access on Roman roads to a *forum* or *macellum* and to the company of others beyond the family circle must have contributed to the spread of ideas: for men, news of actions by the administration, of taxes, of army movements, of government contracts which might be awarded, and so on; and for women, the exchange of remedies for illnesses which may have beset them or their children, and information on the latest in fashions and hair styles or new foods available in the market. In other words, for these women it was probably more a change in attitudes, an increase in knowledge and a lessening of isolation which were the main results of Romanisation, rather than in material comforts or benefit.

Other women of the poorer classes went with their fathers or husbands to live in the emerging towns, and now had to struggle with a money economy rather than subsistence, with living in small houses cheek-by-jowl with their neighbours and the subsequent lack of privacy and space, and with coping from time to time with diseases such as those which periodically swept the empire, striking the towns first.[42] Not for them running water reticulated to private baths suites, or beautiful mosaic floors and frescoed walls. For those pioneering souls who lived in the first Romano-British towns the culture shock must have been enormous, but in time the towns became places of consumer focus, entertainment, even a certain elegance, and it was not until the fourth century that they began to decline, and the population to move back to the country.

Employment opportunities were greater in the towns, where the presence of the wealthy created service jobs and the emergence of small shops provided openings for the lower classes, even if they were much fewer for women. The shops were often owner-occupied with a dwelling at the back, or took up a small space rented from the owner of a courtyard-style house, opening on to the street. Inscriptions at Rome list the kinds of jobs for women there, and similar jobs would be found in Britain: fishmongers, greengrocers, and sellers of grain, salt and other commodities; gold workers also worked from a shop, and an example of a young (male) slave working in such a shop is known from Britain.[43] Other female occupations recorded included physicians, nurses, midwives or wet-nurses, teachers, porters, woolworkers ('wool weighers' as well as weavers), hairdressers, seamstresses or dressmakers and laundresses. There were also prostitutes, actresses and musicians. Little differentiated these last three: at Rome, jobs on the stage were only for the lowest classes, and actresses and musicians also doubled up as prostitutes. The well-known graffito from Leicester, 'Verecunda the actress (loves) Lucius the gladiator' is evidence of this occupation in Britain and of the people with whom actresses associated.[44] Undoubtedly prostitution flourished in Britain under the Romans, and it did in all other parts of the empire. Brothels were a common feature of towns, often located near baths or inns:

'Innkeeper, my bill please!'
'You had one *sextarius* of wine, one *as* worth of bread, two *asses* worth of relishes.'
'That's right.'
'You had a girl for eight *asses*.'
'Yes, that's right.'
'And two *asses* worth of hay for your mule.'
'That damn mule will ruin me yet.'

(*CIL* 9.2689)[45]

As for the upper class Romano-British woman, there was probably little difference in her lifestyle whether she lived in her rich town house or her extensive country villa. The appointments would be much the same, and the activities similar: supervising slaves and running a large household, assisting her husband with entertaining, bearing children and having, to some extent, the oversight of their education and upbringing and, of course, 'working with wool'. Her life would not be so crowded with effort that she did not have time to avail herself of the various forms of entertainment and leisure activities available.

Leisure and entertainment

Our wealthy Romano-British woman would probably not need to visit the public baths in the nearest city, as rich villas were equipped with their own baths suites. But the lower classes in the towns certainly made use of such amenities, not only to wash but also to exercise, socialise, gossip and gamble. Women bathed in the morning and the men in the afternoon, unless there were separate facilities for males and females; mixed bathing was forbidden by law in the second century. The fact that this law was re-enacted by later emperors suggests that it was not scrupulously observed.[46] Provided by funds from wealthy locals, the baths must have been a popular addition to the amenities available to Romano-Britons. They were established in all the major towns, and in many of the smaller ones as well in *vici* associated with military establishments and in the forts themselves.[47]

The most celebrated of public baths in Britain were those at Bath (*Aquae Sulis*), begun in the Neronian period and in use throughout the Occupation. Others were less elaborate, but still contained the same basic facilities: an exercise area (*palaestra*), change room (*apodyterium*), dry heat room (*laconicum*), warm bath (*tepidarium*), sweating room with hot bath (*caldarium*) and cold plunge bath (*frigidarium*). If reasonably well off, a woman was accompanied to the baths by a slave who was to be responsible for guarding her mistress's clothing while she was bathing. Theft was very common, as the curse tablets from Bath attest. Following an exercise routine the woman oiled her body, and after leaving the hot chamber she scraped off the excess dirt and sweat with a strigil – or this was done by her slave, an attendant or an accompanying friend.

(A charming terracotta lamp in the British Museum depicts such a scene.) She then entered hot and tepid baths and, if brave, the cold plunge bath. All the while the visit would be an occasion for social intercourse and pampering. Rooms were set aside as massage and beauty parlours, and for meetings or similar small gatherings. Even as early as the second century BC, the playwright Plautus was making fun of women for the time spent at the baths:

> DINARCHUS: I believe fish, whose life is one long bath, take less time in bathing than Phronesium. If women would let you love them for as long a time as they take over their baths, their lovers would all become bath-keepers.
>
> (*Truc.* 322–5)[48]

Other occasions for social interaction between men and women occurred at the theatre and the amphitheatre. Theatres were not a major feature of the Romano-British urban landscape – few have yet been discovered, and it may be that there were, in fact, few ever erected in Britain. Four are known: at Brough-on-Humber, Canterbury, Gosbecks at Colchester, and Verulamium. The action in the theatre was not as popular as that in the amphitheatre or at the racetrack, but even so it is possible that performances were subsidised or at least patronised by the emperor – so Juvenal's 'bread and circuses' (*Sat.* 10.77–81), and also Fronto in the second century AD, who considered that it was politic for the emperor to promote the theatre, as well as the arena and the circus (*Elements of History* 17).

The seeming lack of theatres in Britain may point to a lack of public interest in matters theatrical. For young women of careless reputation looking for male company, this might be regretted because, Ovid (*Ars. Amat.* 3.633) tells us, the theatre was the place to go for assignations. But women were also attracted to those who participated in the theatre: actors, pantomimes and musicians. Mention has already been made of the empress Flavia Titiana's fascination for a flute player; there were also the liaisons of Messalina with the actor Mnester, and Domitia and the pantomime Paris.[49]

There was more opportunity for meeting people at the amphitheatres, especially during breaks in the activities when people would promenade.[50] If elsewhere in the western part of the Empire is a guide, the games were embraced by both men and women. At least 12 amphitheatres are known in Britain, and there were probably others. From a gladiator's helmet found in Sussex and the Leicester graffito mentioned above, it is clear that gladiatorial shows as well as wild animal shows (with untrained fighters) and public executions were staged for the entertainment of the masses. A fresco depicting a wounded and defeated gladiator from Colchester painted not long after the Boudiccan destruction of the town is evidence of the attraction of the arena from an early period – and Colchester was home to many veterans from AD 49 when the *colonia* was first established. At the time of Tiberius, a law was passed forbidding men and women of upper class families down to four generations to be actors or gladiators; and this prohibition also applied to free men under the age of 25 or women under the age of 20.[51] This was probably an attempt to prevent the continuation of a practice that was already occurring. But women were not just fascinated by the games;

the gladiators themselves were the object of adoration and fantasy ('It's the sword they're in love with!': Juvenal *Sat.* 6), in the first/second century AD, makes a scathing attack on women gladiators, and of the deliciously scandalous behaviour of a rich Roman woman who left her senatorial husband for a gladiator. The attraction to women of sports stars in the modern world is an apt comparison.

It is not known how many games would be put on in the various amphitheatres in Britain in any year. It has been calculated that, at the time of the Claudian invasion, in the Roman calendar there were 159 days of the year expressly designated as holidays, and of these 93 were given over for games at state expense.[52] But that was Rome, and Britain was probably very different, and there was also far less disposable wealth. The fact that so many arenas existed in Britain might suggest that there was a strong demand for this type of entertainment, with or without the gladiators; but the ones so far uncovered are not large, and there is no certainty that all were in use across the same time period.

There were probably sufficiently wealthy people to stage periodic shows in the amphitheatres and racetracks, if on a modest scale. It is unlikely that there would be any Roman Briton who could afford games on the imperial scale: on his return from Dacia, the emperor Trajan staged games that lasted for 123 days, and involved 11,000 wild animals and 10,000 gladiators (Dio 69.15.1). It is also unlikely that chariot races would commonly be staged in Britain, and to date no racetracks have been discovered. Initially all spectacles had to be paid for out of private purses. At Rome in the early imperial period it was the financial responsibility of the praetor, and in the provinces the *decuriones*, and while these men might have had the money to put on races teams of four, six, eight and up to twelve horses, their families may have been reluctant for them to part with it. Martial (10.41) has a witty tale of a wife who divorced her husband when she found he had been elected to the praetorship at Rome. The poet commends her: 'This is not divorce, Proculeia: it is good business.' As a modern historian has commented wryly, 'The search for popular favour was not cheap.'[53] While staging spectacles was very costly, the expense was seen as a way of building up one's clientele, and thus political influence; so from the time of Domitian on they could be given only by the emperor, or if in the provinces, with official approval.

The theatre, games and probably the circus, then, were grafted onto Romano-British society, and of all the innovations introduced by the Romans perhaps these sat least comfortably on Late Iron Age Britain, a society in which the only known leisure pursuits seem to have been feasting, hunting and perhaps religious rituals. The theatre could at least be merged with religion, and into local beliefs and attitudes. It is doubtful, however, that the activities of the arena or the racetrack gripped the imagination of Romano-British men or women to the extent that they did in Rome. At all events, many of the venues were abandoned well before the Romans left Britain.

Education

Very little can be extracted from the sources on the education of the women of early Britain. As with many aspects of this study, analogies have to be drawn from the

Continent, or from Rome itself. It is likely that, even in late British Iron Age, upper-class women in tribes with close ties to Rome would have been exposed to Roman-style education, and that during the Occupation women from this old aristocracy received the type of education that their Roman contemporaries were given.

From Caesar's account of the war with Gaul, we find that it was a Celtic custom to take the children of the leaders of the enemy as hostage not only when they were defeated, (e.g. *B.G.* 1.31), but also as a means of ensuring that allies stayed friends (e.g. *B.G.* 1.9). Such a strategy had also been employed in classical Greece to ensure a particular outcome: the Spartan king, Cleomenes, took the children of Hippias hostage to ensure that the tyrant and his family left Athens in 510 BC (Hdt. 5.65.1). The practice of taking as hostage the children of an enemy or potential enemy was adopted by the Romans, not only as a method of control but also as a means of developing in the young hostages a knowledge of and taste for the Roman way of life. They would be taken into the families of the leading senators (and after 31 BC, into the imperial family), where they received a thorough Roman education and upbringing, and subsequently were loyal allies of Rome. This would include learning the Latin language, and absorbing Roman *mores*.

Such hostages could well include the sons of British allies, and it may not be too fanciful to propose that the boy portrayed on the Ara Pacis in Roman dress with a Celtic torc around his neck was a son of Tincommius, the chieftain who owed his position as ruler of the Atrebates tribe to Augustus, and who later fled to Augustus when he was usurped by his brother, Eppillus, around 7 BC (*R.G.* 32). It was this type of young man who, on returning to Britain, would himself become a tribal leader, and who would enthusiastically encourage his own sons to learn Latin and wear the toga; and if, as argued earlier (see Chapter 2), women held considerable status in pre-Roman society, the daughters as well as the sons of the tribal aristocracy would be exposed to Roman education. Suetonius (*Aug.* 21) relates that Augustus took women as hostages as well as men and while it cannot be known if this did happen in respect of Britain, it is likely that even before the Conquest there would have been women among the British upper classes who were educated and articulate.

Education for women of the Roman upper class evolved over time from the schooling provided first by the mother at home to a more formal arrangement. From about the age of seven to eleven, girls went along with boys to elementary schools set up in a small shop space or under an awning in the forum, and run by an educated slave or freedman (*litterator*). Having learnt the basics of reading at home, the children would now obtain skills in reading, writing and arithmetic. Learning was by rote, and much emphasis was placed on memorising the Twelve Tables – Rome's original written laws. A *paedagogos* or educated slave would accompany the child to school and help with the lessons at home. From about the ages of 12–15, girls and boys attended secondary school, conducted by a *grammaticus*, who introduced the classical texts of Greek and Latin. These would be studied in detail, and a facility in both languages was the hallmark of an educated Roman. Language, grammar, history, science, mythology and general knowledge gleaned from these texts all provided girls with an educational basis for their future lives as wives and mothers of leaders in the community. They did not progress further, however. Tertiary education was the prerogative of males only, and besides, many girls were already married at 15. If they were lucky, as was the young wife of Pliny the Younger (*Epist.* 4.19), their husbands might continue their education either themselves, or provide private tutors. A very few might even get to study rhetoric or philosophy, as their brothers did.

Of the Roman women who came to Britain (see Chapter 3), many were from the senatorial or equestrian order. It must be assumed that the women of the local ruling classes were, or became, their equals in social graces and education. Of women of the lower classes, little can be said. It is doubtful, despite the need for Latin as the language of the army and of commerce in Britain, that even moderate facility in the spoken word would transfer to the written word. The numbers of errors in stonemasons' efforts suggest that their mastery of written Latin was far from complete; and these men (and their womenfolk) would at least have had the advantage of mixing with people for whom Latin was a first language. How much less facility with the language would the women of rural Britain have, with little opportunity to increase their linguistic skill when living in small farmsteads remote from urban centres. For them a Roman-style education was beyond reach – and perhaps irrelevant.

Life on the frontier

Women associated in some way with military establishments would have fared better in gaining, if they did not already have it, facility in the Latin language because Latin was so widely spoken there. But it remains to be seen whether their lives would have been more comfortable or fulfilling on the whole than those from civilian sites. Much would depend on the class from which the women came.

The main legionary fortress sites of Roman Britain were Caerleon, Chester, Colchester, Exeter, Gloucester, Inchtuthil, Lincoln, Usk, Wroxeter and York. Colchester was the first fortress established, in AD 43, and during the Occupation up to three legions were based in Britain. By the end of the Roman period, only one legion was left, the Sixth Legion *Victrix* at York, although there were still forts based on Hadrian's Wall and beyond it, and others along the Saxon Shore. Many of the fortresses were occupied for a limited time, and all except Inchtuthil and Usk became towns of some size after the army had moved on. York was promoted to the status of *colonia* and was the capital of Britannia Inferior in the first division of Roman Britain, but it remained a garrison town to the end, and the cemetery evidence points to a considerable imbalance between males and females (see Chapter 3). A regular civilian settlement grew up on the other side of the River Ouse from the fortress, and since it had all the features of a Romano-British town, it cannot be considered in this study as a 'frontier town' where women had to live in army-type accommodation, and be denied the conveniences of urban living. We must look further, to the frontiers.

There is no doubt that women travelled with the army, probably from the time it first arrived in Britain. As shown earlier, it was customary for the wives of generals and their senior officers to accompany their husbands on campaign. For the wives of lower ranks, imperial policy forbade the marriage of legionary soldiers, and so if they had been married, on enlistment they would be divorced. Thus one might expect few women, Roman or otherwise, in army establishments. But army camps attracted female followers, and the growth of settlements (*vici* or *canabae*) outside the military base containing shops, inns, brothels and houses. Soldiers came to form liaisons with local women which became more permanent unions. They established 'family' homes in these *vici*, far from their native lands and any previous relationships.[54]

Many inscriptions from military sites are military in content: dedications to the emperor, dedications to the gods in fulfilment of vows (for deliverance from the enemy?), milestones and so on. But a number of them also record the names of women, some of whom were introduced in earlier chapters of this work, but whose lives might with profit be revisited.

From the inscriptions and literary material we have met the wives of several governors who probably went to Britain on campaign with their husbands. They would have lived initially in army quarters, but it is almost certain that, as peace was achieved and the legions moved further out from the southeast, a provincial capital was set up with a suitable gubernatorial residence – first in Colchester, and then in London. We have also met the wives of four legionary commanders of the Sixth *Victrix*, whose sojourn in Britain would not have been such a great hardship, based as they were at York, though still in the commander's residence or *praetorium*.

The wives of officers commanding units in the north of the province must have had a much more isolated existence, days' travel from urban centres and the amenities they offered. Yet they did not seem to have led a cloistered life. They brought their slaves with them, and entertained visiting dignitaries and socialised among themselves. Such activity would have included the birthday party for which Sulpicia Lepidina had received an invitation from her friend, Claudia Severa. The women also seem to have exchanged visits, despite the dangers of living on the frontier.[55] There would be little to do in places such as Vindolanda, and it is clear that military wives became adept at making their own amusement. Marriage to a professional soldier would mean a very different life from the one many women had experienced as single girls. It is interesting to note that, in the earlier survey of the wives of provincial governors, many of those women were in fact the daughters of men who had also been governors. For them there could be few surprises in the provinces.

Garrison commanders were provided with a residence for a family, and the archaeological material recovered from various sites confirms that women and children did live there. The food available was more than adequate: the diet of the Roman army has been studied in some depth, and the results show that those living in army establishments had good nutritious food with reasonable variety. While the facilities provided were fairly basic, and not in the class of a Romano-British villa, they would have been reasonably spacious and comfortable. The *praetoria* excavated at Housesteads and Chesters had running water, a baths suite and several rooms heated by a hypocaust system. This last would be a source of great comfort on long, cold, northern winters' nights.[56]

Those women who lived in the settlements outside the fort had less luxury. The *vici* grew up haphazardly, with no planning input from the military, even though they were close by. Too often the army moved on before any development could occur. Some, on the other hand, benefited considerably from the association: as at Catterick, which had begun its life as a settlement outside an Agricolan fort, had been involved in supplying commodities to Vindolanda, and had subsequently gained a water supply, baths and temples. Its position on the Great North Road also led to the establishment of a *mansio*, or government inn/staging post.[57] The residents of Catterick were lucky. Such facilities were rare in a *vicus*.

From the inscriptions, it seems that not just family units were found at military sites. The extended family of husband, wife, children and mother-in-law was discussed earlier. Three other inscriptions, from Northumberland, involve sisters: one set up by Aurelia Caula for her 'very dear sister' Aurelia S[...]illa, who died at the age of 15, one by Aurelia Pusinna to her 'most devoted and very much missed sister', Aurelia [...], and another to Aelius Mercurialis, a *cornicularius*, by his sister Vacia.[58] It would be of interest to know the circumstances of these burials, and whether the young women would now be left all alone in Britain. Isolation and the problems which that brings would be one of the greatest hardships for women in army establishments in Roman Britain.

Various aspects of the daily life of women in the Late Iron Age and Roman Britain have been examined here, from the point of view of class and also of location. Housing, food and its service, occupations, leisure and entertainment, and education were examined, as well as the life of women whose lives were bound up with the army. It is clear that there were considerable benefits to be derived from Roman-style housing, particularly in the provision of running water, and buildings that were better lit and ventilated; for women they were generally more attractive places in which to live. But there is no certainty that the majority of the population actually adopted such houses, the furnishing that went them, or the new foods which were imported to supplement the staples – which continued to be consumed, and to provide an adequate if unadventurous diet. Women's occupations and leisure activities were more varied in the Roman period, but the participation in them by the poorer or more isolated Britons would be limited, as would the concept of a Roman-style education. In sum, while daily life of women in the major towns, the villas and the army establishments changed in appearance and quality for the well-to-do and it may have improved the lot of the urban poor, in the rural areas the poor and isolated were only superficially touched by Rome.

Notes

1 See Haselgrove 1994.
2 The dating of Cunliffe 1995: 69 is taken here.
3 Beds: Polyb. 2.17, Diod. Sic. 5.28, Strabo 4.4.3; seats, tables, hearths, spits, cauldrons: Diod. Sic. 5.28, Athen. 4.151e; torches Tac, *Ann.* 14.30.
4 The average diameter of a roundhouse was *c.*6 m (Wacher 2000: 24).
5 Reynolds 1994; and information from internet site: 'Butser Ancient Farm': http://www. butser.org.uk/iafias_hcc.html (24/05/04).

6 Magiovinium: Neal 1987; Ewe Close: Wacher 2000: 124; Odell: Hingley 1989: 33–4; Chysauster; Cunliffe 1997: 226, 262 and plate XXIII.

7 It is estimated that there were probably around 1000 Romano-British villas in Britain. This compared with the c.100,000 farm houses of native style (James 1993: 147). On courtyard houses see Jones 2004.

8 So Jones and Mattingly (1990: 222), who also consider mosaic floors 'a testimony to the wealth, snobbishness and taste for conspicuous consumption of the provincial élite'.

9 On mosaics in Roman Britain, see Neal 1981.

10 On wall paintings in Roman Britain, see Davey and Ling 1982.

11 Stools: Liversidge 1955: 29–32. Couches at Verulamium: Niblett 1999: 173–5; at Colchester: Crummy 2003.

12 Liversidge 1955 *passim*, and figures a, c, and plates 22, 38, 44–50.

13 *RIB* 562, 563, 688.

14 The fresco is now in the National Museum at Rome.

15 See also Balsdon 1962: 271.

16 London water pipes: Williams 2003. Wroxeter public water access (White and Barker 1998: plate 12).

17 Examples of villas with baths include: Eccles (Kent), Ashtead (Surrey), Beauport Park (East Sussex), Bignor (West Sussex), North Wanborough, Sparsholt and Rockbourne (Hants.), Littlecote (Wilts.), Holcombe and Lufton (Devon), Gorhambury and Gadebridge Park (Herts.), Brixworth (Northants.), and Norton Disney (Lincs.). For private baths in London: Milne 1995: 53.

18 If the growth of villas (domestic establishments in the countryside which had evidence of investment of considerable surplus wealth) and the development of local market centres were the criteria for defining wealth, then the failure for these to develop might indicate poverty. However, it has been shown that this was not necessarily so, that 'non-villa settlements' could actually make a contribution to the rural economy and that, despite their appearance, Romanisation was indeed a factor in their prosperity. Such failure would be the result of several interconnected factors: the geographical and physical condition of the area, the presence of large estates, and the actual social organisation pertaining in the area (Hingley 1989: 11–12, 21–24).

19 For Iron Age pottery, see Cunliffe 1991, especially appendix A.

20 James 1993: 111, 113; Cunliffe 1991: 460–1; Collis 1994.

21 See Chapter 4, on glass beads and vessels in graves. Deposits of glass vessels were always rare: in a summary of the finds in the cemeteries of London, Hall (1996) records a total of 56 glass objects (including 16 beads) as compared with 341 of terracotta.

22 Jones and Mattingly 1990: 214; Barber and Bowsher 2000: 127.

23 Of the London burials, one was sexed F, the other 'unknown' (the skeleton was incomplete), but having two bracelets and a pin among the grave goods.

24 Rock 1869; Wallace and O'Floinn 2002: 132 and plate 4.22.

25 Thetford Treasure: Johns and Potter 1983; Mildenhall: Painter 1977a; Water Newton: Painter 1977b; Canterbury: Painter 1965; Hoxne: Bland and Johns 1993. See also Sherlock 1973.

26 The *Lex Fannia* of 161 BC (Aulus Gellius *Attic Nights* 2.24).

27 Athen. 4.152d–f; 4.150d–f. See Arnold 1999 on Celtic feasting and its political implications.

28 As yet not fully published. See Boyle 2004.

29 See Alcock 2001 on food in Roman Britain. It has been heavily used for this part of the chapter. See also Jones and Mattingly 1990: 196–7 on trade with Britain in the AD 40s.

30 Maltby 1996 on animals, and Jones 1996 on plants.

31 See King 1999; Grant 2004.

32 Cf. Alcock (2001: 81), who believes that a garum factory had been set up in London in the third century and possibly another in Kent, and sees this as evidence of the popularity of

the sauce in Britain by this time. I would argue, however, that this demand is only reflecting the taste of the cosmopolitan population of the south-east.

33 See Hawkes 2001.

34 *RIB* 1129; Tomlin 2003; *RIB* II.7.2501.586.

35 Cunliffe (1995: 113) refers to a 'sufficer' economy which became, with the growth of agricultural outputs, a 'maximiser' economy which would support an increased population occupying the same land.

36 *IG* III.iii.69.

37 Suggested by Cunliffe 1995: figure 85.

38 See Chapter 5. In Greece and Rome, spinning and weaving were considered womanly pursuits, even for upper class women (although male weavers were known in Egypt). Among the better known literary examples was Penelope, wife of the hero Odysseus, in Homer's *Odyssey*, and in Roman historical times Cornelia, mother of the Gracchi, and Livia, wife of Augustus.

39 Orr and Crummy 20.4. My thanks to Mr Philip Crummy from Colchester Archaeological Trust for this information, and for showing me this second find, as yet not conserved (May 2004).

40 See Wacher 1995, 67–8, 238–9, 285, 318.

41 On this aspect, see Carcopino 1941: 201–3, who argues that women in Roman times did not form a large part of the labour force and, on the basis of the paintings from Pompeii and Herculaneum, that men did the shopping. (In Apuleius's *Metamorphoses* 1.24.5, Lucius does his own shopping.) Women were not often seen in the streets as they preferred the 'sheltered security' of their own homes. He does admit, however, that the women portrayed are from the upper class, who would be unlikely to be carrying shopping bags and baskets.

42 Such as that which swept the empire in AD 166: SHA: *Ver.* 8.

43 At Malton, Yorks (*RIB* 712).

44 *RIB* II.7 2501.586

45 Trans. in Shelton 1998: 327. From Aesernia, Italy. Note four *asses* = one *sestertius*.

46 SHA: *Had.* 18.10; *M. Aurel.* 23.8; *Alex. Sev.* 24.2.

47 Towns in Roman Britain: Wacher 1995; small towns: Burnham and Wacher 1990.

48 Trans. T.R. Riley (adapted).

49 SHA *Pertin.* 13; Tac. *Ann.* 11.28; Suet. Dom. 3.

50 It is not known whether Augustus's laws on segregated seating and special places for matrons applied in the provinces.

51 Helmet: Wacher 1995: 49, figure 18; fresco: Crummy 1997a: 85. *Année Epig.* 1978, 145.

52 Carcopino 1941: 226.

53 Jones 1992: 105.

54 However, from the evidence of Vindolanda, it has now been proposed that married quarters may have been provided for these soldiers, and also for auxiliaries who had 'families' (Hassall 1999). This would raise many questions, including whose responsibility it was to feed these 'families', whether the practice was known elsewhere or whether it was only at Vindolanda, where there would be limited access to markets, etc.

Hassall has also proposed that, at Colchester and Gloucester, both Roman colonies, the barracks at the respective fortresses provided quarters for veterans – presumably when they had been demobilised, and perhaps even after they married.

55 Birley 2002: 123–37.

56 Food: Davies 1971; King 1984, 1999. *Praetoria*: Allason-Jones 1989: 56; Johnson 1990: 26.

57 Burnham and Wacher 1990: 111–17.

58 *RIB* 1745, 1829, 1742.

7

RELIGION

The native religion in early Britain was for both men and women a combination of superstition, fear, awe, pragmatism and a modicum of faith. Because the gods were not anthropomorphic they could be anywhere, but particularly in trees, animals, birds, water or in the earth, and could cause havoc at any time among unsuspecting humans. Thus they had to be propitiated with offerings or rituals, knowledge of which resided in the priests or Druids. Such knowledge was power, and it is not surprising that the Romans saw the Druids as subverting the authority of the state, and as being a focus for resistance to Romanisation in Gaul and Britain. Their eradication was driven by politics, rather than religion. The Romans brought their own gods to Britain, but as their religion was an amalgam of Greek, Etruscan, oriental and native Roman deities, it was not difficult to absorb the religion of yet another culture, and to see it through Roman eyes. That the native Britons did not necessarily do so was unimportant, intent as the Romans were on creating another part of the Empire on the edge of the Ocean. With the Roman world edging closer to chaos in the third century, religions which offered hope, not in this world but in the next, appealed to many. So it was that Christianity, which had suffered several severe persecutions in the almost 300 years of its existence, was able in 313 to be free of the stigma of a proscribed religion and openly to attract converts to a religion which offered salvation and hope for life after death. Its future for the next millennium and a half was secured when, in 391–92, the emperor Theodosius I closed the temples and banned all pagan cults. Christianity became the religion of the State.

In an earlier publication it was concluded that the religion of the Late Iron Age was an integral part of the life of the community; and while the Roman deities might have an attraction to the native leaders – and for the imperial cult, and then Christianity, the attraction was more likely political – in the end when the western Empire was breaking down and the Romans were leaving British shores, it was to the old gods and the old sacred sites that they returned.[1] Many abandoned their flirtation with Christianity, which was left to flounder with little leadership, less organisation and only a few petty political champions until resuscitated in the late sixth century.

The role of women in the religion of early Britain is examined in this context. While any position in leadership became limited over time, their involvement was always considerable. This is seen in their active contribution to the various cults as priestesses, worshippers and benefactors. Their burials are also examined briefly.

Priestesses and cults

While the Druids were the spiritual leaders or priests, it is likely that women participated in some of the ritual and perhaps even in the leadership of the native religion. Tacitus (*Ann.* 14.30) has them in a frenzied role in the Roman attack on the sacred grove and the slaughter of the Druids at Anglesey; and later sources mention Druids in Gaul (Britanny) and 'Druidesses' in Gaul and Germany Inferior.[2] It has been argued that these women underwent the same lengthy training which, according to Caesar (*B.G.* 6.13–14) the men received,[3] and thus had a similar role, although there is no indication of this from the classical sources. Druids were from the upper class in Celtic society and while there is also no evidence that they were connected with specific cults, they were closely associated with the leaders of the tribes. Divitiacus, a Druid of the Aedui, for instance, was the brother of the king, Dumnorix (*B.G.* 1.16–10; Cic. *de Div.* 1.41.90). Druidic power was undoubted. The mention in the later sources of Druids and Druidesses is an indication that, despite official attempts from the time of Augustus on to suppress and then to eliminate them as religious leaders, they still operated as figures of influence in the community. It is reasonable to suppose that if they were found among those continental tribes close to Britain later in the imperial period, they would also be in Britain. The discovery of headdresses or crowns and other ritual objects at Romano-Celtic temples at Farley Heath, Wanborough and various other sites well after the coming of Rome gives some weight to this view.[4]

Cults relating especially to women must have existed in pre-Roman Britain, but are hard to define because the deities themselves are rarely able to be defined. As in all societies, women would have been particularly concerned with their own health and that of their family, and with fertility and surviving the perils of childbirth. This was reflected in the rituals: as mentioned earlier, the deposition of a woman's skull in the pelvic girdle of a horse at Odell in Bedfordshire has been seen as a fertility rite. Such concerns and resultant relationships with the gods were long lasting. Sites extending from the Iron Age to beyond the Roman period which were possibly dedicated to gods of healing and/or fertility, along with other attributes, include Frilford II, Henley Wood, Maiden Castle I and Woodeaton.[5] It is only in the Roman period that deities especially favoured by women can be identified with confidence. They are examined below.

The role of women in early British religion might be compared with the situation at Rome. The most prestigious women were the Vestal Virgins who kept alight the eternal flame at Rome, the survival of which was essential to the welfare of the state. They were priestesses of Vesta, goddess of the hearth, in a cult which had supposedly been established by the second king of Rome, Numa Pompilius (Plut. *Numa Pomp.* 9–10). The Vestals served the State for 30 years and were given high honour and privilege, not the least being the *ius liberorum* whereby they were independent of a male guardian. They had great status and, at times, political influence in the state.[6] Other priestesses were known, but for them there is little suggestion of political input. They were appointed for specific cults such as that for the Empress Livia, deified by her grandson Claudius, or for the worship of the Bona Dea (Good Goddess), or they were associated with the Imperial cult.

The Imperial cult, involving worship of the emperor's *numen* or spirit, was established by Augustus as a means of uniting the empire with the emperor himself as the focus. Worship of a ruler as a god was not an incomprehensible or unacceptable concept in the eastern (Greek) part of the empire and in Egypt, and cults to the emperor were established there. In the west, rulers had to be more careful and in Italy no promotion of the emperor as a god was attempted immediately after the establishment of the cult. But further west at Lyon (*Lugdunum*) in Gaul, away from the critical eyes of the Roman senate, a cell of the cult and an altar to Rome and Augustus were set up (12–10 BC), and celebrated on coins from the mint at Lyon.[7] The cult expanded as various emperors were deified after their death, and continued until the reign of Constantine I. Elsewhere dedications to the emperor's *numen* were by both sexes, but in Britain there was only one to the emperor by a woman, at Risingham, in fulfilment of a vow to his fortune (*fortuna*).[8]

Colleges of six *seviri* or *Augustales* were established as priestesses and priests. The Imperial cult was the one opportunity for ambitious freedmen or women to hold coveted municipal or even provincial positions. In Britain, it was established early, focusing on the temple of the Divine Claudius at Colchester which was rebuilt after the Boudiccan revolt. London soon had its own branch. Further temples were constructed in the major cities in due course, with locals holding priesthoods. Only two are known. Their names suggest a Greek (servile?) origin for one, and a native British origin for the other: Marcus Verecundus Diogenes from the *colonia* of York and Marcus Aurelius Lunaris, *sevir* of both York and Lincoln. Others, including women, are certain, if the female *sevirales* from Lycia and Pompeii are an indication.[9]

In Britain, only one priestess is known by name. Diodora was not a priestess of the imperial cult, but of the cult of Heracles (Roman Hercules) of Tyre. Her name is Greek, and the name of the god is the Greek form, so it is extremely unlikely that there was actually a cult of Hercules at Corbridge where the inscription was found. However, it was suggested earlier (see Chapter 3) that, since priests and priestesses were normally from the upper classes, Diodora could well have been the wife of an army officer from the eastern part of the empire. Hercules was a god favoured by military men.[10]

There were other cults which Roman women might join. Some had mixed membership, as for the worship of Demeter (the Eleusinian Mysteries, a Greek cult which was adopted by upper class Romans) and of Cybele, the Magna Mater, from Asia Minor. Others, like the Bona Dea, were for women only. Little is known about the mystery cults, except what has been portrayed in art: the frescoes in the Villa of the Mysteries in Pompeii are a well-known example. Cults such as these were invariably associated with fertility and regeneration – of the land, of humans and of animals, but later ones came to be more focused on the individual and the hope of a happy afterlife. Of these, only Mithraism was not open to women.

It is not always easy to identify cults for women in Britain. The worship of Cybele is suggested by an inscription from Carrawburgh, where Tranquila Severa set up an altar on behalf of herself and her family in gratitude to the goddess; more certain evidence of the existence of an actual cult organisation is the small pot found at Dunstable, inscribed 'Regillinus presented the pot of the *dendrophori* of Verulamium'. The *dendrophori* were minor office-bearers in the cult of Cybele, and Dunstable is less than 20 km north of Verulamium, where a temple to the goddess has been identified. At Colchester, two pairs of finger cymbals found in a child's grave point to the cult of the Magna Mater there.[11]

It might be expected that London would be home to other foreign deities: in the Watling Street cemetery the cremated burial of a woman contained a lamp with the head of the jackal god, Anubis, who was part of the cult of the Egyptian goddess, Isis. Other objects relating to Isis confirm the presence of a cult and temple in London.[12]

Native gods were not neglected. At Bath the goddess Sulis was conflated by the Romans with Minerva, and honoured with a classical-style temple. Women were among the many petitioners who deposited *defixiones* in the sacred pool over several hundred years. And at Thetford, the cult of Faunus, an old Latian deitiy, was given Celtic epithets such as Crani(us) = perhaps 'accumulated treasure', and Medugen(us), 'the mead begotten'.[13] The inscribed spoons here included the names of several women members of the cult.

Deities

The deities which women favoured did not necessarily have to be female, although it is known from Dio Cassius (*Epit.* 62.6.2) that Boudicca sacrificed to the goddess Andraste who was probably a goddess of victory. But, as might be expected in an age with little medical knowledge, gods of healing were more popular with women. Apollo, brought from Greece to Italy as early as the Etruscan period, was identified as the god of prophesy and medicine or healing (Macrob. *Sat.* 1.17.15). He, his son Asclepius (Aesculapius in the Latin form), and Hygieia the daughter of Asclepius were transported to Britain, where there are inscriptions to all three, including one to both Asclepius and Hygieia. A number are to Apollo alone, but on occasion he is conflated with a native god as Apollo-Maponus or Apollo-Grannus. Neither Maponus nor Grannus appears to reflect strongly Apollo's attribute of healing, but it has been shown that there were links between Maponus and the Matres (discussed below), and that Grannus was a god of healing on the Continent. Furthermore, at Nettleton an altar was erected to the god Apollo-Cunomaglos by a woman named Corotica, daughter of Iutus; and Cunomaglos, meaning 'hound prince', had associations with the sun, hunting and healing.[14]

There were dedications to the Celtic god Nodens at Lydney, a temple site which remained in use until the latter part of the fourth century. One of the attributes of Nodens was the dog, regularly seen as having a healing role. Nine figures of dogs were found at this site, as were numerous (320) women's dress pins. It is believed that the temple was for a healing god, one of whose attributes was the care of women in childbirth. General health was not neglected by the god. An ex-voto of a hand found at the shrine has concave fingernails – a condition known as koilonychia, the result of iron deficiency. The shrine was located beside a deposit of iron-bearing gravel, and it has been suggested that drinking the water in small quantities would have had beneficial effects on the red blood cell count.[15]

Mars, the Roman god of war, is a somewhat surprising recipient of women's devotions. One inscription, set up by Simplicia at Martlesham, Suffolk, combines him with a native god, Corotiacus; the purpose of the dedication is unclear, as nothing is known about Corotiacus. However a dedication by a woman at Ribchester to Mars perhaps clarifies the first: a vow is fulfilled to Mars, 'the Peace-bringer', by the setting up of an altar.[16] Mars was a very ancient god, the father of Romulus and Remus and thus progenitor of the Roman people. He was a god of agriculture, shepherds and seers. He could evidently bring peace as well as war. There is also the hint of a link with fertility in his association with farming.

The goddess Fortuna has been mentioned earlier (see Chapter 3) in relation to the dedication by Sosia Juncina, and it was suggested that this dedication related to fertility. A further dedication to Fortuna may have had a similar genesis: 'To Fortune and Bonus Eventus, Cornelius Castus and Julia Belismicus, husband and wife, set this up.'[17] It would be pleasant to think that the 'happy event' was the birth of a child.

Fortuna had ancient associations with fertility and childbirth, but the goddesses from whom most women would seek comfort and aid were the deities known as the Deae Matres, Mother Goddesses or Mothers. These usually came in threes (e.g. Plate V), but there is a group of four on a relief in the Museum of London (Plate X). They were represented with attributes such as a baby or child, a cornucopia, bread or fruit, or a dog,

Plate X Four mother goddesses (*Matres*) (London Museum).

all suggesting fertility. Their origins are obscure, and the cult may have come from Europe. Even so, there was at least a perception that they were native: an inscription from Winchester is a dedication to the Matres of Italy, Germany, Gaul and Britain. Dedications were made by both men and women, and one is by a couple: 'To the Mother Goddesses Ollototae, Julius Secundus and Aelia Augustina (set this up).' A second inscription gives more an idea of what was expected of the Matres: 'To the Mother Goddesses, (and) to the Fates, for the welfare of Sanctia Gemina.'[18] Here the motive for the dedication was fertility and successful birth. The Latin name for the Fates, *Parcae*, was originally *parica* meaning 'child-bearing', and the association between the Mothers and the Fates is thus quite clear.

The Nymphs, found in a number of dedications by women, are more enigmatic. They were the daughters of Zeus (Jupiter) – mortal, though very long living. Found usually in the sea, rivers and springs, they could also be in trees, woods and mountains. They are often associated with Apollo or Asclepius and thus had healing aspects, and they could also inspire humans to poetry or prophesy. Generally they were benign, but were known to punish lovers who were unfaithful to them. It is not possible to determine the rationale behind the three dedications by women to the Nymphs in the Romano-British inscriptions: one was found by a bridge, so was probably related to water and healing; the provenance of the other two is not known. It may not be coincidental, however, that of the three dedications, two were by mother-and-daughter devotees.[19]

Mention should also be made of the deity honoured at Coventina's Well. Coventina's origins and attributes have been the subject of much debate for many years, without resolution. She was evidently considered by her votaries to have a high standing in the pantheon, as she was given the epithet Augusta on two inscriptions, and on others referred to as nymph or goddess. One votary made sure he would get it right by calling her a goddess-nymph.[20] All known dedications were by males, mainly soldiers whose units originated in the north-west provinces. This does not mean, of course, that the soldiers involved actually came from those areas. The place of origin of only two soldiers is known.[21]

Coventina has been seen as a goddess of healing, and as having some connection with death. But other attributes may have been equally important. From a first look at the inscriptions, they seem to be the usual bland formulae recording the name of the goddess and the dedicator, or those details plus the information that he was fulfilling a vow. A closer examination shows that, in two instances, Coventina was being thanked by the soldiers for looking after their welfare (*pro salute sua*).[22] It is, therefore, likely that some of the other dedications to Coventina apart from these two were for soldiers' safety in combat, rather than for their recovery from ill health. After all, a fort in the wilds of the north would hardly be the place for soldiers to recover from illness or battle wounds. The objects found in the well, however, support the view of healing as at least one of Coventina's attributes, as does a dedication to Minerva (Medica?) at the same site; they also show that there were some women at the fort or surrounds.

That there were few women at Carrawburgh is understandable. That even the women who dedicated an altar there did not choose Coventina reinforces the view that this goddess was not always seen as related to healing or childbirth. The only known inscription from the fort set up by a woman was to the Matres; but there were other inscriptions to the Matres set up by men, suggesting a protective role here, too, rather than a connection with fertility or childbirth.[23]

The role of Sulis-Minerva at Bath was far less equivocal. The presence of medicinal springs had long been known and appreciated by the native inhabitants, and it was in her role as Minerva Medica or goddess of health that the Roman goddess was conflated with the local deity, Sulis. Bath became a popular place for recuperating soldiers, and any dedications to the goddess are by men. However, the names of women are found among the *defixiones*. It has been pointed out that, in an analysis of the curse tablets, while there are appeals to Sulis, Sulis-Minerva or Minerva-Sulis, there is not one to Minerva alone. The same applies to altars found: most are to Sulis, and three are to Sulis-Minerva. In other words, Sulis was recognised as the goddess at the site, and the addition of Minerva was a Roman conceit which probably had little effect on either the Roman visitors or the native inhabitants. Indeed, it is possible that even the Romans did not even know the name of the deity honoured at Bath. Among the altars are dedications to Diana, Loucetius-Mars, Nemetona and, appropriately, the Genius of the Place.

It is likely that the women supplicants whose names were recorded on *defixiones* were not among the richest inhabitants of the town – petitioners included Enica, Oconea, Lovernisca and Cantissena, whose names are not Roman[24] – so the items stolen or lost were fairly insignificant, though doubtless important to those who lost them: cloaks, a bathing tunic, coins, small pieces of jewellery and some household items. The hope was that Sulis would either return them to their owner or punish the thief. There is no indication that any pleas were made to the goddess for good or better health, which is unusual in view of her major role at Bath; but then *defixiones* seemed more aimed at the ill health of the intended victim than the good health of the instigator of the curse.

Lares or household gods were a fundamental part of religion at Rome, but there is little evidence that the practice of worshipping or making offerings to these deities was widespread in Britain. Small figurines interpreted as *lares* have been found in towns such as London, Cirencester and Silchester, but this is limited evidence for the practice. The *lar familiaris* and his place in the household was controlled more by the male head of the house than by his wife; the *paterfamilias* poured a small amount of wine onto the hearth before a meal as an offering.[25]

Offerings to the gods

The usual place to make an offering to a god, apart from the household gods, was at a temple, shrine or sacred place. In the Romano-British period, many temples and shrines were built, either the square-within-a-square type (with variations) or a less elaborate single-celled structure. Finds from these are well documented. But in the Iron Age, few shrines were actually built and offerings to the gods could be deposited in less obvious places. These are more difficult to identify. They included watery contexts such as bogs and rivers, and also shafts in the ground. A further problem for this study is that it is not always possible to determine what offerings might have been made by women.

In an important study of ritual deposits by Gerald Wait, the finds were classified according to location, including 'watery' sites, ritual shafts and Celtic shrines.[26] Possible offerings by women, suggested by women's domestic role, include bronze buckets, cauldrons, spoons (as single deposits or in pairs) and bowls. One deposit, from Lamberton Moor, Berwick, was of four bowls. Some of the more than 100 'ritual shafts' recorded may have been abandoned grain storage pits, while others, on account of their depth, appear to have been deliberately dug for a ritual purpose: the contents of all pits/shafts had a uniformity about them which did not support a domestic interpretation. Shafts which may have related specifically to women were few; but one, at Cadbury Castle Devon, which was 18 m deep, contained among other items 20 bronze and four shale bracelets, one ring and a number of glass and enamel beads. Similar items of personal adornment were found in the burials of women of the Iron Age.

When we look at the Roman period, the evidence reflects to some extent that of the Iron Age. Objects most likely offered by women at Romano-Celtic temple sites are items of personal adornment including hair pins, bracelets, brooches, rings and glass beads, and toilet articles such as tweezers and nail cleaners. Bronze spoons were found at Cold Kitchen Hill, Wiltshire, and at Lamyatt Beacon, Somerset, along with numerous items of jewellery. It is uncertain whether these are connected with men or women, however, because other deposits included iron knives and spearheads. Coins were another non-gender-specific deposit.

An addition to ritual offerings was a figurine of a deity in bronze or pipeclay, frequently representing the goddess Venus. Other goddesses include Minerva and Epona, and seven Deae Nutrices (or Nursing Goddesses) found at Nor'nour on the Isles of Scilly, along with six pipeclay Venuses, a collection of miniature votive pots, 20–30 rings, glass beads, brooches and coins. An interpretation of these as the offerings of women is reasonable.

The healing aspect of deities such as Sulis, Nodens and Apollo has been discussed above. Their shrines yielded objects which were almost certainly deposited by women. Hundreds of hair pins, items of jewellery and other personal effects were found at Bath, but among the most telling was the pair of carved ivory breasts,[27] a reminder that women's complaints, such as cancer of the breast or mastitis have a very long history, and that it is only of recent times that drugs have been able to make a difference. An appeal to the goddess may have been the last resort for the sufferer.

Nodens at Lydney received similar votives, including 270 bronze bracelets and 320 hair or dress pins. There were also several Roman spoons, as well as tweezers and nail cleaners. Nettleton, which had two phases of pagan use, had the same types of offerings to Apollo: 66 bracelets of bronze or shale, 138 pins, 28 spoons and several toilet items. But conclusive evidence for the offerings of women came in the form of 25 spindle whorls.[28]

Mars, the god of war, was mentioned earlier as having some connection with fertility, although that would not normally be seen as his main attribute. But it is interesting to look at the finds at the temple at Harlow, a temple probably dedicated to Mars. While there were items of military equipment and horse trappings, there were also numerous bronze and bone pins, items of jewellery and toilet implements; and an iron wool comb was an almost certain female offering.[29]

Mercury (Greek Hermes) also seems, like Mars, to have been a god preferred by males, but at Uley it is quite clear that women approached him as well – either as a suppliant making a request on a *defixio*, or as a devotee making an offering. One curse tablet, in the name of Saturnina, asks for help in recovering a linen cloth she has had stolen, and offers one third of it to the god if the cloth is recovered. Votive offerings which probably came from women include miniature pots, beads, bracelets, necklaces, earrings, rings and pins. There were also toilet articles, spoons and, significantly, spindle whorls. Similarly the Chelmsford temple, probably dedicated to Mercury, yielded one spindle whorl, three loom weights and a wool comb. The appeal of Mercury to women is somewhat complex, and probably based on the confusion between a Roman goddess, Maia, who was worshipped on the same day as Mercury, that is, 15 May, and the ancient Greek Maia, the mother of Mercury/Hermes – a much earlier goddess whose name means 'mother' or 'nurse'. This would thus put Mercury/Maia within the group of fertility/nurturing gods which had special appeal to women.[30]

A collection of artefacts relating to women, including earrings and spindle whorls, was found at Ivy Chimneys, Witham, and while water was a feature of the site, the identity of any associated healing deity was not firmly established.[31] What is of interest here, and at some other sites above, is the incidence of quite valuable offerings, such as gold and silver earrings and rings. This is in contrast to the modest grave goods for women in the Roman period, and suggests that different forces of logic were at work in women's attitude towards the gods above and below the earth.

At Great Dunmow, on the other hand, while there were offerings to a unknown local deity which included a spindle whorl and an iron wool comb, the jewellery was fragmentary. This is more like the grave deposits found in the late Roman period. It is probably significant that the shrine at Great Dunmow dated to the late fourth century.[32]

Burials

Burials other than Christian may be considered briefly here, for the sake of completeness. Graves and grave goods for women were considered in some depth in Chapter 5, but the actual disposal of their bodies was dealt with only in passing when determining the use of coffins. Burial and religion are closely intertwined and the problem of interpretation is that it cannot be known to what extent a woman was buried according to her own wishes, that is reflecting her own religious beliefs, and how much the method of burial reflected the wishes of those who buried her.

In the Late Iron Age some women could have high status burials – with chariots, with imported grave goods, and buried in wide and deep graves. Others received less ceremony, interred mainly in a foetal position with few if any grave goods apart from a brooch which probably held the burial garment in place, a pot, or animal or bird remains. In the Roman period, the move to coffins and to supine and extended burial was almost immediate, to be replaced within the century with cremations, and then a return to inhumation by the mid-third century. In non-Christian graves, the appearance in graves of hobnails was also almost immediate, signifying the burying of Roman-style footwear with the deceased. The most common grave goods in female graves after hobnails were pottery, coins, items of personal adornment and bird or animal remains, although grave goods progressively declined in quality and number over the centuries of Roman rule. Prestige burials were marked instead by stone and lead coffins and 'plaster' packing.

The bodies of certain women as well as men were subject to particular burial rites for reasons which are difficult or impossible now to recover. It has been argued that decapitated burials were a means of releasing the soul which resided in the head to allow it to migrate another body – perhaps even a newborn. The literary and archaeo-logical evidence supports the view that post-mortem decapitation was not a form of punishment. Prone burials are not yet able to be explained satisfactorily; but it has been noted that, of the female burials in the cemetery at Bath Gate, Cirencester, exactly one-third were prone. Further research may unlock the secret of this strange rite which occurred late in Roman Britain and continued into the Anglo-Saxon period. Neither decapitated nor prone burials could be acceptable to Christianity, which had its own identifiable methods of burial.[33]

Christianity[34]

This chapter on religion in early Britain concludes with a brief account of the rise and decline in influence of women in the Christian church generally, before identifying some Christian women in Roman Britain and suggesting others. The restrictions of the evidence – literary, epigraphical and prosopographical – mean that only a few women can be identified by name. Because of the type of evidence, it will be seen that most of these would have come from the wealthier classes. The poor left little but their remains in cemeteries.

It is known from a study of the books of the New Testament that women were among the followers of Christ, and were held in esteem and even occupied positions of leadership in the early Church. Women were present at the crucifixion, and were the first to bear witness to the resurrection.[35] They were also very active in the spread of the new religion. Some, at least, were of high rank.[36] In his letters, Paul mentions a number of women by name – at Philippi, Corinth and, especially important for the purposes of this study, at Rome.[37] They included women who were clearly leaders: women such as Priscilla (Prisca) who, with her husband Aquila, a Christian Jew, had been involved in establishing the religion in Rome, and who had in AD 49/50 been expelled from the city by Claudius. It is known that, after travelling to Corinth, the couple went with Paul to Syria, where they once again set up a house church.[38]

As the infant Church grew, women came to have formal roles as deacons, presbyters and teachers, as well as status as virgins, or in 'orders' of widows.[39] Even Tertullian, who railed against any role for women in the church,[40] lists widows and virgins among its leaders: ... *si episcopus, si diaconus, si vidua, si virgo, si doctor* ... , '... whether bishop, deacon, widow, virgin, teacher ... '[41] Such status may have reflected the position of certain women in the Jewish religion.[42] By the fourth century, the predominance of males in the Church was assured. An acceptable role for women was by this time only as benefactors, as members of religious orders, or as (often anonymous) members of a congregation,[43] and a series of Church Councils in the fourth and early fifth century confirmed this relegation to a secondary position.[44]

It is against this background that we look for Christian women in Roman Britain. Christianity probably came to Britain before the end of the second century, and had individual followers well before that. It is known that there was a considerable Christian presence in Gaul, as evidenced by the number of martyrs put to death at Lyon in 177 (Euseb., *H.E.* 5.1), and it is very likely that there were converts in Britain at or around the same time. Tertullian (*c.*160–240) says that Christianity was in parts of Britain beyond Roman settlement (*Adv. Iud.* 7), and Origen (185–255) describes the religion as a unifying force there (*Hom. 4 on Ezek.*). In view of the threat of persecution, Christians had a very low profile until the early fourth century, but that some in Britain were known and put to death is certain, even from as early as mid-third century.[45] These would include women because women martyrs are known from elsewhere. Indeed, among the most prominent of the 48 martyrs at Lyon had been the slave girl, Blandina, and her Gallo-Roman mistress.

Once Christianity was no longer a proscribed sect following the Peace of the Church in 313, its members were free to build churches and to bury their dead separately from non-Christians in designated cemeteries. Under the patronage of the emperor Constantine, large and splendid churches were built in parts of the Empire, especially at Rome and Jerusalem, but in Britain there is little evidence of such wealth. Christians first assembled in private houses, and the first recognisable church, built on the plan of the Roman basilica, was probably that at Colchester around 320. Recognisable Christian cemeteries were noteworthy, among other aspects, for their inclusion of infants given the same respect as adults. For those cemeteries which continued into the fifth century (and dating of these is difficult, because of the absence of grave goods in a Christian cemetery), they are also noteworthy for the equality in numbers of males and females buried there. It was argued earlier in this work (see Chapter 4) that female infanticide, which had been practised as a result of Roman influence, was not carried out by Christians, and that the numbers of males and females in the population approached equality at the end of the Roman period as Christianity became more widespread.

Women as well as men made their contributions to Christianity, and were from the ranks of both the rich and the poor, but it is only from the upper classes that we have any hope identification. The difficulties are considerable. None have been specifically mentioned in the ancient sources, and only a handful are known from inscriptions on artefacts. Nevertheless, it is possible that the identity of other Christian women from Roman Britain can be teased out from the evidence we do have.

Those who are known from the Water Newton hoard bore the names Innocentia, Viventia and Ianicilla. The names of the first two are engraved on a silver bowl from a set of Communion plate dated to the fourth century. The inscription begins with the Christian symbols Alpha Chi-Rho Omega, and continues: INNOCENTIA ET VIVENTIA ... RVNT, which can be interpreted as 'Innocentia and Viventia, being ..., (gave this)'. Ianicilla's name appears on a silver 'votive leaf' or plaque above Christian symbols in the inscription, (I)ANICILLA VOTVM QVOD/PROMISIT CONPLEVIT, 'Ianicilla has fulfilled the vow which she promised.' The names Innocentia and Viventia are Roman, but are more common in Christian inscriptions. Ianicilla is probably a variant of Ianilla, which is only found in a Christian context. The value of these gifts precludes their being offerings by poor women. Most likely they were donations from wealthy women in the Christian community. It has been argued that for a religious institution there was actually much more *kudos* to be gained from the patronage of a wealthy person than in receiving gifts from the poor.[46]

The motives behind women's donations to the Church might be queried. It was suggested above that, with leadership positions being out of the question, women might see the giving of gifts as a substitute for giving of actual physical service to the Church. On the other hand, it may be that women made donations in the hope of something in return, be it intercession by the priests on their behalf, a promise of salvation, or even material goods. In Ireland, for instance, St Brigit gave to the poor and received gifts from the wealthy. In other words, when donations were made, it was with the expectation that there would be some kind of return. If we transfer this concept to the Water Newton benefactions, the transaction is in many ways similar to the 'contract' which was thought to exist between gods and humans in the pagan Roman religion, especially if valuable gifts were offered. St Patrick deplored the actions of wealthy women who threw gifts and their jewellery onto the altar in his church, seeing this perhaps as a form of bribery or the 'buying of indulgences' – the source of monumental problems in the Church many centuries later. According to Patrick, his returning the unsolicited donations to their donors caused considerable uproar, apparently because such gift-giving (and, presumably, the anticipation of a reward) was considered normal (*Conf.* 49).[47]

Not far from Water Newton is Mildenhall, where another notable hoard has been found. While in this case the treasure was not Christian plate, the hoard has Christian associations as well as undoubted pagan iconography. Five silver spoons were found, three with a *Chi-Rho*, and two inscribed with a personal name and the invocation VIVAS = 'May you live (long)'. One of these was of a woman, Pascentia, a name which is known only in a Christian context. The Chi-Rho is undoubtedly Christian, the VIVAS (by the fourth century) most likely so, as was shown in an earlier study.[48] From the wealth displayed by the hoard, Pascentia and her companions were obviously among the wealthier members of Christian society in Roman Britain in the late period. In view of the non-Christian objects in the hoard, however, Pascentia and her household had no problem in blending the iconography of pagan Greece and Rome with that of Christianity. This was so often the case in fourth century Britain, and leads one to question the depth of commitment of these wealthy women or indeed their concept of Christianity.

The members of a cult of Faunus, whose ritual objects and treasure were found at Thetford, were also wealthy. It is very likely that this cult emerged in the second half of the fourth century, when paganism revived under the rule and with the encouragement of the apostate emperor, Julian (360–63); the practice was not officially condemned by his Christian successors until 391 when Theodosius I banned pagan cults. The Thetford hoard is notable for the mix of pagan and Christian associations, and it has been argued elsewhere that some of the people whose names appear on the inscribed utensils were in fact 'lapsed' Christians. Two of these were women. There are two spoons in the hoard inscribed with the words SILVIOLA VIVAS 'Silviola, may you live (long)' one also inscribed with a Greek cross; another spoon has the legend PERSEVERAVITVIVAS which has been explained as an engraver's error, the correct reading being PERSEVERA VTI (= VT) VIVAS, Persevera [I wish] that you may live (long)'.[49] While Silviola may be an appropriate name for a devotee of a rural god, the name is in fact known in inscriptions only in a Christian context at Rome; so, too, Persevera is found only in Christian inscriptions. There is thus a very strong probability that these women were, at least for a time, part of a community of wealthy Christians in Britain in the fourth century.[50]

Even later than the Mildenhall hoard was that found at Hoxne, in Suffolk, which could have been deposited as late as the mid-fifth century. The coins include two of the usurper Constantine III (AD 407–11) and more than 2000 from the reign of the emperor Honorius (393–423). Amongst the finds were items of women's jewellery which had undoubted Christian associations: a gold necklace the clasp of which had a monogrammatic cross imprinted, and the pierced-work bracelet, mentioned earlier, fashioned with the words VTERE FELIX DOMINA IVLIANE (sic), 'Use (this) happily, Lady Juliana'. Juliana may have been the wife of Aurelius Ursicinus, whose name is inscribed on a set of ten silver spoons included in the hoard. The name of another woman, Silvicola, also appears on a spoon. The Chi-Rho symbol is found on two others, and the monogrammatic cross on a set of ten spoons and ten ladles. A further spoon is engraved VIVAS IN DEO, 'May you live in God'.[51] The Christian ownership of the treasure is, therefore, not doubted; and the find is proof that wealthy Christian women still lived in Britain right to the end of Roman occupation, and perhaps even after the Romans had left.

Identification of Christian women on artefacts with Christian symbols is a relatively simple matter. Much more difficult is the task of identifying them from the works of the ancient writers and from the inscriptions of Roman Britain.

It is suggested that the wife of Aulus Plautius, the first governor of Britain, may have been a Christian. Her story was told earlier (see Chapter 3), but will be recapitulated briefly. Pomponia Graecina, a woman of aristocratic birth and connections with the imperial family, was, some ten years after her husband's term in Britain 43–47, accused of having practised a foreign religion. For this she was subjected to trial by her husband in the presence of the males of her family, but was acquitted.[52] She died some time around AD 80. While it has on occasion been speculated, but rejected, that this *externa superstitio* might have been Druidism, it could have actually been Christianity: it is of considerable interest to note an early inscription in the catacomb of Callistus at Rome, begun in mid-second century, for one Π[O]ΜΠΩΝΙΟC ΓΡΗ[ΚΕΙΝΟ]C (Pomponius Grecinus), who is believed to belong to the same family as our Pomponia Graecina.[53] Furthermore, the members of the *gens* Pomponia were connected to the equally noble Caecilii, and it was from this latter family that one of the most famous third-century Christian martyrs, St Caecilia, was to come. It is possible that Pomponia Graecina was Christian, since at the time of Nero there were converts at least among the freedmen in the imperial household, and it is known that by the end of the century certain members of the aristocracy had become Christians.[54]

Among other early converts to Christianity was the (unnamed) wife of Claudius Hieronymianus, legionary legate of the Sixth Legion at York in the 170s (see Chapter 3). According to a stone inscription, her husband was a devotee of Serapis. She became a Christian some time between the York appointment and his final posting in Cappadocia. It will be recalled that he was a victim of the plague, and converted to Christianity on his deathbed.[55]

From other inscriptions there are a further three females women who may have been Christian. In all cases the inscription begins with an invocation to the spirits of the departed (*Dis Manibus*) or at least the letters DM, which is typical of Roman (pagan) burials. However, by the later Roman period the DM may have become just a meaningless formula on tombstones: there are many instances of the letters on undoubted Christian inscriptions in the catacombs at Rome.[56] Other features suggest that the three Romano-British burials were, in fact, Christian.

The first, suggested as Christian by Thomas, was that of a child at York: little Simplicia Florentina died at the age of ten months, mourned by her father who was a soldier of the Sixth Legion.[57] In a well-formed inscription on the lid of a stone coffin, she is referred to as a 'most innocent soul', a term which might be seen as appropriate for a Christian child; and the name Simplicia is known in Christian contexts. The burial was set in gypsum, and such 'plaster' burials are often thought to indicate a Christian identity, although this is certainly not always so.[58]

The second inscription, carefully formed, is on a tombstone from Roman Carvoran, Northumberland: 'To the spirits of the departed: and to Aurelia Aia, daughter of Titus, from Salona, Aurelius Marcus of the century of Obsequens (set this up) to his very pure wife, who lived 33 years without any blemish.' There are several reasons for believing that this inscription is Christian. Aurelia Aia was evidently the freed slave, then wife, of Aurelius Marcus, a Roman soldier. She came from Salona. This was a town on the Adriatic coast which had been home to eastern missionary-traders in the third century, and from the early fourth century became a large centre of 'red hot (Christian) fanaticism', drawing pilgrims to the tomb of the bishop-martyr Domnio who died in the Great Persecution around AD 304.[59] The name of Aurelia Aia's father, Titus, while that of a first century emperor, was also the name of one of St Paul's closest associates. That earlier Titus travelled with Paul to Crete, and became the island's first bishop (Paul, *Titus* 1.5). Even today there is a large church dedicated to him there. Titus would thus be an appropriate name for a Christian convert.[60]

Aurelia Aia herself is referred to as having lived 33 years 'without blemish' (*sine ulla macula*), which has led E. Birley to suggest she was a Christian.[61] This premise is a very reasonable one, as the expression is found in a number of places in the

New Testament.[62] One further argument which may point to a Christian identity is that the age of Aurelia Aia is given only in years, rather than the more common Roman practice of giving the age in years, months and days. But this was not necessarily always so, and while the seeming lack of concern for the precise age could be seen as an indicator of Christianity, the argument is not conclusive.[63] Christians' exact ages were also noted on occasion: for example, in his letter to (Julia) Eustochium on the death of her mother, Paula, St Jerome gives Paula's age at death in years, months and days (*Epit.* 108). She had been an early leader in women's monasticism at Rome and Jerusalem.

A similar argument for the absence of exact age at death could be advanced for our third inscription, from York. It is found on a particularly elegant tombstone, the inscription itself flanked by two winged *putti* (angels?). It reads, 'To the spirits of the departed (and) to Eglecta, aged 30, here buried beside their son Crescens, aged 3; Antonius Step(h)anus had this set up to his wife.' There are, however, more compelling reasons for a Christian identification, based on the actual names in the inscription. That Stephanus is Greek is true, and that it was known well before the Christian period (e.g. Demosthenes 45 and 46). But Stephen was the name of the first Christian martyr (Acts 6–7), and even today is a popular name in Roman Catholic and Orthodox families. The names of Stephanus' son and wife, too, are significant. While Crescens is common enough as a Roman *cognomen*, it was also the name of one of Paul's followers who accompanied him to Rome (2.*Tim.* 4.10). With regard to Eglecta, it is not a Latin name and comes from the Greek ἐκλέγω = 'to choose', which gives in the New Testament οἱ ἐκλέγτοι 'the chosen ones'.[64] Eglecta can readily be seen as a Christian name. The combination in the one inscription of three names which are found in Christian contexts is fairly convincing evidence for a Christian identity for that inscription, despite the presence of the ubiquitous 'DM'.

If Eglecta is taken as a Christian name, then another from Roman Britain is possible: Fabius Honoratus, tribune of the First Cohort of Vangiones and his wife, Aurelia Eglectiane erected an altar-shaped tombstone for their 'most sweet daughter'. The stone can be dated to the third century or later, since the First Cohort of Vangiones is known to have been based at Risingham in the third century. The combination of Latin and Greek names for the mother is not unknown, though somewhat rare in Roman Britain, and could indicate a servile origin.[65] Eglectiane may have been the daughter of a freed Greek slave. In this case, however, little more can be extracted to support a Christian identity.

There are undoubtedly other inscriptions from Roman Britain which were erected to women who were Christians, but there is at present no way that they can be positively identified.[66] The pity is that the stones were found and recorded long before the importance of archaeological context was recognised. To date no tombstone has been found in a cemetery identified with any certainty as Christian.

From the material above, it is clear that few names of Christian women can be known to us and, because of the nature of the evidence such as inscriptions on silver spoons and stone, of those who are known to us, most are from the wealthier classes, either Roman or British. Undoubtedly in Britain, as in other parts of the Empire, women of wealth continued to be attracted to the faith. Christianity did not appeal only to the wealthy, but we are destined never to know the names of countless women from the lower classes who were baptised and died as Christians in Britain. We can meet *them* only through archaeology – and it is to the burial evidence that we will now briefly turn.

Cemeteries for use by Christians were provided in the Roman empire from an early period, but not until the fourth century do they appear in Britain. It is possible to identify these cemeteries, and thus identify the Christian women buried in them. A set of criteria was developed some years ago to be applied to the archaeological evidence. The most important were: Christian evidence *in situ*; west-east burial; body placed supine and extended; graves undisturbed by others; presence of a contemporaneous and clearly pagan cemetery in the same locality; presence of neo-natal or very young infants in the cemetery given equal respect as adults; an absence of decapitated or prone burials; and a general absence of grave goods, but particularly items which would suggest sacrifice such as animal or bird remains.[67]

This is not to say that Christian burial could not occur without all or most of these criteria, but their presence is undoubtedly a fairly conclusive indicator, and a single burial would be much harder to classify as Christian. There is little doubt about one such burial at York, however. A woman found in stone coffin with rich grave goods including a glass vessel and numerous beads, bracelets and earrings, was accompanied to the grave by an openwork bone plaque reading SOROR AVE VIVAS IN DEO, 'Hail, sister, may you live in God'. A Christian identity for this unnamed wealthy Romano-British woman of York is undoubted.[68]

From the study by the author published in 1991, it was concluded that there were 13 cemeteries in fourth-century Britain which might be seen as Christian. To that list might now be added the cemeteries at Bletsoe, Newarke Street Leicester, and Shepton Mallet. One lives in hope that some day a cemetery – meeting the above criteria – will be discovered, complete with inscription detailing the name and a little of the life of a Romano-British Christian woman.

Religion was an integral part of the lives of the women of early Britain. Over time the focus on nature and on natural phenomena of the pre-Roman period came to be replaced by more anthropmorthic deities; cults and ritual became more regularised, and offerings more personal. Women did make their mark on the religion of early Britain. They were involved as priestesses, devotees and donors, and while any leadership role may have been restricted to a few of the upper classes, their needs and desires ensured that deities were created or evolved to meet those needs, be they emotional, spiritual or practical. Rituals, votives and *defixiones* were the conduit to the gods who would, if the formulae were right, grant them husbands returned from war, revenge on enemies, and lost property recovered; but what they sought from the gods above all was a fertile, healthy body able to cope with the rigours and dangers of pregnancy and childbirth. Only with the advent of the salvation cults and then Christianity did the focus shift from their well-being in this world to their fate in the next.

Notes

1 Watts 1998.
2 SHA *Numer.* 14; *Aurel.* 63.4.5; *Alex. Sev.* 59.9; Ausonius (*Commem. Profess.*) 4.7–10, 10.22–30.
3 Ross 1999: 17. On the Druids, see also Chadwick 1997; Piggott 1974.
4 Bird 1996 and references.
5 Watts 1998: figure 6.
6 A well known example is the attempt of the Senior Vestal, Vibidia, to save the empress Messalina's life when her adultery and sham marriage to C. Silius was disclosed to Claudius (Tac. *Ann.* 11.26–38).
7 *BMC* 565.
8 *RIB* 1211. For the Imperial cult, see Fishwick 1987.
9 London: *RIB* 5; Diogenes: *RIB* 678; Lunaris: *JRS* 40 (1921) 21; Lycia: Lalla, from Arnaea, 'priestess of the Emperor's cult' (Pleket 13); Pompeii: Eumachia, 'public priestess' who built and dedicated a porch to Concordia Augusta and to Pietas (*CIL* 10.810) and Mamia, 'public priestess' who built a small temple to the genius of Augustus (*CIL* 10.816).
10 *RIB* 1129.
11 *RIB* 1539; Matthews 1981; Niblett 2001: 85, 110; Crummy 2004.
12 Henig 1984: 113–14; Wardle 2000.
13 Jackson 1983.
14 Asclepius and Hygieia: *RIB* 609; Apollo: *RIB* 1120, 2132 and MacCulloch 1911: 125; Wedlake 1982: 135–6; Ross 1992: 299, n. 41. See also Green 1996.
15 Wheeler and Wheeler 1932: 40–2; Wells 1982: 187.
16 *RIB* 213, 584.
17 *RIB* 318.
18 Henig 1984: figure 10; *RIB* 88, 574, 951; Robertson 1970.
19 *RIB* 744, 1228, 1789.
20 Allason-Jones 1985: 3–11; *RIB* 1523–35.
21 *RIB* 1525, 1526.
22 *RIB* 1532, 1533.
23 *RIB* 1539, 1540, 1541.
24 *Tab. Sul.* 59, 60, 61, 63.
25 Henig 1984: 169; on *lares*, see Alcock 1986.
26 Wait 1986. Cunliffe (1995: 10) has noted that the preponderance of finds in rivers was in those which flowed to the east.
27 Cunliffe 1984c: Figure 50.
28 Wheeler and Wheeler 1932: 41, 82; Wedlake 1982: *passim.*
29 France and Gobel 1985: 82–91; Wickenden 1988: 56.
30 Rose 1970; Wickenden 1992: 88, plate X; Tomlin 1993a: 121–2.
31 Turner 1999.
32 Wickenden 1988.
33 Decapitated burials: Watts 1998: 74–89. Bath Gate: Anderson 1987.
34 This section is a later version of a paper presented at the Roman Archaeology Conference at Leicester in April 2003.
35 For example, Luke 23.49–55, 24.10.
36 For example, Acts 13.50, 17.12.
37 Philip. 4.2; Rom. 16.3–15; 2 Tim. 4.19–21.
38 Suet. *Claud.* 25; Rom. 16.3–5; Acts 18.2, 18, 26; 1 Cor. 16.19; 2 Tim. 4.19. On the expulsion from Rome, Suetonius (*Claud.* 25) tells us that the usually tolerant Claudius expelled all Jews at this time on account of riots 'at the instigation of Chrestus'. This points to conflict between Jews and Christians even at this early date.
39 Pliny *Epist.* 10.96; 1 Tim. 5.9–10.

40 *De Bapt.* 17; *De Virg.* 9; and later John Chrysostom *On the Priesthood* 3.9.

41 *De Praes. Haeret.* 3.

42 As argued by Brooten (1982: *passim*). Women in positions of authority in the Jewish and Christian religions is a matter of considerable debate. For a summary of the evidence, see Kraemer 1992: 174–90.

43 I am indebted to Ms Elizabeth Vine for references here.

44 For example, Canon 19 of the Council of Nicaea (325), Canon 26 of the Council of Orange (411), and the general tone of the Council of Nîmes (394).

45 For a discussion of the evidence for martyrs in Britain see Watts 1991: 9–10.

46 Painter 1977b; Kajanto 1982: 252, 274, 212; Bitel 1984.

47 Bitel 1984.

48 Painter 1977a; Watts 1991: 153–5.

49 A later reading by Tomlin (1993b), PERSEVERANTI VIVAS = 'Long life to you, Perseverantius', is less convincing.

50 Johns and Potter 1983; Watts 1988.

51 Bland and Johns 1993.

52 Tac. *Ann.* 13.32.

53 Marucchi 1974: 244, no. 300.

54 Philippians 4.22; Marucchi 1974: 240–81 gives examples.

55 *RIB* 658; Tertullian *Ad Scap.* 3.4.

56 For example, an inscription found in the Vatican Cemetery, which has, besides D-corona- M, depictions of fish and anchor and the words ΙΧΘΥC ΖΩΝΤΩΝ ('The fish of the living') (Marruchi 1974: figure 52).

57 *RIB* 690.

58 Thomas 1981: 128; Green 1977, cf. Watts 1988: 59–61.

59 Salona was originally part of the Greek world, but was raised to the status of Roman *colonia* (the *colonia Martia Julia*) at the time of Caesar. According to the archaeological evidence, the Christian community initially built or used modest premises. The first ecclesiastical buildings were constructed in the last years of the third century in the same places (Dyggve 1951: figure 6–13).

60 *RIB* 1828; Dyggve 1951: 8–9; Frend 1996: 164.

61 Cited in commentary on *RIB* 1828.

62 For example, 1 Peter 1.19; 1 Tim. 6.14; Eph. 5.27.

63 Toynbee 1953. See, for example, *RIB* 955, which has no specific indicators for a Christian identity.

64 *RIB* 695; for example, Acts 9.15; 1.Peter 2.9; Eph. 1.4; Rom. 16.13.

65 *RIB* 1482.

66 A possible Christian inscription, suggested in the relevant commentary, is *RIB* 955. Septima D . . . is the name of the woman. See also Handley 2000.

67 Watts 1991.

68 RCHM 1962: 73.

8

CONCLUSIONS

Sed haec prius fuere
But all this is over now.
(Catullus 4)

This study has ranged over almost five centuries, discussed the lives of perhaps a hundred women and looked at the archaeological remains of thousands more. It began in Iron Age Britain and dashed briefly into the mists of Celtic Ireland and western Europe before planting itself firmly among the Roman *matronae* of Britannia. We have met women riding chariots and women buried with chariots; governors' wives and shopkeepers, virgins and prostitutes. We have been with them as they went to the baths wrapped in cloaks which were later stolen, and entered temple precincts to make offerings to gods. We have seen them eat, drink, live, pray and die. It is time now to put the pieces of the picture together.

Barry Cunliffe looked at the progress in the Iron Age up to the Roman Conquest and concluded that life in Britain at that time would be unrecognisable from seven centuries earlier, at the end of the Bronze Age. Changes in social organisation and control and in land management and production, advances in technology particularly in the use of iron, and the focus of religion directed away from the forces of nature and on to the fertility of the land and its inhabitants, all contributed to the world which Caesar encountered in 55–54 BC.[1] It might be thought that the coming of Rome had a similar effect on the next 450 years, but this may have been more apparent than real. The Roman way of life was embraced by the wealthy, and those living in the new towns. That influence spread into the countryside with ever diminishing impact, although even in the most remote corners of the province the organised and practical Romans would have ventured to survey the wealth for taxes or, by the fourth century, to enlist men for the mainly home-grown army. Roman roads snaked across the island, assisting first the movement of the legions, and then commerce and communication. The lives of British women were touched to a greater or lesser extent, depending on wealth and geography.

From the evidence of archaeology and of the sometimes problematic literary sources, women in the pre-Roman Iron Age enjoyed relatively high status, and some had genuine power. There were more or less equal numbers of adult males and females in the various tribal communities, thus it does not seem that female infanticide was practised as a general rule. There may have been some regional variations in burial practice, however.

Women's health and nutrition were not inferior to men's, nor does it appear that they were subjected to domestic violence – at least of the kind which would result in broken bones. If they survived the perils of childbirth, they lived to the same age as males, even if not in the same numbers. But some died in childbirth, and others of post-natal complications. Other diseases such as tuberculosis were detected, but the most common and probably the most debilitating affliction was arthritis. Malnutrition had probably been a problem in their childhood, and was due more to a failure to eat the right foods rather than deprivation of food. This affected later growth and stature.

Their bones showed the effects of a lifetime of heavy physical effort. 'Working with wool', as the Greek and Roman women were wont to do, was but part of what would have been for many women of Iron Age Britain women a life of hard labour. Houses were simple, but stout and practical. For much of the year, they would not have been the focus of the women's day; their work involved the outdoors as much as indoors in the planting and harvesting seasons. Slaves were probably only the prerogative of the rich.

In life these women observed the local deities, making offerings of objects of long-lasting materials such as bronze or glass, objects with which the god could associate them; almost certainly there were other offerings of organic material such as foodstuffs, which have long since gone. Their greatest concerns brought before the gods centred on their fertility and that of their animals and crops, and the health and welfare of themselves and their families. In death, they were honoured with graves as deep and as large as men's, and accompanied by similar grave goods. Women of the native aristocracy were given prestige burials along with men, and the incidence of women's chariot burials is a good indicator of the status of women within a tribe. Imported prestige grave deposits from across the Channel confirmed that, for some women at least, there was a little luxury in their lives.

The impact of Rome on the women of Britain was, over time, far reaching. The most immediate and visible result would be the emergence of the Romano-British town, with its forum, basilica, temples and shops, and the Roman-style houses which became part of the towns. While these catered for the citizens of Rome who had ventured to British shores, or for veterans who, on discharge, found a home alongside old army colleagues, the houses were also occupied by native Britons. The womenfolk of the former native ruling classes, whose sons were quick to 'wear the toga', themselves adopted Roman dress and hairstyles, jewellery and luxury items. In their houses they had all the facilities that might be found at Rome; the poor gained little except access to running water at a communal source – no mean benefit – and to the baths which sprang up in every town which had Roman pretensions.

In the country, the wealthy members of the old native aristocracy adopted the symbols of Romanisation: the villa with its private baths suite, mosaic floors and frescoed walls. These establishments reflected the comforts that the same families had in the towns. Women from these families would be adept at running households in both town and country. Slaves kept both in good order, with a bailiff in charge when the master and mistress were absent.

Women whose husbands were part of the provincial administration would have found life very trying at first; but with the establishment of fortresses and a governor's *principium*, Roman convenience and practicality ensured that life became easier. Most of those whom we have identified as the wives of governors, senior officers or procurators ultimately found themselves in London, a city which provided the facilities, resources and entertainments that might be found at Rome. Away from London, those women who were the wives of army officers would not have had great inconvenience, apart from the isolation. Quarters for officers, and particularly the commanding officer, were far from meagre – the governor's headquarters of the VI *Victrix* at York a virtual home-away-from-home with its fine frescoed walls. All these women, in their own way, contributed to the Romanisation of the province.

The women who lived in *vici* outside army forts and in small towns generally did not experience many luxuries, and were in a similar position to the poorer classes who lived in the various large towns. Some facilities were available, and the attraction of shops and baths, introduced by the Romans, would be unlikely to pale. There is, too, no evidence that the standard of living or of the health of the inhabitants in towns deteriorated during the years of the Occupation. Women lived to the same age as they had previously in the Iron Age, or even older, and to about the same age as men, although they were fewer in number. Nutrition was probably helped by the increased variety of foods available, and the average height was greater.

Women's role in religion was never as high as men's, although there is the possibility that there were Druidesses, both in Britain and on the Continent, well after the establishment of the province. The gods favoured by women remained the same as in the Iron Age, relating particularly to personal and family health and welfare, fertility and safety in childbirth. The introduction, around the third century, of gods of a salvation type attracted women converts from both rich and poor classes. This was reflected also in Christianity, which may have come to Britain as early as the end of the second century. Women were among the Christian converts, and wealthy women among the benefactors, but any role they may have had in the Church hierarchy – a matter of considerable debate – was gone by the fourth century. On the other hand, women could be priestesses in the Imperial cult, focusing on the emperor, a cult which continued until the time of Constantine I.

There was a reverse side to this Roman coin. From the archaeological evidence, it is clear that women's status progressively declined. The cemetery data show that there were fewer women than men buried in Romano-British cemeteries, and this was believed to be the result of female infanticide, a practice common the Roman world. The graves of women show a decline in status also: the early graves are equal to or larger and deeper than males', while those later in the Roman period became smaller and shallower. Grave goods show a similar decline. While females had the majority of burials which indicated status – stone or lead coffins, plaster or step burials, which ultimately would be hidden in the ground – it was the Romano-British male who was most often found in that most prestigious and visible of burials, the mausoleum.

Two main themes have emerged in this summary. The first is that the role and status of women declined from the Late Iron Age to the end of the Roman period. The second is that, while Roman women contributed to the Romanisation of the province, the influence of Rome on British women was not universal; it was most felt on those who were among the wealthy classes, both in the town and country, and in places where Romanisation was at its most pervasive – that is, in the Romano-British towns and in the areas closely associated with them.

* * *

For those whose interests centre on Late Iron Age and Roman Britain, it might be useful to suggest areas for further research which have been revealed during the course of the research for this present work. The most obvious is on cemetery remains, not just on the bones of women, but of all burials. Children have been dealt with here in the inscriptions, and not in the analysis of cemeteries. With the advances in techniques for the sexing of children some progress can be anticipated here – not only in scientific analysis, but also in the sociological/historical aspects of cemetery studies. There is also a great need for the remains from earlier sites, such as Trentholme Drive at York and Bath Gate, Cirencester, to be re-examined in the light of scientific advances, especially in DNA studies. Family groups might be studied – this would complement the work done by archaeologists such as Nina Crummy at Butt Road, Colchester, and the work on the Roman family by Suzanne Dixon.[2]

Some of the more recent reports, such as Poundbury, have sought to identify the origins of people from their bones, for example, oily diet = Mediterranean origin. This is, as far as the writer knows, a first attempt. Such studies have become as important as those which first collated basic cemetery data. We now have more than 6,000 burials, most reasonably well-documented, which have given a general picture of burial practices in Late Iron Age and Roman Britain. The logical move forward is to look at the more complex sociological picture.

That is not to say, however, that researchers cannot benefit from the publication of more well-documented cemeteries. It has been one of the frustrations of this present work that three very important sites are still not fully published. The excellent Lankhills report which came out in 1979 still awaits its companion volume on the skeletal remains, and the Ancaster and Ashton burials have as yet had only fragmentary publication in the works of various writers. These two sites are of vital interest not just for the cemetery material, but as part of a composite which includes associated settlements, and any religious material.

It is now some years since Charles Thomas's work on Christianity in Roman Britain was first published, and archaeological finds since then have multiplied.

An updated record of such finds and a good bibliographical record would be of considerable assistance, as would a revised and expanded study of the temples of Roman Britain. Michael Lewis's classifications may need some modification, but his record of temples, published almost 40 years ago, is still a sound basis for such a work.[3]

Women, too, could be dealt with from the point of view of artefacts. Some work has already been published, such as that by Sonia Puttock, and more research is under way. Catalogues are important, but the social, historical and religious background is also important in such a study. Owing to various constraints, this was an aspect of the present work which could be dealt with only in discussions on grave goods. A more specialised approach is highly desirable.[4]

Despite such shortcomings, this study has, it is hoped, put the women of early Britain into their historical perspective, progressing – if that is the right word – from many rural groupings dominated by land-controlling native aristocracies to a combination of a relatively few Romanised urban communities and a much larger number of rural communities of diminishing Romanisation, ruled from a place thousands of kilometres away. It has also shown the deterioration of the status of women under Roman rule. One wonders if that feisty female who saw the one age end and the other begin, Queen Boudicca, would have been amused.

Notes

1 Cunliffe 1995: 112–13.
2 Crummy *et al.* 1993; Dixon 1992.
3 Thomas 1981; Lewis 1966.
4 Puttock 2002.

REFERENCES
Archaeological and secondary sources

Alcock, J.P. (1986) 'The concept of Genius in Roman Britain', 113–33 in M. Henig and A. King (eds) *Pagan Gods and Shrines of the Roman Empire*, Oxford: OUCA.

——— (2001) *Food in Roman Britain*, Stroud: Tempus.

Allason-Jones, L. (1989) *Women in Roman Britain*, London: British Museum Press.

——— (1999) 'Women and the Roman army in Britain', 41–51 in A. Goldsworthy and I. Haynes (eds) *The Roman Army as a Community*, Portsmouth, RI: J. Roman Archaeol.

——— (2004) 'The family in Roman Britain', 273–87 in M. Todd (ed.) *A Companion to Roman Britain*, Maldon, MA: Blackwell.

Anderson, T. (1987) 'Cirencester: an osteo-archaeological analysis of the Bath Gate cemetery', Unpublished project report in partial completion of requirements for MA, Department of Archaeology and Prehistory, Sheffield University.

Arnold, B. (1999) '"Drinking the feast": alcohol and the legitimation of power in Celtic Europe', *Cambridge Archaeol. J.*, 9.1: 71–93.

Arnold, C.J. (1995) 'The archaeology of inter-personal violence', *Scottish Archaeol. Rev.*, 9 and 1: 71–79.

Balsdon, J.P.V.D. (1962) *Roman Women*, London: Bodley Head.

Barber, B. and Bowsher, D. (2000) *The Eastern Cemetery of Roman London: Excavations 1983–1990*, London: Museum London Archaeol. Service.

Beard, M. (1990) 'Priesthood in the Roman Republic', 17–48 in M. Beard and J. North (eds) *Pagan Priests: Religion and Power in the Ancient World*, New York: Cornell University Press.

Berresford Ellis, P. (1995) *Celtic Women*, London: Constable.

Billington, S. (1996) 'Fors Fortuna in Ancient Rome', 129–40 in S. Billington and M. Green (eds) *The Concept of the Goddess*, London: Routledge.

Bird, J. (1996) 'A Romano-British priestly head-dress from Farley Heath', *Surrey Archaeol. Collections*, 83: 81–9.

Birley, A. (1981) *The Fasti of Roman Britain*, Oxford: Clarendon.

Birley, E. (1935) 'Three Roman inscriptions', *Archaelogia Aeliana*, 4th ser., 12: 195–203.

Birley, R. (1997) 'The Vindolanda bonfire', *Current Archaeol.*, 153: 348–57.

——— (2002) *Garrison Life at Vindolanda: A Band of Brothers*, Stroud: Tempus.

Bitel, L. (1984) 'Women's donations to the churches in early Ireland', *J. Royal Soc. Antiq. Ireland*, 114: 5–23.

Black, E.W. (1983) 'Ritual dog burials from Roman sites', *Kent Archaeol. Rev.*, 71: 20–2.

Bland, R. and Johns, C. (1993) *The Hoxne Treasure*, London: British Museum Press.

Boddington, A. (1986) 'Raunds, Northamptonshire: analysis of a country churchyard', *World Archaeology*, 18: 411–25.

Borrill, H. (1981) 'Casket Burials', 304–18 in C. Partridge (ed.) *Skeleton Green A Late Iron Age and Romano-British Site*, London: Soc. Prom. Roman Stud.

Boswell, J. (1989) *The Kindness of Strangers. The Abandonment of Children in Western Europe from Late Antiquity to the Renaissance*, London: Allen Lane/Penguin.

Boyle, A. (2004) 'Riding into history', *British Archaeol.*, 76: 22–7.

Brooten, B.J. (1982) *Women Leaders in the Ancient Synagogue*, Atlanta, GA: Scholars Press.

Buchet, L. (1993) 'Les habitants de la Gaule rurale, société des motes, société des vivants: apports de l'anthropologie', 17–22 in A. Ferdiere (ed.) *Monde des Mortes, Monde des Vivants en Gaule Rurale* (Actes du Colloque ARCHÉA/AGER, Orléans, Conseil Régional, 7–9 February 1992) Tours: La Simarre.

Burnham, B.C. and Wacher, J. (1990) *The 'Small Towns' of Roman Britain*, London: Batsford.

Carcopino, J. (1941) *Daily Life in Ancient Rome*, London: Penguin.

Chadwick, N. (1997) *The Druids*, 2nd edn, Cardiff: University Wales Press.

Chambers, R.A. (1987) 'The late- and sub-Roman cemetery at Queensford Farm, Dorchester-on-Thames, Oxon', *Oxoniensia*, 52: 35–69.

Champion, S. (1995) 'Jewellery and adornment', 411–19 in M. Green (ed.) *The Celtic World*, London: Routledge.

Cherici, P. (1994) *Celtic Sexuality*, London: Duckworth.

Clark, G. (1993) *Women in Late Antiquity: Pagan and Christian Lifestyles*, Oxford: Oxford University Press.

Clarke, G. (1979) *Pre-Roman and Roman Winchester Part II: The Roman Cemetery at Lankhills*, Winchester Studies 3, Oxford: Clarendon.

Collard, M. and Parkhouse, J. (1993) 'A Belgic-Romano-British cemetery at Bledlow-cum-Saunderton', *Rec. Buckinghamshire*, 35: 66–75.

Collis, J. (1968) 'Excavations at Owslebury, Hants: an interim report', *Antiq. J.*, 48: 18–31.

—— (1970) 'Excavations at Owslebury, Hants: a second interim report', *Antiq. J.*, 50: 246–61.

—— (1977) 'Owslebury (Hants) and the problem of burials on rural settlements', 1–13 in R. Reece (ed.) *Burial in the Roman World*, London: CBA.

—— (1994) 'An Iron Age and Roman cemetery at Owslebury, Hampshire', 106–8 in A.P. Fitzpatrick and E.L. Morris (eds) *The Iron Age in Wessex: Recent Work*, Salisbury: Trust for Wessex Archaeology/Assoc. Française D'Etude de L'Age du Fer.

—— (2003) *The Celts: Origins, Myths and Inventions*, Stroud: Tempus.

Cooper, L. (1996) 'A Roman cemetery in Newarke Street, Leicester', *Trans. Leicestershire Archaeol. and Hist. Soc.*, 70: 1–90.

Cox, M. (1989) 'The human bone from Ancaster', *Ancient Monuments Laboratory Report 93/89*.

Croom, A.T. (2000) *Roman Clothing and Fashion*, Stroud: Tempus.

Crummy, N. (2004) 'Music and dancing at St Mary's', *The Colchester Archaeologist*, 17: 29.

Crummy, N., Crummy, P., and Crossan, C. (eds) (1993) *Excavations of Roman and Later Cemeteries, Churches and Monastic Sites in Colchester, 1971–88*, Colchester: Colchester Archaeol. Trust.

Crummy, P. (1997a) *City of Victory*, Colchester: Colchester Archaeol. Trust.

—— (1997b) 'Colchester, the Stanway burials', *Current Archaeol.*, 153: 337–44.

—— (2003) 'The western suburb: excavations on the site of the former Victorian workhouse at St Mary's Hospital', *The Colchester Archaeologist*, 16: 10–15.

Cunliffe, B.W. (1984a) *Danebury: An Iron Age Hillfort in Hampshire, Vol. 2 The excavations, 1969–1978: The Finds*, London: CBA.

—— (1984b) 'Relations between Britain and Gaul in the first century BC and early first century AD', 3–12 in S. Macready and F.H. Thompson (eds) *Cross-Channel trade between Gaul and Britain in the Pre-Roman Iron Age*, London: Soc. Antiq.

—— (1984c) *Roman Bath Discovered*, revised edn, London: Routledge and Kegan Paul.

—— (1991) *Iron Age Communities in Britain*, 3rd edn, London: Routledge.

—— (1995) *Iron Age Britain*, London: Batsford/English Heritage.

—— (1997) *The Ancient Celts*, Oxford: Oxford University Press.

Davey, N. and Ling, R. (1982) *Wall Painting in Roman Britain*, Gloucester: Sutton.

Davies, R.W. (1971) 'The Roman military diet', *Britannia*, 2: 122–42.

Dawson, M. (1994) *A Late Roman Cemetery at Bletsoe, Bedfordshire*, Bedfordshire Archaeol. Monograph 1.

deJersey, P. (1993) 'The early chronology of Alet, and its implications for Hengistbury Head and cross-Channel trade in the Late Iron Age', *Oxford J. Archaeol.*, 12: 321–35.

Dent, J.S. (1982) 'Cemeteries and settlement patterns of the Iron Age on the Yorkshire Wolds', *Proc. Prehist. Soc.*, 48: 437–57.

—— (1983) 'A summary of the excavations carried out in Garton Slack and Wetwang Slack 1964–1980', *East Riding Archaeol.*, 7: 1–14.

—— (1985) 'Three cart burials from Wetwang, Yorkshire', *Antiquity*, 59: 85–92.

Derbyshire, D. (2001) 'Chariot queen's grave unearthed', *Electronic Telegraph*, 2143, 7 April 2001 (www.telegraph.co.uk).

Dixon, S.M. (1992) *The Roman Family*, Baltimore: Johns Hopkins University Press.

Dobson, B. (1974) 'The significance of the centurion and 'primipilaris' in the Roman army and administration', 392–434 in H. Temporini (ed.) *Aufstieg und Niedergang der römischen Welt*, II.1, Berlin: deGruyter.

Dyggve, E. (1951) *A History of Salonitan Christianity*, Oslo: Aschehoug; Cambridge, MA: Harvard Univerity Press.

Ehrenberg, M. (1989) *Women in Prehistory*, London: British Museum.

Farley, M. (1983) 'A mirror burial at Dorton, Buckinghamshire', *Proc. Prehist. Soc.*, 49: 269–302.

Farwell, D.E. and Molleson, T.I. (1993) *Excavations at Poundbury 1966–80, Volume II: The Cemeteries*, Dorchester: Dorset Nat. Hist. Archaeol. Soc.

Fishwick, D. (1987) *The Imperial Cult in the Latin West. Studies in the Ruler Cult of the Western Provinces of the Roman Empire*, Leiden: Brill.

Fitzpatrick, A.P. (1997) *Archaeological Excavations on the Route of the A27 Westhampnett Bypass, West Sussex, 1992, Vol. 2: The Late Iron Age, Romano-British and Anglo Saxon Cemeteries*, Salisbury: Wessex Archaeology.

Fitzpatrick, A.P. and Crockett, A.D. (1998) 'A Romano-British settlement and inhumation cemetery at Eyewell Farm, Chilmark', *Wiltshire Archaeol. Nat. Hist. Mag.*, 91: 11–33.

Fox, C. and Lethbridge, T.C. (1926) 'The La Tène and Romano-British cemetery, Guilden Morden, Cambs.', *Proc. Cambridge Antiq. Soc.*, 27: 49–71.

France, N.E. and Gobel, B.M. (1985) *The Romano-British Temple at Harlow*, F.R. Clark and I.K. Jones (eds), Gloucester: West Essex Archaeol. Group.

Frend, W.H.C. (1996) *The Archaeology of Early Christianity*, London: Chapman.

Frere, S.S. (1983) 'Roman Britain in 1982: sites explored', *Britannia*, 14: 279–356.

—— (1984) 'Roman Britain in 1983: sites explored', *Britannia*, 15: 255–332.

—— (1987) *Britannia*, revised edn, London: Routledge and Kegan Paul.

Gordon, R. (1990) 'Religion in the Roman Empire: the civic compromise and its limits', 233–55 in M. Beard and J. North (eds) *Pagan Priests: Religion and Power in the Ancient World*, New York: Cornell University Press.

Grant, A. (2004) 'Domestic animals and their uses', 371–408 in M. Todd (ed.) *A Companion to Roman Britain*, Malden, MA: Blackwell.

Grasby, R.D. and Tomlin, R.S.O. (2002) 'The sepulchral monument of the procurator C. Julius Classicianus', *Britannia*, 33: 43–75.

Green, C.J.S. (1977) 'The significance of plaster burials for the recognition of Christian cemeteries', 46–53 in R.Reece (ed.) *Burial in the Roman World*, London: CBA.

Green, M. (1995a) *Celtic Goddesses*, London: British Museum Press.

—— (1996) 'The Celtic goddess as healer', 26–40 in S. Billington and M. Green (eds) *The Concept of the Goddess*, London: Routledge.

Greenwell, W. (1906) 'Early Iron Age burials in Yorkshire', *Archaeologia*, 60: 251–324.

Gregory, A. (trans.) 1902 *Cuchulain of Muirthemne*, n.p., John Murray, reprinted 1970, Gerrards Cross: Colin Smyth.

Hall, J. (1996) 'The cemeteries of Roman London', 57–84 in J. Bird, M. Hassall, and H. Sheldon (eds) *Interpreting Roman London*, Oxford: Oxbow.

Handley, M. (2000) 'The origins of Christian commemoration in late antique Britain', *Early Medieval Europe*, 10.2: 177–99.

Hanson, W.S. (1988) 'Administration, urbanisation and acculturation in the Roman West', 53–68 in D. Braund (ed.) *The Administration of the Roman Empire 241 BC–AD193*, Exeter: University Exeter.

Hassall, M. (1999) 'Homes for heroes: married quarters for soldiers and veterans', 35–40 in A. Goldsworthy and I. Haynes (eds) *The Roman Army as a Community*, Portsmouth, RI: J. Roman Archaeol.

Haselgrove, C. (1994) 'Social organisation in Iron Age Wessex', 1–3 in A.P. Fitzpatrick and E.L. Morris (eds) *The Iron Age in Wessex: Recent Work*, Salisbury: Trust for Wessex Archaeology/Assoc. Française D'Etude de L'Age du Fer.

Henderson, J. (1991) 'Industrial specialization in late Iron Age Britain and Europe', *Archaeol. J.*, 148: 104–48.

Henig, M. (1984) *Religion in Roman Britain*, London: Batsford.

Hill, J.D. (2001) 'Romanisation, gender and class: recent approaches to identity in Britain and their possible consequences', 12–18 in S. James and M. Millett (eds) *Britons and Romans: Advancing an Archaeological Agenda*, York: CBA.

Hingley, R. (1989) *Rural Settlement Roman Britain*, London: Seaby.

—— (1997) 'Resistance and domination: social change in Roman Britain', 81–100 in D.J. Mattingly (ed.) *Dialogues in Roman Imperialism*, Portsmouth, RI: J.Roman Archaeol.

Holder, P.A. (1982) *The Roman Army in Britain*, London: Batsford.

Hood, S. and Walton, H. (1948) 'A Romano-British cremating place and burial ground on Roden Downs, Compton, Berkshire', *Trans. Newbury District Field Club*, 1: 10–62.

Hope, V.M. (1997) 'Words and pictures: the interpretation of Romano-British tombstones', *Britannia*, 28: 246–58.

Jackson, K. (1983) 'The inscriptions on the silver spoons' 46–8 in C. Johns and T. Potter (eds) *The Thetford Treasure*, London: British Museum Press.

James, S. (1993) *Exploring the World of the Celts*, London: Thames & Hudson.

Jenkins, F. (1957) 'The role of the dog in Romano-Gaulish religion', *Latomus*, 16: 60–76.

Johns, C. (1996) *The Jewellery of Roman Britain*, London: University College London Press.

Johns, C.M. and Potter, T.W. (1983) *The Thetford Treasure: Roman Jewellery and Silver*, London: British Museum Press.

Johnson, J.S. (1990) *Chesters Roman Fort*, London: English Heritage.

Jones, B. and Mattingly, D. (1990) *An Atlas of Roman Britain*, Cambridge, MA: Blackwell, reprinted 2002, Oxford: Oxbow.

Jones, B.W. (1992) *The Emperor Domitian*, London: Routledge.

Jones, M. (1996) 'Plant exploitation' 29–40 in T.C. Champion and J.R. Collis (eds) *The Iron Age in Britain and Ireland*, Sheffield: Collis Publications.

Jones, M.J. (2004) 'Cities and urban life', 162–92 in M. Todd (ed.) *A Companion to Roman Britain*, Malden, MA: Blackwell.

Jones, R. (1975) 'The Romano-British farmstead and its cemetery at Lynch Farm, Near Peterborough', *Northamptonshire Archaeol.*, 10: 94–137.

Kajanto, I. (1982) *The Latin Cognomina*, Rome: Bretschneider.

Keegan, S.L. (2002) *Inhumation Rites in Roman Britain: The Treatment of the Engendered Body*, Oxford: Hadrian Books.

Keys, D. (2001) 'Warrior queen and her Iron Age chariot unearthed on a building site', *Independent*, 7 April 2001 (electronic version: www.independent.co.uk).

King, A.C. (1984) 'Animal bones and the dietary identity of military and civilian groups in Roman Britain, Germany and Gaul', 187–217 in T. Blagg and A. King (eds) *Military and Civilian in Roman Britain*, Oxford: BAR.

—— (1999) 'Animals and the Roman army: the evidence of animal bones', 139–150 in A. Goldsworthy and I. Haynes (eds) *The Roman Army as a Community*, Portsmouth, RI: J. Roman Archaeol.

Kraemer, R.S. (1992) *Her Share of the Blessings*, New York: Oxford University Press.

Leach, P. and Evans, C.J. (2001) *Excavation of a Romano-British Roadside Settlement in Somerset. Fosse Lane Shepton Mallet 1990*, London: Soc. Prom. Roman Stud.

Leech, P. (1981) 'The excavation of a Romano-British farmstead and cemetery on Bradley Hill, Somerton, Somerset', *Britannia*, 12: 177–252.

Lethbridge, T.C. (1936) 'Further excavations in the early Iron Age and Romano-British cemetery at Guilden Morden', *Proc. Cambridge Antiq. Soc.*, 36: 109–19.

—— (1937) 'Romano-British burials at Linton, Cambridgeshire', *Proc. Cambridge Antiq. Soc.*, 37: 68–71.

Lewis, M.J.T. (1966) *Temples in Roman Britain*, Cambridge: Cambridge University Press.

Liversidge, J. (1955) *Furniture in Roman Britain*, London: Tiranti.

—— (1959) 'Roman burials in the Cambridge area', *Proc. Cambridge Antiq. Soc.*, 67: 19.

Lloyd-Morgan, G. (1995) 'Appearance, life and leisure', 95–120 in M. Green (ed.) *The Celtic World*, London: Routledge.

MacCulloch, J.A. (1911) *The Religion of the Ancient Celts*, Edinburgh: Clark; reprinted 1991, London: Constable.

Mackinder, A. (2000) *A Romano-British Cemetery on Watling Street: Excavations at 165 Great Dover Street, Southwark, London*, London: Museum London Archaeol. Service.

McWhirr, A., Viner, L., and Wells, C. (1982) *Romano-British Cemeteries at Cirencester*, Cirencester: Cirencester Excavation Committee.

Magie, D. (1950) *Roman Rule in Asia Minor to the end of the Third Century after Christ*, Princeton: Princeton University Press.

Maltby, M. (1996) 'The exploitation of animals in the Iron Age: the archaeozoological evidence', 17–27 in T.C. Champion and J.R. Collis (eds) *The Iron Age in Britain and Ireland: Recent Trends*, Sheffield: Collis Publications.

Marucchi, O. (1974) *Christian Epigraphy*, (trans. J.A. Willis), Chicago, IL: Ares.

Matthews, C.L. (1981) 'A Romano-British inhumation cemetery at Dunstable', *Bedfordshire Archaeol. J.*, 15: 4–137.

Mays, S. (1998) *The Archaeology of Human Bones*, London: Routledge.

Megaw, R. and Megaw, V. (1996) 'Ancient Celts and modern ethnicity', *Antiquity*, 70: 175–82.

Millett, M. (1990) *The Romanization of Britain: An Essay in Archaeological Interpretation*, Cambridge: Cambridge University Press.

Milne, G. (1995) *Roman London*, London: Batsford/English Heritage.

Morris, I. (1992) *Death Ritual and Social Structure in Classical Antiquity*, Cambridge: Cambridge University Press.

Neal, D.S. (1981) *Roman Mosaics in Britain*, Gloucester: Sutton.

—— (1987) 'Excavations at Magiovinium, Buckinghamshire, 1978–80', *Rec. Buckinghamshire*, 29: 1–124.

Niblett, R. (1999) *The Excavation of a Ceremonial Site at Folly Lane, Verulamium*, London: Soc. Prom. Roman Stud.

—— (2001) *Verulamium: The Roman City of St Albans*, Stroud: Tempus.

Orr, K. and Crummy, P. (2004) 'New light on old problems', *The Colchester Archaeologist*, 17: 2–7.

Painter, K.S. (1965) 'A Roman silver treasure from Canterbury', *J. Brit. Archaeol. Assoc.*, 3rd ser. 28: 1–15.

—— (1977a) *The Mildenhall Treasure*, London: British Museum Publications.

—— (1977b) *The Water Newton Early Christian Silver*, London: British Museum Publications.

Pare, C.F.E. (1992) *Wagons and Wagon Graves of the Early Iron Age in Central Europe*, Oxford: OUCA.

Parfitt, K. (1995) *Iron Age Burials from Mill Hill, Deal*, London: British Museum Press.

Parkin, T.G. (2003) *Old Age in the Roman World*, Baltimore, MD: Johns Hopkins University Press.

Partridge, C. (1978) 'Excavations and fieldwork at Braughing, 1968–73', *Hertfordshire Archaeol.*, 5: 22–108.

—— (1981) *Skeleton Green A Late Iron Age and Romano-British Site*, London: Soc. Prom. Roman Stud.

Patterson, J.R. (1987) 'The Italian *alimenta*', *Papers British School Rome*, 55: 124–46.

Pflaum, H.G. (1974) *Abrégé des Procurateurs Equestres*, (French adaptation S. Ducroux and N. Duval), Paris: E. de Boccard.

Philpott, R. (1991) *Burial Practices in Roman Britain*, Oxford: Tempus.

Piggott, S. (1974) *The Druids*, Harmondsworth: Penguin.

Pinter-Bellows, S. (1993) 'The human skeletons', 62–91 in N. Crummy, P. Crummy, and C. Crossan (eds) *Excavations of Roman and Later Cemeteries, Churches and Monastic Sites in Colchester, 1971–88*, Colchester: Colchester Archaeol. Trust.

Puttock, S.L. (2002) *Ritual Significance of Personal Ornament in Roman Britain*, Oxford: Archaeopress.

RCHM (1962) *Eburacum Roman York*, London: HMSO.

Raepsaet-Charlier, M.-T. (1987) *Prosopographie des Femmes de l'Ordre Sénatorial (Ier–IIe siècles)*, Louvain: Aedibus Peeters.

Rahtz, P.A. (1977) 'Late Roman cemeteries and beyond', 53–64 in R. Reece (ed.) *Burial in the Roman World*, London: CBA.

Rahtz, P.A., Hirst, S., and Wright, S.M. (2000) *Cannington Cemetery*, London: Soc. Prom. Roman Stud.

Rankin, D. (1996) *Celts and the Classical World*, London: Routledge.

Rankov, B. (1999) 'The governor's men: the *officium consularis* in provincial administration', 15–34 in A. Goldsworthy and I. Haynes (eds) *The Roman Army as a Community*, Portsmouth, RI: J. Roman Archaeol.

Redfern, R. (2002) 'Sex and the city: a biocultural investigation into female health in Roman Britain', 147–70 in G. Carr, E. Swift, and J. Weeks (eds) *TRAC 2002 Proceedings of the Twelfth Annual Theoretical Roman Archaeology Conference*, Oxford: Oxbow.

Reynolds, P. (1994) 'Butser ancient farm', 11–14 in A.P. Fitzpatrick and E.L.Morris (eds) *The Iron Age in Wessex: Recent Work*, Salisbury: Trust for Wessex Archaeology/Assoc. Française D'Etude de L'Age du Fer.

Richardson, J. (1976) *Roman Provincial Administration*, Bristol: Macmillan; reprinted 1978, Bristol: Class. Pr.

Roberts, C. and Manchester, K. (1995) *The Archaeology of Disease*, 2nd edn, Stroud: Alan Sutton.

Roberts, C. and Cox, M. (2003) *Health and Disease in Britain from Prehistory to the Present Day*, Stroud: Sutton.

—— (2004) 'The human population: health and disease', 242–72 in M. Todd (ed.) *A Companion to Roman Britain*, Malden, MA: Blackwell.

Robertson, N. (1970) 'Fate', 430–2 in N.G.L. Hammond and H.H. Scullard (eds) *The Oxford Classical Dictionary*, 2nd edn, Oxford: Clarendon.

Rock (Canon) (1869) 'Celtic spoons', *Archaeol. J.*, 26: 35–51.

Rodwell, K. (1987–8) *The Pre-historic and Roman Settlement at Kelvedon*, London: Chelmsford Archaeol. Trust/CBA.

Rose, H.J. (1970) 'Maia', 640 in N.G.L. Hammond and H.H. Scullard (eds) *The Oxford Classical Dictionary*, 2nd edn, Oxford: Clarendon.

Ross, A. (1992) *Pagan Celtic Britain*, revised edn, London: Constable.

—— (1999) *Druids*, Stroud: Tempus.

Ryder, M.L. (1993) 'Wool at Danebury: a speculation using evidence from elsewhere', *Oxford J. Archaeol.*, 12: 305–20.

Rynne, E. (1974–75) 'Ancient burials at Ballinlough, Co. Laois', *J. Kildare Archaeol. Soc.*, 15: 430–3.

Savunen, L. (1995) 'Women and elections in Pompeii', 194–206 in R. Hawley and B. Levick (eds) *Women in Antiquity: New Assessments*, London: Routledge.

Schutkowski, H. (1993) 'Sex determination of infants and juvenile skeletons: 1. Morphognostic features', *Amer. J. Phys. Anthrop.*, 90: 197–205.

Shelton, J. (1998) *As the Romans Did*, 2nd edn, New York: Oxford University Press.

Sherlock, D. (1973) 'Zu einer Fundliste antiker Silberlöffel', *Bericht der Römisch-Germanischen Kommission*, 54: 203–11.

Sherwin-White, A.N. (1973) *The Roman Citizenship*, new edn, London: Oxford University Press.

Sparey Green, C.J. (1993) 'The mausolea painted plaster', 135–40 in D.E. Farwell and T.I. Molleson (eds) *Excavations at Poundbury 1966–80, Volume II: The Cemeteries*, Dorchester: Dorset Nat. Hist. Archaeol. Soc.

Stead, I.M. (1986) 'A group of Iron Age barrows at Cowlam, North Humberside', *Yorkshire Archaeol. J.*, 58: 5–15.

—— (1991) *Iron Age Cemeteries in East Yorkshire*, London: English Heritage.

Stead, I.M. and Rigby, V. (1986) *Baldock: The Excavation of a Roman and Pre-Roman Settlement, 1968–72*, London: Soc. Prom. Roman Stud.

—— (1989) *Verulamium: The King Harry Lane Site*, London: English Heritage/British Museum Publications.

Stirland, A. (1989) 'The cremations from the Iron Age cemetery', 244–9 in I.M. Stead and V. Rigby (eds) *Verulamium: The King Harry Lane Site*, London: English Heritage/British Museum Publications.

Struck, M. (2000) 'High status burials in Roman Britain (1st–3rd centuries AD) – potential of interpretation', 85–96 in J. Pearce, M. Millett, and M. Struck (eds) *Burial, Society and Context in the Roman World*, Oxford: Oxbow.

Thomas, C. (1981) *Christianity in Roman Britain to AD 500*, London: Batsford.

Thompson, H. (1993) 'Iron Age and Roman slave-shackles', *Archaeol. J.*, 150: 57–168.

Tierney, J.J. (1960) 'The Celtic ethnography of Poseidonius', *Proc. Royal Irish Acad.*, 60: 189–246.

Toller, H. (1977) *Roman Lead Coffins and Ossuaria in Britain*, Oxford: BAR.

Tomlin, R.S.O. (1988) *Tabellae Sulis: Roman Inscribed Tablets of Tin and Lead from the Sacred Spring at Bath*, Oxford: OUCA.

—— (1993a) 'Roman towns and Roman inscriptions of Britain, 1939–89', 134–46 in S.J. Greep (ed.) *Roman Towns: The Wheeler Inheritance*, York: CBA.

—— (1993b) 'The inscribed lead tablets: an interim report', 113–30 in A. Woodward and P. Leach (eds) *The Uley Shrines*, London: English Heritage/British Museum Press.

—— (2003) ' "The girl in question": a new text from Roman London', *Britannia*, 34: 41–51.

Toynbee, J.M.C. (1953) 'Christianity in Roman Britain', *J. Brit. Archaeol. Assoc.*, 3rd ser., 16: 1–24.

—— (1964) *Art in Britain under the Romans*, Oxford: Clarendon.

—— (1971) *Death and Burial in the Roman World*, Baltimore: Johns Hopkins University Press.

Turner, R. (1999) *Excavations of an Iron Age Settlement and Roman Religious Complex at Ivy Chimneys, Witham, Essex 1978–83*, Chelmsford: Essex County Council.

Turner, R.C. and Rhodes, M. (1992) 'A bog body and its shoes from Amcotts, Lincolnshire', *Antiq. J.*, 72: 76–90.

Ucko, P.J. (1969–70) 'Ethnography and archaeological interpretation of funerary remains', *World Archaeol.*, 1: 262–77.

Wacher, J. (1995) *The Towns of Roman Britain*, 2nd edn, London: Routledge.

—— (2000) *A Portrait of Roman Britain*, London: Routledge.

Wait, G. (1986) *Ritual and Religion in Iron Age Britain*, Oxford: BAR.

Wallace, P.F. and O'Floinn, R. (2002) *Treasures of the National Museum of Ireland: Irish Antiquities*, Dublin: Gill & Macmillan.

Wardle, A. (2000) 'Funerary rites, burial practice and belief', 27–30 in A. Mackinder (ed.) *A Romano-British Cemetery on Watling Street: Excavations at 165 Great Dover Street, Southwark, London*, London: Museum London Archaeol. Service.

Warne, C. (1872) *Ancient Dorset* (privately published).

Warwick, R. (1968) 'The skeletal remains', 113–216 in L.P. Wenham (ed.) *The Romano-British Cemetery at Trentholme Drive, York*, London: HMSO.

Watson, S. (2003) *An Excavation in the Western Cemetery of Roman London: Atlantic House, City of London*, London: Museum London Archaeol. Service.

Watts, D.J. (1988) 'The Thetford Treasure: a reappraisal', *Antiq. J.*, 58: 55–68.

—— (1989) 'Infant burials and Romano-British Christianity', *Archaeol. J.*, 146: 372–83.

—— (1991) *Christians and Pagans in Roman Britain*, London: Routledge.

—— (1998) *Religion in Late Roman Britain*, London: Routledge.

—— (2001) 'The silent minority: women in Romano-British cemeteries', *Archaeol. J.*, 158: 332–47.

Wedlake, W.J. (1982) *The Excavation of the Shrine of Apollo at Nettleton, Wiltshire, 1956–1971*, London: Soc. Antiq.

Welinder, S. (1988–89) 'An experiment with the analysis of sex and gender of cremated bones', *Tor*, 22: 29–41.

Wells, C. (1976) 'The human burials', in S. West (ed.) 'The Romano-British site at Icklingham' *East Anglian Archaeol.*, 3: 63–236.

—— (1978) 'Human remains', in C. Partridge (ed.) 'Excavations and fieldwork at Braughing, 1968–73', *Hertfordshire Archaeol.*, 5: 85–7.

—— (1982) 'The human burials', 135–202 in A. McWhirr, L. Viner, and C. Wells (eds) *Romano-British Cemeteries at Cirencester*, Cirencester: Cirencester Excavation Committee.

Wenham, L.P. (1968) *The Romano-British Cemetery at Trentholme Drive, York*, London: HMSO.

West, S. (1976) 'The Romano-British site at Icklingham', *East Anglian Archaeol.*, 3: 63–126.

Wheeler, H. (1985) 'The Racecourse cemetery', *Derbyshire Archaeol. J.*, 105: 222–80.

Wheeler, R.E.M. (1943) *Maiden Castle, Dorset*, London: Soc. Antiq.

Wheeler, R.E.M. and Wheeler, T.V. (1932) *Report on the Excavation of the Prehistoric, Roman and Post-Roman Site at Lydney Park, Gloucestershire*, London: Soc. Antiq.

Whimster, R. (1981) *Burial Practices in Iron Age Britain*, Oxford: BAR.

White, R. and Barker, P. (1998) *Wroxeter: Life and Death of a Roman Town*, Stroud: Tempus.

Wickenden, N.P. (1988) *Excavations at Great Dunmow, Essex*, Chelmsford: Essex County Council.

—— (1992) *The Temple and Other Sites in the North-eastern Sector of Caesaromagus*, Chelmsford: Chelmsford Museums Service/CBA.

Wiedermann, T. (1989) *Adults and Children in the Roman Empire*, London: Routledge.

Wild, J.P. (2004) 'Textiles and dress', 299–308 in M. Todd (ed.) *A Companion to Roman Britain*, Malden, MA: Blackwell.

Williams, T. (2003): 'Water and the Roman city: life in Roman London', 242–50 in P. Wilson (ed.) *The Archaeology of Roman Towns: Studies in honour of John S Wacher*, Oxford: Oxbow.

Wilson, D. (1968) 'An early Christian cemetery at Ancaster', 197–9 in M.W. Barley and R.P.C. Hanson (eds) *Christianity in Britain, 300–700*, Leicester: Leicester University Press.

Woolf, G. (1990) 'Food, poverty and patronage: the significance of the epigraphy of the Roman alimentary schemes in early imperial Italy', *Papers British School Rome*, 58: 197–228.

NAME AND PLACE INDEX

Emp. = emperor; IA cemetery = Iron Age cemetery; leg. = legendary; R-B cemetery = Romano-British cemetery; St = saint

164

SUBJECT INDEX